THE DIARIES OF
Marya Zaturenska
1938–1944

· · ·

EDITED BY
Mary Beth Hinton

WITH AN INTRODUCTION
AND BIOGRAPHICAL NOTES BY
Patrick Gregory

SYRACUSE UNIVERSITY PRESS

The paper used in this publication meets the minimum requirements of American National Standard for Information Sciences—Permanence of Paper for Printed Library Materials, ANSI Z39.48-1984.∞™

Library of Congress Cataloging-in-Publication Data

Zaturenska, Marya, 1902–

    The diaries of Marya Zaturenska, 1938–1944 / edited by Mary Beth Hinton; with an introduction and biographical notes by Patrick Gregory.—1st ed.

    p. cm.

    Includes index.

    ISBN 0-8156-0714-8 (alk. paper)

    1. Zaturenska, Marya, 1902—Diaries. 2. Poets, American—20th century—Diaries 3. Women immigrants—United States—Diaries. 4. Russian Americans—Diaries. I. Hinton, Beth. II. Gregory, Patrick. III. Title.

    PS3549.A77 Z464 2001

    818'.5203—dc21

    [B]   2001049409

Manufactured in the United States of America

Contents

Illustrations

Mary Beth Hinton has an M.A. in English Literature from Syracuse University. She is editor of the *Syracuse University Library Associates Courier,* in which she has published excerpts from the depression-era diary of Marya Zaturenska.

Patrick Gregory, the son of Marya Zaturenska, was born in New York City in 1932. A former book editor in New York and Boston, he now lives in Northampton, Massachusetts, with his wife, the classicist Justina Gregory.

Preface

A few years ago a friend of Syracuse University Library, the writer Robert Phillips, suggested that I publish excerpts from the diaries of Pulitzer Prize winning poet Marya Zaturenska (1902–1982) in the *Syracuse University Library Associates Courier.* That journal, of which I am the editor, contains articles related to the holdings of the library's Department of Special Collections. Zaturenska's diaries, book and essay manuscripts, holographs of poems, correspondence, and memorabilia are kept there with the papers of her husband, the poet and critic Horace Gregory (1898–1982).

I went to the closed stacks and lifted M. Z.'s diaries out of the darkness of an archival box—and out of a half-century of silence. She had covered the diary notebooks with flower-printed cloth, and, except for some newspaper clippings about family members and literary friends, she had filled every inch of every page with words. Reading those words, I felt that she had strained with all her energy to reach unattainable ideals of beauty, integrity, friendship, and health. Yet, in spite of her poverty as an immigrant child, her at times incapacitating anxieties as an adult, and her less than robust health, she created lasting works of art and scholarship. Also important, she was a loving wife and mother. A symbol of that love still lies between the pages of her depression-era diary: it is a lock of brilliant red-gold hair that belonged to her child Patrick Gregory.

After Dr. Robert Mandel, then the director of Syracuse University Press, expressed interest in publishing a book of selections from Marya Zaturenska's diaries, I talked to Patrick Gregory, who is literary executor of his mother's estate. He not only agreed to the project but became an essential collaborator. We decided to use selections from the years 1938 to 1944, when M. Z. was fully mature as a poet and the world was shattered by war. I transcribed three diary notebooks from this period—more than 800 manuscript pages—and together Gregory and I made the selections, cutting the text by half. As I edited the material, he reviewed the various drafts, answering many queries about his mother and her circle. Having known most of the people mentioned in the diaries—albeit as a child—Gregory wrote the biographical notes, as well as the introduction.

The selections were made with three main criteria in mind: 1) to include material of possible interest to historians of the period, particularly literary historians; 2) to present an honest, reasonably well-rounded portrait of the diarist; and 3) to offer the reader a coherent and entertaining narrative. We did not attempt to expurgate the material, though we deleted a couple of remarks that might have caused pain to living people. We omitted repetitive material that would have impeded the narrative and added little to the text: M. Z.'s frequent outbursts of maternal feeling and her reiterated expressions of anxiety about financial and professional matters. For the sake of brevity much peripheral material—consisting of war news, reflections on the weather, second- and third-hand literary gossip—has been removed.

The notebooks are dated from August 1938 to December 1940, from December 1940 to May 1942, and from May 1942 to September 1944.* M. Z. wrote in pen in longhand, leaving no margins. At the beginning of each new year, she recorded the day, month, and year. Otherwise, her dating—consisting of day, month, and sometimes day of the week—is intermittent and occasionally out of sequence. Under one date there may be many passages, each separated from the next by a line (in this edition represented by a bit of space), so that one cannot tell whether the passages were all written at one sitting or over the course of days. After checking her out-of-sequence dates against a perpetual calendar, I silently corrected many of them and deleted a few that eluded reasonable guesses. The section on the Gregorys' trip to Europe in 1939 constitutes an anomaly in the diaries in that it was recorded all of a piece after their return home.

In editing the diaries I have tried to preserve the authenticity of the original text while making it more readable. M. Z. was erratic, though generally

---

*Each notebook contains 201 pages. The first, 1938 to 1940, measures 33 mm x 21 mm; the second, 1940 to 1942, measures 13.4 mm x 21 mm; and the third, 1942 to 1944, measures 55 mm x 23.5 mm.

sparing, in her use of punctuation. I attempted, therefore, to follow her pattern, but with consistency. My editing tasks included correcting or supplying factual information, such as names, dates, and titles of works.

I would like to thank Stacie Gillian, my research assistant, for the many hours she spent gathering and checking facts. Alexandra Shedlovsky Dove and Rosanna Warren graciously provided photographs of their mothers. I would also like to acknowledge the support and kindness of Sanford Sternlicht, Justina Gregory, Robert Phillips, John W. Crowley, Randall Brune, John Elliott, David H. Stam, Peter S. Graham, Mark F. Weimer, Kathleen Manwaring, and the staff of Syracuse University Library's Department of Special Collections.

Permission for the photograph of Horace Gregory was granted by the estate of Helen Merril, Maurice C. Greenbaum, Executor. Permission for the photograph of Norman Holmes Pearson was granted by Pearson Papers, Beinecke Library, Yale University.

Mary Beth Hinton

Syracuse, New York
June 2001

Introduction

I

When Syracuse University Press requested permission to publish excerpts from my mother's diaries, my immediate, instinctive response was less than enthusiastic. The reluctance sprang, I think, from two sources: one critical, the other sentimental. In regard to her poetry, my mother took great care in preparing her work for public viewing. Each poem went through numerous drafts, which were often put away in a drawer for proper aging and meditation before being reworked into final versions. Even after a poem had appeared in print, she often found herself dissatisfied with it, and the poem would be quietly eliminated from subsequent selections or collections of her verse.

In contrast, the diaries were never prepared by her for publication. The only signs of her critical intervention are some very occasional annotations or additions—usually no more than a few words reflecting a subsequent, undated reaction to a passage—and the deletion of certain references either by blacking out in ink, or cutting away whole pages from the notebooks. The sentences are often elliptical, the punctuation erratic or nonexistent (in some of the notebooks she uses hyphens to separate phrases), and there is careless repetition of words and phrases. In short, these pages, even at their most fluent and eloquent, clearly represent for the most part nothing more than preliminary notes for the first draft of a finished text, and in permitting their publication I worried that I would be unnecessarily exposing my mother to undue criticism by unsympathetic readers.

So much for my critical concerns. As for the sentimental ones, they are more complex and, I suppose, harder to justify. On rereading these diaries I found myself overcome at intervals by two emotions: first, deep pain at the evidence of my mother's great and continual unhappiness; and second, a great, an instinctive, urge to come to her protection.

The latter impulse was something new and unexpected in our relationship and caught me off guard. It was, I reflected, closer in nature to a parental response than that of a child, and seemed to constitute a strange reversal of roles. But then, it is true that the young woman in the earlier diaries was young enough to be my daughter, and I felt an old man's yearning to pour forth the full treasure of my poor arsenal of advice, to murmur dire warnings, to somehow shield her from harm. But of course if parental advice can seldom be conveyed directly from one living generation to the next, what chance has it to transcend the grave? Besides, as we all know, there comes a time when each generation must go its own way unencumbered by parental love.

My mother possessed the usual repertoire of human failings: she was vain, jealous, self-pitying, prone to anger, envy, and despair. Whether her portion of these failings was greater than those possessed by you and me I cannot venture to say. But what most of us manage to conceal by one means or another, she chose to display conspicuously in her diaries. One of her greatest and most painful social liabilities, her irrepressible indiscretion, she hereby turned on herself.

Marya Zaturenska was not what most people, including herself, would define as a "nice" person. And she would acknowledge this fact without arrogance or apology:

> Dinner with Sarah Lawrence people. Very nice people—nicer than we've ever known before—nicer than the dreadful "literary" crowds we've known. Yet Horace, though I know he's an excellent teacher, feels as I do. "They don't really speak our language." Why do we feel more at home with people interested in writing good poetry or prose (though as *people* we may dislike them) than with *these* people, intelligent, decent, kind? (March 10, 1939)

The precise relationship between "niceness" and literary ability, between virtue and genius—between personal integrity and literary integrity—is a question of passionate interest to her that reappears in numerous forms throughout these diaries. And I would like to think that it serves as the basis of her predilection for literary gossip.

Private diaries (along with suicide notes and deathbed confessions) enjoy a privileged status that is, I believe, wholly unmerited. Their authority rests largely on a general mistrust of all public utterances, and on the bare fact that they admit of no rebuttal. Yet their truthfulness is no more certain than that of a novel or a letter to the editor, and can only be judged by the same critical processes. The more eloquent the diarist, the more deeply "personal" his or her revelations, the more ready we are to accept the story as true. John Murray has been much abused for flinging Lord Byron's memoirs into the fireplace grate on the urging of the poet's widow, but though the loss to literature was prodigious, the loss to history was less than certain, and I heartily sympathize with the human aspect of his dilemma.

As far as I can determine, these pages present an accurate picture of events as my mother felt and interpreted them; her honesty here is only too apparent. But the diaries do not, I insist, offer the reader a true portrait of her. Like most diarists, she had recourse to her diary only in certain moods—almost invariably those of melancholy and dejection. The closest one comes here to encountering her social personality is in the critical comments on her reading: in them we see her wit, her quickness, her original and often surprising turns of phrase. In them we get a clue as to why many people regarded her as such a stimulating and exhilarating conversationalist—and why we find so many younger writers and would-be writers seeking out her company. What on the whole is missing from these pages is my mother's pleasure in people. All too often her recorded reactions to social occasions are those of "the morning after": the inevitable sense of letdown after high expectations, of lost opportunities, failed gestures, and squandered intimacies. Yet her desire to please was surely one of her more attractive social traits, even though the effort left her with a sense of dissipation and despair.

References to her state of health, both physical and psychological, appear frequently throughout the diaries. The physical illnesses were very real, though inadequately diagnosed and treated by a long procession of "literary" doctors and dentists; among the ailments that are beginning to emerge in these pages are incipient diabetes and thyroid malfunction. Her psychological illness at this period of her life manifested itself in "phobias": a terror of crossing streets and a fearful reluctance to venture far from home without someone accompanying her. "Perfectly alright until I step out of the house," she confided to her diary (June 11, 1942). Although the Riverside Drive apartment house was fortunately contiguous to a small park where she could walk on her own, yet she wrote that the "park has become a prison" (May 27, 1942). When she went shopping or visited friends or went to see her publisher she was at this time invariably accompanied by her husband or one of the children or by a friend. (Ironically, this was a slightly less extreme form of the agoraphobia that made a virtual recluse out of her beloved teacher and friend William Ellery Leonard in Wisconsin.) The move to Palisades was clearly made in part to allow her more space without the intimidation of urban traffic and in the hope that a change of scene would prove beneficial.

Her illnesses, her financial worries, her sense of inadequacy as a housekeeper, parent, and wage earner, coupled with her anxieties about her writing, her painful bouts of writer's block, and her growing feeling of failure as a player on the literary scene—all this contributes naturally enough to a deeply melancholy cast to the diaries. Yet the same acute critical sensibility that told her how deeply she was out of sympathy with the literary currents of the time also afforded her continual delight and stimulation in her wide reading and provided her with an inner conviction that her own writings, however dissatisfied she felt with them, were interesting, original, and worth the terrible emotional cost that accompanied their production and reception. Somewhere concealed beneath the surface of these pages lurks my mother's hidden joy in living. And as one turns from the diaries to her poetry, this joy burgeons forth in full flower.

II

Marya Zaturenska kept diaries throughout most of her adult life. The selections published here were drawn from three diary notebooks dated respectively August 1938 to December 1940, December 1940 to May 1942, and May 1942 to October 1944. These volumes were chosen because of what the editors considered their combined interest as biography and history. They were written during a critical period of their author's personal and literary life, a period when, in spite of illness, acute depression, and near despair, she was beginning the work that was to constitute her most enduring legacy as a poet. They also reflect with a remarkable sense of immediacy the tumultuous historical events of the time. In these pages the connection between poetry and politics is made real, and the focus of literary history shifts, as it were, from the poet's living room to the battlefield, and back. "The war is too large, too dreadful, too heart-breaking," she wrote. "I am not fit to touch a theme of such scope and tragedy—only a little of the sadness and terror bit by bit, almost unconsciously, can appear in my poems." Above all, these notebooks record one woman's perilous journey, *nel mezzo del cammin de nostra vita,* through that dark wood where the straight way was all but lost.

Childhood and Youth

Marya Zaturenska was born in Russia and emigrated to America with her family when she was about seven years old. The exact date of her birth is uncertain, but she recalls seeing the year 1902 on some official document in her family's possession, and from early on she gave her birthday, a bit arbitrarily perhaps, as September 12, 1902. Her parents were Jewish, and her father, who was a tailor by trade, settled his family in a Henry Street tenement on New York's Lower East Side. Shortly after the family's arrival Marya's mother died, and her father remarried. She seldom discussed those early years in any but the darkest, most allusive terms; the memory of them was agonizing to her even in her later life, and she chose not to share the pain with anyone. It was not so much a question of concealing her past as of discovering how to deal with it. Her poems are haunted by the reflected terrors of those years, and the diaries make frequent references to them; they pervaded her outlook on life.

As a girl Marya's greatest yearning was to flee the suffocating confines of her environment. She found an escape of sorts in her reading—and in her passionate love affair with the English language. Her father looked dimly on such distractions. Fortunately for her, others did not. She must have been an extraordinarily precocious—and attractive—young girl, for while still in her mid-teens she was taken up by a group of settlement house ladies, including the poet Jeanne Foster, who encouraged her early efforts at poetry, introduced her to several prospective literary patrons—including Vachel Lindsay and Willa Cather—and subsequently helped her to obtain a scholarship to Valparaiso University in Indiana. From there her poetry publication served to win her a Zona Gale Fellowship to study at the University of Wisconsin.

Before she was twenty Marya Zaturenska's poems had appeared in numerous periodicals, including *Poetry: A Magazine of Verse,* edited by Harriet Monroe, who was to remain a good friend and supporter. By the time she transferred to the University of Wisconsin she was recognized as something of a prodigy. While there she was befriended by the poet and noted Latinist William Ellery Leonard. Her coeditor on the university literary magazine was a fellow student and poet, Kenneth Fearing, who was to introduce her in New York to a recent Wisconsin graduate, Horace Gregory. Marya and Horace married within a few weeks of their first meeting, in 1925.

Marriage

Horace Gregory's childhood experience differed from that of his wife. His father was a successful Milwaukee businessman of Anglo-Irish descent; his mother (nee Heinkel) was Bavarian by birth, and Lutheran in upbringing and outlook. Horace was born with an undiagnosed birth defect that left him partially crippled throughout his early childhood (he later walked with a slight limp), and with an occasional tremor in his hands. He was a cheerful, bookish child, much loved and much worried over by his family. Because of his physical frailty, he was taught at home by private tutors, until in his teens he managed to persuade his parents to allow him to attend a local prep school. It was with a good deal of reluctance that his father (who had intended him for the family business) gave him permission to attend the University of Wisconsin at Madison. At Madison he became a prize student of William Ellery Leonard, under whom he discovered *De Rerum Natura* of Lucretius (which was to play a lasting role in his intellectual and spiritual outlook), and began the English version of the poems of Catullus that later comprised his first published book.

Horace's flight to New York resembled Marya's flight from the city a few years before in that both young people sought to free themselves from what they perceived as parental oppression. But whereas Marya was leaving a squalid, poverty-stricken environment wholly unsympathetic to her ideals, Horace was fleeing the comfort and security of an all-too-caring family in order to strike out on his own.

The young couple must have presented an interesting contrast in temperaments. Horace possessed the charm, innocence, and the easy self-confidence that are often peculiar to somewhat spoiled children newly entered into adulthood. Shocked and indignant at the spectacle of poverty and injustice he encountered on his rambles through the city, he was drawn inevitably toward left-wing political ideologies. Marya, though vivacious and capable of soaring flights of gaiety, was subject to fits of depression, and tended to be distrustful of herself, her friends, and the world at large.

Physically, at the time of their marriage they were both slight and somewhat fragile looking, and Marya's dark, exotic beauty was highlighted by

Horace's blond, Celtic features. In those flapperish years of the 1920s, Marya went in for long flowing dresses and colorful attempts at finery that tended to give her more of a gypsyish look than the desired one of elegance. Horace, something of a dandy, was always meticulously attired in well-tailored tweeds, and he handled his walking stick—a necessary appurtenance given his unsteady gait—in such a way as to make it seem like a playful affectation. During the late 1930s, Marya began rather suddenly to put on weight. The change in her appearance shocked, pained, and disoriented her, for she had always seen herself as ethereal and waif-like. The diaries contain a number of despairing allusions to her "loss of looks."

The Gregorys had two children: Joanna and Patrick, born in 1927 and 1932, during the young couple's most trying period financially. Horace's appointment to the faculty of the newly founded Sarah Lawrence College in 1934 gave them for the first time at least the illusion of some sort of financial stability.

That their marriage was to be an enduring one, in spite of its stresses and conflicts, is made clear in these pages. And its effect on Zaturenska's creative development as a poet was important and generally beneficial. Horace's background in the classics of English and Latin literature was secure, and he was able to contribute his prodigious reading to Marya's own wide-ranging stock of literary exemplars. He deeply admired her gifts—so very different from his own—and was an encouraging and sympathetic critic of her work. There was never the least sense of rivalry in the respective careers. And though Horace tended to view their various setbacks and disappointments with a certain philosophic detachment that Marya attributed, with irritation, to his "fatal Irish optimism," they took great pride in each other's triumphs and accomplishments.

Friendships

Indeed, Horace was among the few poets of her acquaintance with whom Marya managed to sustain a long-term relationship free of rivalry. Just as Horace seemed to have a natural talent for making friends, Marya possessed a near genius for converting friends into enemies—if only in her own imagination. Certainly she was impossibly demanding of her friends, requiring a loyalty and an attentiveness to her emotional needs that would have tried the patience of a saint in a circle that boasted few aspirants to saintliness. The mere fact that one of her present friends could consort with one of her former friends she regarded as an act of terrible "betrayal"—a word repeated all too often in these pages. Clearly there was something amiss in this over-possessiveness, and those interested in psychological diagnoses will find sufficient material in the diaries to formulate any number of plausible theories. But without delving into causes, we can readily see the effects: she suffered greatly through long periods of her life from a sense of loneliness, isolation, and self-doubt. Nonetheless, she was fortunate in having a few longtime acquaintances who obstinately refused to quarrel with her or to withdraw their affection, and who stayed with her to the end. For Marya Zaturenska was, in spite of her disturbing fits of temperament, capable of inspiring love.

New York: The War Years

The Gregorys had moved to Bronxville, New York, in 1935 so that Horace could be closer to his new teaching job at Sarah Lawrence College. Their subsequent return to New York City in 1938 brought them back into the center of the literary scene.

New York, in the years immediately preceding and following the outbreak of hostilities in Europe, was undergoing a vast cultural change. The steadily increasing influx of writers and artists fleeing Nazi oppression abroad gave a new cosmopolitan cast to the intellectual landscape. As the diaries recount, the larger literary parties attended by the Gregorys during the war years were likely to include a smattering of foreign visitors—a French surrealist painter perhaps, along with a couple of English poets, an exiled German critic, and a Central European novelist (as yet untranslated), all conversing in a strange medley of accents with the usual representatives of the left-wing New York intelligentsia, while a few stately remnants of the old literary establishment hovered uncertainly in the background. The introduction onto the scene of new faces, along with fresh outlooks, concepts, and concerns, had an energizing effect on the arts in America, and as the war progressed the increasing number of uniformed guests at these gatherings served as a reminder of broader conflicts beyond the range of literary squabbles. For the time being at least New York City seemed to have replaced Paris as the artistic capital of the Western world.

The diaries suggest that the Gregorys' apartment on Riverside Drive became a regular port of call for poets and writers newly launched onto the treacherous waters of the New York literary scene. Young people were drawn to the Gregorys because of the diversity of their respective work, the wide range of their literary interests, and above all because of their contagious enthusiasm for whatever works of poetry had at the moment caught their attention. Since neither Marya nor Horace belonged to any recognized echelon of the literary establishment, there was no need to stand on ceremony with them or hesitate to take yet one more drink before leaving. Indeed, to judge from these pages, people seemed to arrive—sometimes unannounced—at all hours, and to linger late into the night. The gatherings were generally lively, and opinions forthright. When tempers began to fray, Horace usually read a poem or prose passage from a work he or Marya had just unearthed—something culled from a literary magazine newly arrived in the mail, or, more likely, some obscure poet from the distant past whom they were eager to introduce to their youthful guests. They particularly favored poets whose work they felt was unjustly neglected and deserved another look. Marya and Horace seldom read their own work, nor did they encourage their guests to do so. As the diaries show, attempts at self-promotion usually resulted in one of Marya's notorious outbursts of "indiscretion" or cutting irony.

The Changing Face of American Poetry

The diaries bear witness to the changes taking place in American poetry during this period, whose full force was to be felt shortly after the end of the war. To some extent these changes represented the normal effort of an emerging generation of poets to find their own voice, yet in retrospect, the dynamics of these changes clearly reflected a reaction against the war. Among younger poets, public utterances and social causes now seemed tainted by the rhetoric of propaganda, and poetry was to be best preserved for private, more intimate concerns. The new "confessional" poetry centered on the individual rather than society, on psychology rather than nature. Its most prominent proponents were critics and teachers who claimed their sources in the English metaphysical poets, borrowing the latter's reliance on irony and intricate conceits but for the most part dispensing with their religious and transcendental beliefs. In the early 1950s the confessional establishment, by then securely entrenched in the universities, was challenged by the Beats, who found their inspiration in Whitmanesque celebration of the self. The two tendencies flowed together to form the mainstream of contemporary American verse, swelled by an infinite number of rushing tributaries. All this took place in the decade immediately following the last entries in this diary, but already in these pages one can discern the swirling shifts in the current.

Marya Zaturenska, whose work had never belonged to any discernible fashion or trend, felt increasingly unsympathetic to these new poetic sensibilities, and in turn was viewed as an increasingly distant outsider, whose intensely lyrical voice was sounding from some strange out and beyond. Her later poems, concerned as they were with time and loss, and often dealing with netherworlds of history and the imagination, seemed almost perversely self-effacing. And because her own literary influences sprang from out-of-the-way, unfashionable sources, her remoteness from the poetic establishment continued to increase. The diaries record this distancing in painful detail.

The History of American Poetry

From 1940 to 1942 the Gregorys worked together on a collection of essays that was to become their *History of American Poetry, 1900–1940*. It was a project that appealed greatly to both of them since it combined their love of poetry as a mode of expression and their fascination with history and the historical process. In writing about living poets the Gregorys had decided beforehand to treat them as figures in some indefinite historical past. The perspective afforded by such an approach was undoubtedly informative, but often unflattering to the poets discussed. As the diaries make plain, Marya's reading at this time, besides those works connected directly with the History, was largely in poets of the previous centuries, along with Hardy, Rilke, and Yeats. Few of her contemporaries could survive the sort of comparisons the Gregorys had lodged in their minds, and all too often it was a case of breaking butterflies on wheels. Besides, as any experienced reviewer knows, the slightest critical strictures or reservations tend to outweigh in the subject's eyes any portion of praise. In their innocence—or naïveté—the joint authors failed to recognize that in writing about one's contemporaries the appropriate literary form is journalism, not history. As a result, the book—in spite of its enduring merits—was at the time a tactical error that had an immediate deleterious effect on their careers. And its publication, as the diaries show, did nothing to alleviate Marya's growing sense of isolation.

Zaturenska's Religious Beliefs

In conclusion a few words must be said about Zaturenska's religious beliefs, though these words must be framed with caution, for her beliefs were clearly shifting and their theology overshadowed by emotion. As a teenager in New York she was baptized in the Episcopal Church. Undoubtedly this was done in willing compliance to the wishes of the settlement house ladies who helped to spring her release from the Henry Street ghetto, as well as out of an adolescent yearning for some sort of spiritual renewal. Nominally she remained a Christian throughout the rest of her life, and she and Horace attended church with some regularity during their stay in New York City during the late forties and fifties. But Zaturenska's Christianity was shot through with backslidings and doubts, and when a close friend, perceiving the genuineness of Marya's religious impulses, attempted to win her to Roman Catholicism, she found a fervent listener but unwilling convert. Though much intrigued by Modernist Catholic theology (particularly the writings of Baron von Hügel), she ultimately sided with Simone Weil and replied that if conversion meant in any sense a renunciation of her racial origins she could not comply. Her heart went out to the Christian message of redemption and forgiveness, but she bore within her the legacy of her Jewish past. The diary records, sometimes openly, sometimes between the lines, this passionate dialogue. And the dialogue is important in that it is reflected in the "mystical" element discernible in many of the poems, in the frequent recurrence of religious imagery and symbols, and in the poet's preoccupation with the hauntings of history. In attempting or choosing to overlook Marya Zaturenska's profoundly religious response to life, the critic of her work risks rejecting the inner tension that vitalizes many of her poems.

A Note on the Biographical Notes

The literary scene of the late 1930s and early 1940s was, like all previous literary scenes, populated for the most part by men and women whose work has gradually drifted out of print and whose names are familiar only to those with a vested interest in literary history or with a passion for literature that prompts them to venture beyond the frontiers of contemporary fashion. Some of these figures enjoyed a certain prominence in their time—poets like Edgar Lee Masters, John Gould Fletcher, and William Rose Benét—while some were yet to come into prominence: Theodore Roethke, Elizabeth Bishop, Robert Fitzgerald. And there were some, almost totally forgotten now, who brought with them into a room the bright aura of promise and the irresistible self-confidence of youth. In attempting to recapture the atmosphere of the social occasions recorded in these pages it is important to remember that the present obscurity of many of the figures did not cast its shadow over their activities, and that they moved through the scene in the full light of their perceived achievements and proclaimed ambitions. In short, all the people here avidly partook of those prerogatives that the living exact from the dead.

In compiling the brief biographical footnotes of the book's *dramatis personae* (starred at first mention in the text), I have tended to favor the more obscure figures. There are, for example, no entries for Robert Frost or T. S. Eliot or Marianne Moore. I only regret that the biographical data relating to some of these people eluded my researches and that I could do little more than once again invoke their names.

Patrick Gregory

Northampton, Massachusetts
June 2001

The Diaries of Marya Zaturenska, 1938–1944

_1 9 3 8_

As the diary begins, Marya, her husband, Horace Gregory, and their children, Joanna and Patrick, were on a family holiday. They had met their friend Norman Pearson in Denver.

August 22, 1938, Boulder, Colorado

The immensity and inhuman beauty of the mountains and the scraggly Velasquez-like landscape. Austere—half desert, half treeless plain, closed in by mountains.

Illness—the same pain, a continual pressure behind the eyes. Not a day spent without pain. The doctors say nonchalantly that it is not serious—that everything will clear up—but months pass, all is the same, and the world grows terrifying seen with eyes that are strange to me.

Horace and Marya had moved to Bronxville in 1935 after Horace got a job teaching at Sarah Lawrence College. They moved back to New York City in 1938.

September 25, Bronxville

Working like mad. Obsessed by new poems, writing and rewriting difficult, aware of one's limitations. _To surmount one's limitations._ That's the great secret.

Norman Pearson* aristocratic, sensitive. His half-tendency toward fascism, his exquisite courtesy to all who worked for him, his generosity to the poor, his kindness and feeling of responsibility to servants. B. the Communist brutal to his servants, robbing the sick who were dependent on him as a doctor, saying that since we live under a corrupt system one must be corrupt too. His intense racial consciousness—awkwardness, fear, servility and contempt towards gentiles. *When he talks of Mary he means Moses.* Would really be happier as a Zionist. Wants a world where the Jews can live in a golden unmolested ghetto. N. P.'s attitude of tolerance and sympathy towards the Jewish problem. But he dislikes Jews and wouldn't have one too close to him. Yet he would die defending them from persecution—on principle. Neither type is representative of the best or worst of their kind, of course.

The writer of famous children's books Rachel Field. She looked so warm, large, sloppy and motherly in Jim Putnam's* expensive living room. Badly dressed like the mother of a large exhausting genteelly poor family. (She's childless.) I trusted my instinct. I knew exactly what to say to her. I talked eagerly and honestly the way we don't usually do with strangers. But I saw her large body stiffen, her eyes grow blank, shrewd, bright and that unmistakable film of stupidity and self-satisfaction in them. Everything said was wrong. Of course she didn't understand. I had lost my instinct about people. The conversation became banal again but such mistakes are irreparable.

Careful—careful—remember Sophie Brzeska* and Katherine Mansfield. But I forgive K. M. because she was ill, charming, young and sensitively talented. But one shouldn't put oneself at the mercy of *such* women. *Question.* What makes her (R. F.) write for children? I'm sure she doesn't really like them.

Remember Colorado, the university near the mountains. The air electrifying everybody's energies but mine. I sick—sick—always in pain—the bad eye, the round black spot always dancing before me in that incredible sunshine. Altitude-dizziness. Think I may have discovered the cause of everything. Three infected teeth. Will have them out tomorrow. Oh how marvelous it will be to be well—really well. It's years since I've been really well. Then I'll work—and work. I'll do beautiful *strong* work.

The Pulitzer Prize that saved me as a published writer—but made me so self-conscious. I'll have to be damn good now or be laughed at by the people I respect.

October 12, Wednesday

524 Riverside Drive: "The Burrow." The most luxurious place we've ever lived in. And the children received scholarships at the Lincoln School. It's all too luxurious and good. I feel troubled, for even with the scholarships I find the expenses mounting. I think of Heine's "We are living in a beautiful and expensive peace." Horace is delighted at being in New York City again. Early memories weigh on me and I feel as if a rock is slowly dropping, will soon descend, on my head.

Trouble with Covici-Friede due to the firm's bankruptcy. Horace is anxious to sign up with new publishers. It all looks good but until the contract actually comes into our hands—I don't dare to breathe.

October 26, Wednesday

Isolation eating into the nerves. Constant pain. No sleepless nights but bad awakenings. Nightmares.

One dream

I dreamed that H. had disappeared and I felt lost, lonely but resolute. At last I will have to face my destiny. But there was no place to go back to but to my father and mother (who in the dream had grown old together and were living in a place I remember from childhood, a dark two-room flat in a slum tenement near Henry Street). I was not afraid to go back and my parents didn't seem difficult or unkind. But I had gone there carrying a small baby (Pat). Where was Joanna? And I kept saying, "I must earn my living. I *must* pay my way." So I went (still carrying Pat) to the offices of the *Nation* which looked strangely enough like a printing office where I had once held a badly paid and difficult job. M. M. met me and kept prying into my affairs. I hated her now. "I won't give you any reviews," she said, "but I'll try to find you a job." I felt hurt that she had no high opinion of me as a reviewer. Meanwhile I thought of the baby whom I had left in a little crib in another room of the *Nation* offices. I rushed back to see an elderly woman bending over him, looking like Norman Pearson's mother. Before I could stop her she took the baby and disappeared. I tried to run after her but the door was locked. I saw darling Pat being wheeled away by her in a perambulator, he crying for me.

She had dressed him up as a little girl. I tried to scream and awoke. Strong sensation of nausea.

Visit from Norah Hoult.* I like her a lot. Horace and I tired and depressed. Covici's bankruptcy has put his affairs in a fearful tangle. His poetry unless we buy rights will be almost impossible to republish—or reprint. . . .

November 1, Tuesday

Heavy, dull feeling. If one could get the load and weight out of my head and chest. Had lunch with Helen McMaster* at the Stockholm yesterday. Wore my new gray dress with the red buttons, my dizzy red hat with the green feather. When I looked at myself in the mirror I said, "But why did I buy that hat?" It did seem a little too—too much. Felt pleased at being able to move around town again as if one were slowly being sucked into the life-stream again. A good feeling. Fifth Ave. dazzling, crisp, chromium bright. A sort of hard nervous light pouring from it. The most luxurious shops in the world. Jewels, silver, furs, luxurious beyond imagination. Clothes that are works of art, window displays that are poems. Around the corner of our house are the dead-dry tenements of the unpicturesque poor—remember that and look at them very often to preserve your balance.

Dinner with Jack Sweeney* and Norah Hoult at the Brevoort Saturday. We got gay, witty and tight. Norah burst into an eloquent tirade against old William Butler Yeats, disagreed with Horace that he was the representative of Protestant Ireland. *"That* dabbler in the black *arts, that* charlatan and cynic!" Of course she doesn't really know his best poetry. No one in Ireland does. The second-rate minds are most appreciated always. "How superior a man," says Norah, "was A. E. or John Eglinton, how much finer is James Stephens, how more valuable to Ireland, Daniel Corkery. "But," I said, "you see Norah, Yeats has a much greater gift than any of those. His only rival is Joyce." Norah: "I can tolerate Joyce. He has a sense of humor and at heart he's a good Catholic." Marya: "So is Jim Farrell."* Norah: "My God!!!" Conversation closed. But of course I *am* right about Farrell.

Pat refusing to wear his beautiful green beret. "It makes me look like a girl." Joanna: "It makes you look like an artist." Pat: "I don't want to look like an artist. I want to look like a policeman."

November 7

A visit from an old friend, someone who had known me as a child—how far away and long ago God only knows. Felt pains shoot through me at any contact with that period. We never lived long enough in any place to take roots, to make friends. I had but two intimate friends, old M. L.—and Lisa, and they have disappeared from my life without leaving a trace. This girl Dena S. knew them. She remembered my mother, her tall darkness and wildness, high cheekbones, deep-set eyes, always remote, turned inward with a wild unhappiness, her childish voice. D.'s husband turned out to be nice, a neurologist by profession with offices on Park Ave. A fat awkward little man, but rather sweet and sensitive. We thought the evening would be a strain but it wasn't—it was pleasant. Only in the morning after I felt as if all kinds of disease germs, soul-ailments, deep-buried unhappinesses had been stirred up. Dena repeated a remark about me that some distinguished old man (from her description it must have been William Dean Howells—she didn't remember the name) had made about me. I had gone to *Harper's* (or *Scribner's?*) looking for work and had gotten to know him slightly (I was about seventeen). Dena had gotten to know him through me. Meeting her on the street he had inquired about me and said, "Marya is so beautiful and so careless of her beauty."

D. believes that she has always liked me which is absurd. She was unimaginative and aggressive and made trouble between Lisa and myself. And Lisa was my closest friend. However, though I never felt any open resentment my subconscious must have resented her. For half-unknowingly I slipped away from her and forgot her—for years. Dear God what a life that was, hopeless, agonized. Poverty and ignorance from which no one ever hoped to escape. Physical brutality, mental suffering too keen for a child. . . . I never realized what I had escaped from till I had climbed out of the abyss and looked *down,* down. Dena told me how courageous I had been. . . . But no it wasn't courage. It was desperation, there as always, even now—the fear of the abyss.

Friends

No letter from J. W. of whom H. and I are so fond. Haven't heard for a long time or received an answer to our letters.

A silence from X whom I consider my best friend. Though being something of a sadist he has discovered my bad strain of masochism and has, with half-humorous Jesuitical subtlety, wounded me again and again. It is his habit with women he likes and to whom he is attracted. He really doesn't like or want to like women—unless they are old, safe and distinguished. Still he has been generous, affectionate, loyal and kind. I need his friendship. I admire and respect him. . . . But he goads me, I lose my temper, and I let loose in my last letter. Now this silence.

Picked up Kafka's *America* and threw it down again. No good in my present state. It is the lightest of his books. It has a sort of dreadful gaiety, the wit and humor that shoots through a nightmare more dreadful than solemnity. And yes he is a great writer but I am not strong enough to face him.

A note for poets

One of the secrets is to know when and how to lie fallow—to keep silent—to lay down the pen long enough for the seeds to grow, for the trampled grass to revive.

A mournful letter from poor old John Gould Fletcher*—depressing. I remember D. H. Lawrence: "I hate people to whom dreadful things happen." Yes that is the way of the world. I wish Lawrence could have risen above it. But it's hard. It's a truth too dreadful to say out loud. But it's Truth.

November 8, Tuesday, Election Day

Rainy day. Not the mild gentle rains that we have been having lately, but the rain without thunder that seems full of suppressed fury. I feel it in my bones, in my bad cheek and eye.

Dreamed that my mother came to call on me. I was glad to see her though as usual she seemed aloof and indifferent to me, talking and smiling to herself. She asked me to go shopping with her and I went, grateful for her company. After a long time of looking around she suddenly noticed how shabby I was and picked out a black silk chemise and a pink silk dress for me. She told me that I could wear the black silk chemise with my old black chiffon dress and the pink silk dress would just do for the summer. It wasn't exactly what I wanted but still I was glad to get these things.

A visit last week from William Rose Benét* and Marjorie Flack.* Benét graceful, tactful; the words "good breeding" were invented for him. He has been in the literary "racket," knows it's a "racket," has played it as a "racket," and yet has somehow come out unembittered and uncorrupted. Not a brilliant person but very charming.

Some interesting sidelights on Elinor Wylie in the course of the conversation. Benét speaks of her a great deal.

Horace received a summer appointment at Columbia. We drew a sigh of relief for we are swamped, harassed, tormented by doctor bills.

November 14, Monday

The news from Germany. When I read it at the breakfast table, I want to break into a long spell of weeping. Horace's anger as he looks at the headlines seems nothing compared to this chilling silent horror that only a Jew can understand. I have been the least race-conscious person I know and now it's as if a secret wound in my heart has been opened. One feels that it has been bleeding all the time, numbed and unhealed. And there it is now, livid, exposed and shuddering. Perhaps the best interpreter of this was Kafka who felt, foresaw, everything not only as a Jew but as a Central European. He could not, as Matthew Arnold said of Goethe, put his hand on the disease and say, "Here it is," but he felt it intuitively like a dark cloud everywhere, rising slowly—from the war-guilt.

Read Milman's history of the Jews and again was aware of the long hatred of the Western world for the Jews—a people driven mad by God, so obsessed by their mission (which they refused to share with anyone). The sense of spiritual superiority and physical weakness that together spells "danger." There *were* Jews, like Philo, like Herod, who tried to reconcile the one God with the graceful and cheerful Gods of Greece, to clear the dark intensity of the Jewish religion, to lighten it, to bring it into tolerance and joy. But the two forces were irreconcilable. Even the Roman tolerance could no longer endure the cold sneer of superiority that Jehovah's people exuded, that superiority that even conquest couldn't down. And how all the types are there—as always the cosmopolitan first and second. Herod so clever, so intelligent and adaptable—and so Jewish at heart. What I have always hated in my heart is the ghetto psychology, the ghetto mind so narrow and *killing*. I would have wished the Jews out of their ghetto even if it meant assimilation and I realize now that there were others long before me who felt that too, but with such horrors reappearing—what chance is there now for such an ideal?

Dudley Fitts* and Robert Fitzgerald,* Eleanor Green and an exquisite little actress from the Mercury Theatre came down and put on for us an improvised showing of the Fitts-Fitzgerald *Antigone*. They all sat on the floor and read their parts—Dudley as Creon, Robert as all the choruses and extra characters, Eleanor as Ismene and the Queen, the little girl from the Mercury as Antigone. It was lots of fun, and some beautiful poetry—and filled me with a great desire to learn Greek, to read *all* the Greek dramas by myself. Dudley admitted that he found Antigone "very unsympathetic," which may explain why her lines sounded stiffer than some of the other characters and choruses. Dudley's Harvard-Oxford accent as Creon sounded like T. S. Eliot in a rage!

> "Judaism is not a religion, it is a misfortune."
> —Heinrich Heine.

November 22, Tuesday

The news from Germany. As I read the newspaper I feel as if I was slowly being encompassed by a nightmare. Yes one has known these things, one has felt these things were lying dormant all around you. The brutality was there, the bad will, the festering hatred. But somehow I had always felt that an innate human decency and so many years of striving, of struggle to attain liberty, culture, knowledge, had left some mark on our century. Yet didn't the World War disillusion and warn us and show us the dark, steep pits in human consciousness? The abyss was there. It was covered up for a while. Now it opens. That's all.

My bad eye, pain, terror and fear. Small specks flying from it like tiny feathers, like specks of ashes or the shadow of a fly. The doctors say it is not serious. But the pain—the discomfort—the strangeness of it.

My father—the guilt that wears me down.

The children. Love like an obsession. Their health, their futures, the feeling I must not fail them—must never be inadequate. That we must be strong, gay, successful for their sakes. Joanna showing some of my traits causes worry not pride. I want her to be different.

Read Henry Miller's *Tropic of Cancer.* People whisper about it as they used to whisper about *Ulysses.* When one goes to Paris it is quite the *chic* thing to smuggle it in, to show the paper-bound copy around. I felt suspicious—it's the old expatriate thing all over again, I thought. One can't do anything more with the dregs of the expatriate movement. Yes it is the Last Testament of the expatriates—I was right. Like Jim Farrell who has brought a whole school of realistic writing to its final convulsion. "Oh very well," we say. It's *good* but *no more no more.*" There can't be anymore. This is the last of it all. And so of *Tropic of Cancer.* It's the last word on that school, and period—no more now—nothing else is possible. Yet the book has flashes—a lift into poetry, imagination—a *catharsis* that Farrell lacks. Nonetheless I want to cry out, "no more." —Flesh and blood can endure no more.

My poem in the *Atlantic* this month. Looks impressive—Stuffed Shirt somewhat. I can't believe it's my own name printed there. The first stanza is excellent. The rest—not so good. I am not satisfied at all. The poem is a flop but I have a feeling that given strength, health, length of years, etc. I will get there. I'm slowly getting what is good and real.

The granddaughter of the famous English actor Forbes-Robertson. She told me that her grandfather had said that the most beautiful woman he ever met was Dante Gabriel Rossetti's wife, Elizabeth Siddal. She looked like her portraits he had said. But the most striking thing about her was not her hair—or that pensive long throat that became the Pre-Raphaelite models' hallmark, but the curious mouth. I have always been interested in her. The woman Ruskin and Swinburne admired so much was not mediocre. Her little poems, her little pictures have a sort of waxen pathos, stiff yet alive—one feels that if one puts a match to them they would suddenly burn, burn hard and bright. That strange, lifelong, reticent yet fascinating quality about her life and personality. The shop girl who became the grande dame of Bohemia?

November 24, Thanksgiving

Horace's publishing difficulties seem to be settled at last. Heard from his lawyer on the twenty-first, our lucky day.

November 27

Bought such a pretty winter coat with a heavy beaver collar. My old fur coat that I had bought with some of the Shelley Award money (1934) is almost all worn out and Horace insisted that I get a new one. Couldn't afford a fur coat so I got this one instead. It's not expensive but I have a fearful sense of guilt and extravagance and dreamed about it last night. Still it's a good feeling—being able to have nice things exactly when one needs them. It should have happened when I was younger. It would have made another person of me.

The stripped black trees on Riverside Drive leaning into the water, more beautiful than when clothed with leaves. The pure anatomy.

December 1, Thursday

Unable to write, revision so exhausting that I become ill. Read one of those foolish reviews where the reviewer divides all poetry into Personal Poetry, Nature Poetry and Poetry of Social Vision! Angry at the bad journalists-poets who inflict their stupidities on every sensitive, honest poet who can't follow a formula and has no important political job like Louise Bogan* to protect them. Personal Poetry and Nature Poetry is romantic, says the theory. Poetry of S. V. is not (so they say)—but I've seen more romantic nonsense, more flagrant unrealities in poetry of S. V. than in the whole romantic movement. For instance the foolish optimism of the *Daily Worker,* pretending that the Revolution is almost here—when reaction is triumphing almost everywhere. It is silly, dangerous and romantic and based on unrealities.

December 6, Tuesday

Horace home because of a cold. Quiet lovely house. Wrote my customary foolish mournful letter to X and a good letter to Norman Pearson, all about the Oscar Wilde play we saw Saturday. Beautiful acting by a man called Morley as Wilde. The play charmed me in spite of myself, though nothing can convince me that O. W. was a first-rate writer or a really tragic figure. Two years at hard labor was exactly what he needed—but of course the punishment came too late to be of any value.

How times have changed! Blank and Blank famous poets advertise their homosexuality in every line they write—everybody knows—nobody minds. But one of them is a magnificent poet—he has a right to his private life. And he doesn't corrupt starving boys from the slums, disintegrate them with luxuries that they can never have again and then forget about them. That's wicked—the real wickedness. And Wilde deserved punishment for that.

December 8

It's strange, but I find that when I show my poems or read them to people before they are in book form I feel as if some virtue or strength has gone out of them and I find it difficult to get back to writing again. It's like the primitive people who object to being photographed feeling that some inner secret life will be drawn out of them. There's some psychological truth in that fear. I'm convinced of it.

Had a visit from the David Schuberts*—nice kids—but I was a little indiscreet with them and felt worried over it. My wicked careless tongue. When will I learn to curb it? And it's all tongue deep—my bad temper I mean. Once I let it out, I no longer have any bitterness left. Way—way—down I'm not an angry person at all. But O that wicked tongue!

December 14, Wednesday

Endless days in which the tension lifts when dear Horace comes in the house again after a hard day's work. Count the days when the Christmas holidays will begin and we can be together. I feel safe and secure when he is near me.

Saw *Hamlet*—Maurice Evans' version not as good as his *Richard II*. Such sawing of the air and bombastical delivery was never seen, since the great ham-Hamlets of the Victorian era. Of course Evans was doing a masculine Hamlet to Gielgud's neurotic one, but Gielgud caught some of the metaphysical intensity of the play. We took Joanna who quivered with excitement. As Horace says, the play is foolproof. We hear the lines and are carried away. Bad acting—nothing—can take from its greatness.

Saw Jimmy Savio in *The Boys from Syracuse,* mildly bawdy, pleasant songs and dances. Went with the Krecks [neighbors on Riverside Drive] who took us after the show to our first nightclub—quite exciting. A Negro swing king "Fats" Waller was the chief attraction. Magnificent piano playing, dancing and singing. A group of high school kids, obviously from the poorer classes, small, stunted, badly overdressed, doing the "shag" and the "Lambeth" with mechanical vivacity on the floor. A rather depressing sight. These young people seemed a little "sodden" and heavy inside, and all young people on a dance floor should be gay, sparkling, beautiful, healthy, happy and as promising as spring.

Read a new biography of Keats by D. Hewlett, *Adonais*—a mediocre job, but the pathos of the story hit me as if for the first time—it's unbearable. Yet how fortunate Keats was in his one or two loyal friends. How much magnificent work he did in such a short time! Nor did he know the final distress of utter poverty. He was, I know, not rich but he wasn't poor enough to *have* to work for a living—so that the little strength he had was able to go into his poetry. Such courage! manliness. And such a fine mind!

The Leigh Hunt-Hayden set *was* awful, but he was being weaned away from them before the end. Never realized how vicious Byron had been about Keats' work; but then Byron was not a critic. And there was something about Keats' soft luxuriousness that must have seemed a little . . . "tasteless" to people who were brought up on the firm "correctness" and hardness of the school of Pope.

The Dumb-Waiter Shaft. Dreamed that I bent over it and kept falling down and down. But through my panic I kept saying, "I have really escaped—nothing can happen."

December 18

H. has decided to go over to Harcourt Brace. Contract not signed. But hope for the best—whatever place Horace signs up is as they say "alright by me."

K. K. sodden with drink. M., his wife, a former Ziegfeld Follies beauty. Carl Holty,* the artist, back from Europe, and Muriel Rukeyser* last night—quite a party. Holty witty and amusing—half neurotic suddenly about the Jews. His mother a member of a wealthy Milwaukee Jewish family—his father a German actor. He had inherited a great deal of money and lived well and practiced his art in Munich and Paris. He looks like Goering and I doubt if he ever thought of himself as a Jew. But the horrors in Germany have made him conscious of his Jewish blood and brought about a spiritual return to his Jewish mother from whom all his wealth came. He talks Yiddish, tells amusing Jewish jokes, immerses himself in the Cabala and the Talmud. His wit is like Louis Untermeyer's,* a constant nervous crackling, a fear that if he stopped being funny by one-half of a second something fearful might happen—perhaps a hysterical outburst of weeping. Yet in appearance no one is as German, or was as German, in manner and feeling before the Nazis let loose their waves of horror and barbarism.

Muriel's dislike of K. K.'s wife. I realized that even M. K.'s magazine-girl prettiness of the '20s wouldn't help. The type is so completely out of fashion—it's really dated. Even the movie stars of today, the pretty girls on the cover, have an air of decadence, experience, at least a look of awareness. It's no longer the Greek statue but the Egyptian bust of Queen Nefertiti. It's the change from Mary Pickford—to say Joan Crawford—or Garbo—or from Millay to Rukeyser.

1 9 3 9

Fairly pleasant Christmas—the children saying it was the best Christmas they had ever had. Thought of the illness and terror of last year and agreed with them. Still I am not well and everybody is impatient with me. The eye condition continues and one mysterious infection after another crops up. The few friends left are impatient; I don't blame them. A chronic invalid is a bore and a nuisance.

My father called. I was relieved and pleased but we can't talk to each other. Horace gave him a Christmas check and his face lit up like little Pat's when he receives a gift of candy. He became talkative and vivacious. His English becomes more and more difficult to understand. Again I see the abyss yawning, the uncertainty, the fright. Yet no one could have benefited by a good father more than I—always eager to please, to learn—too eager.

New Year's Eve—as always the sense of loneliness and isolation. Dined at the Brevoort with dear Helen McMaster. Ran into old Edgar Lee Masters* and Arthur Davison Ficke,* the last an aging male beauty. Old Masters a bit tight and very melancholy—big sad cynical dark eyes. He was very sweet to me and I devoted all my attention to him, turning my back to Ficke who insisted on calling me "lovely lady." Ficke (quite drunk) became very insulting to me as I left. I felt badly for I knew I had been guilty of bad manners, and therefore felt that I had to condone Ficke's.

Went down to Macmillan with Horace and saw Jim Putnam who gave me the check for the advance on my next book of poems, *Summer to Lapland*. Felt like crying a little for I find it so difficult to write the book, and I also know that if it hadn't been for the Pulitzer, Macmillan would have dropped me. Now I am good for two more books if my next book is fairly well received. Horace will sign up with Harcourt Brace—which cheers us up—as the two places he has depended on for support, the *New Republic* and the *Nation*, are downright hostile. *Poetry* is closed, the *Herald Tribune* impossible.

One can survive only by doing the very finest, the most profound writing and thinking—and then who is the critic now in judgment who is capable of recognizing such values? I know that even X is not to be trusted, the last person who talks to him molds his opinion. He is becoming conscious of the political powers ranged against him—and is eager to placate them. He will be very discreet about Horace for H. is not popular with the people X wants to conciliate.

When I read the *Nation* or the *New Republic* now—wave after wave of sadness and then anger comes over me. They might have been so important as molders of liberal political opinion, and upholders of strict and impartial literary values. Instead they have become tools for the airing of grievances by squabbling minority factions.

The Corot landscape of the Riverside Drive waterfront, the stripped trees, the gray sky-like water. Then all of a sudden the quick noise of a steamboat or in the evening the gold flash of an electric sign.

Saw *The Lady Vanishes*, a quick-paced movie at the Globe Theatre, very exciting and bright—like an Auden poem.

Picked up a nice old edition of Lionel Johnson whose work I used to like. Read it with growing distaste. The diction is nice but a little ornate rather than (as I once found it) austere. The influence of Walter Pater—rather than of Walter Savage Landor as I once thought. His Catholicism of the peculiar 1890 "aesthetic" variety makes me crawl. It's a little fishy—posed. I don't believe in his piety. Also the overuse of certain words, "chaunting," for instance, drives me mad. Yet again I see in his work qualities that molded the early Yeats. None of these people knew the real Catholic poet of the period—Gerard Manley Hopkins. Coventry Patmore did—but missed his opportunity. But how genuine Hopkins' religious intensity is. How he must have disliked them all—Wilfrid Meynell's polite pieties, Francis Thompson's elaborate banalities (if he had seen them), Lionel Johnson's affected religiosity. He was right in turning to Patmore with respect. Patmore was the one Man among them. He had a vigorous and manly mind—and Hopkins understood that.

January 19, Thursday

Horace exhausted with overwork. When he returns he talks over and over again of the difficulties and strains at the school. It's as if he couldn't shake off the load from his shoulders.

A pleasant evening with Muriel Rukeyser, R. Pitts, and Eleanor Clark* last Monday. They stayed till midnight. Muriel has gotten a splendid job with *Life* magazine on an enormous salary. She's becoming very good-looking and distinguished in appearance. Good fortune at the right time does wonderful things for a woman's looks.

January 21

Joanna's birthday. My father called. Have a great yearning and affection for him, but find it difficult to talk to him. To be old, poor, lonely, alien—this seems to be the ultimate lot of most of my family—or as in my mother's case to die young, having known little of what makes life not merely pleasant but simply endurable. I have really been fortunate. I have pulled myself out of a deep abyss—but wore out my energy doing it.

January 26, Thursday

Wasted lonely days. Fierce cold, a wind that howls along the Drive and freezes the water and the air. Unbearable to walk out. News of Barcelona's fall. Felt as if I couldn't go on working on my little poems—when so much horror is going on. An intense hatred for Father Coughlin [radio broadcaster supporting pro-Fascist Christian Front] whose influence has done a lot to defeat the lifting of the embargo. "See," I want to say to people who laughed at him, "clever people laughed at Hitler who seemed as mad and foolish as Coughlin was."

Where was Russia? Why doesn't she help the refugees from Central Europe, why hasn't she given more help to Spain? Russia is indeed, in the words of Alexander Bloch, turning to Europe "her hostile Asiatic face." More and more I feel the horror and danger of all totalitarian states.

January 30, Monday

Horace home today, completing a Sarah Lawrence job. Pleasant to have him home on a day like this, dull, damp and rainy. Last night Horace, Helen McMaster and I had dinner and a great many drinks at a little Italian restaurant near our house. The drinks went to my head and I became argumentative and emotional, but they did me good. They lifted me out of this heavy-painful body and gave me a rare sense of well-being. "Artificial happiness," Shaw calls it.

Old William Butler Yeats's death announced today. A foolish misinformed article in the *New York Times*. Only Shaw is left of the great Victorians. "All the Olympians a thing never seen again." He was doing his best and greatest work. Given ten years more I think he would have added ever greater magnificence and light to our times. I wish that the Irish would bury him at St. Patrick's with Swift—but religious bigotry and ignorance being what it is in Ireland, I would not be surprised if a public funeral were denied him. The hatred felt for him by the little poets in Ireland was all the more malicious for being half-disguised. Only a week ago Norah Hoult, who had dinner with us again, burst into a tirade against him—insisting that he was inferior to A. E. or Stephens. Like most men who have achieved full development after years of struggle, he had no sympathy with those who had never matured as artists or men. And he showed it sometimes and sent the envious pack after him. Hiding their jealousy behind religious or political cloaks, they slandered or spread malicious stories about him. Now that he is dead, the Colums,* the O'Sullivans, the Gogartys, the Austin Clarkes, etc., will say the decent words and be glad that the Great Shadow is not overwhelming their houses. But they will dwindle into oblivion and Yeats will remain still towering over Ireland. He had one opponent worthy of his steel—George Moore—and I've never liked Yeats kicking him when he was dead and couldn't answer with his wit, as incomparable as Yeats's own.

I expect to see the journalists' elegies begin soon in this country. Louise Bogan will burst a blood vessel expressing adoration for all the qualities she really fears and disowns in her own life. Her literary passion for Yeats is strangely similar to Elinor Wylie's adoration for Shelley. With both women it is a case of self-identification rather than understanding. In both cases their feelings are and were more fitted for psychiatry than literary criticism.

The fall of Barcelona. I didn't see the Spanish war as a fight for Communism against Fascism so much as a desperate battle between progressive forces and the deep-rooted old feudalism.

Decided to call my new book of poems *Grass Is My Garland* instead of *Summer to Lapland,* which seems too reminiscent of Prokosch's eternal travel poems and Auden's *Letters from Iceland. Grass is my Garland* is certainly more in my style.

February 8, Thursday

Halfway through from a bad attack of grippe. Horace and the children had it badly too and now Mary, the girl who helped us with the housework. I feel helpless without Mary and resentful—I don't want to be dependent on servants. My conscience troubles me about it. My inefficiency gnaws at my pride.

Called for little Pat at the Lincoln; the school has a pleasant, happy atmosphere. I want so much for the children to have a decent start in life. But even with the scholarship the strain on our health and finances is terrific. I try saving money but, although my only real extravagance is the maid for the housework, I find it almost impossible to put anything away.

We've never known such loneliness and isolation. In the last few months I haven't received a single letter addressed to myself. Old doctor bills pressing in and my eye condition still strange and troubling. Can't afford further treatment. I keep indoors till the world narrows down to a frightening speck, a vague shadow seen through window glass.

Nostalgic fake-spring weather. Vague memories, desires, a feeling that something wonderful, glowing and happy could be recalled—if I tried hard.

But when I tried—nothing but sadness. Frightened childhood, lonely and difficult, an adolescence devoted to looking for jobs. No amusement, no real friends or directed studies. Courtship period—lonely and bitter—a little normal life at Madison—then poverty again and early married days full of poverty, worry, no holidays, frustrated ambitions. Then a fierce rush of ambition—half successes—then just as life became pleasant and I was learning to adjust myself—the dammed illness that aroused my worst phobias. And now this shut-in feeling from which I can't escape—and these fears!

The young couple on the street evidently from Columbia, gay, vivid, healthy, her face petulant and young like an early-spring flower, thick, careless hair around a well-shaped little head. Alive, alert, drinking in life as if it would never end. This is what we should have had. And Horace and I had charm at that age and I was lovely. But the ragged clothes, the worry, the strain, and always for us the bad health, for neither of us was ever really well—well in a real sense of physical well-being.

This is a bad complaining entry. I think of Yeats and his death often and feel that his was a beautiful, rich, poet's life, that such a life will never be lived again by a poet in our times—the changing world will not allow it.

February 19, Sunday

For the first time in my life I'm gaining weight. It's as if my sluggishness, my continual depression, my inaction physical and spiritual are beginning to affect my looks. I'm really horrified and upset at this. Even a ring that I've worn on my small finger has suddenly become too tight. Haven't I always known that there are no secrets from nature? Your inner life, your private habits, your secret thoughts mold your body, make your personality, and betray you to the world.

Dinner at the Helen and Robert Lynds' (the authors of *Middletown*). Very fine, remarkable people. Eager, searching minds; they have a moral and physical dignity that makes one respond and feel as if one were worthy indeed to have been admitted to their company.

Max Lerner* and Anita there. Anita very lovely again since the birth of her baby. She has a gift of saying the wildest, the most indiscreet things with an air of disarming innocence, and Max brilliant, vigorous, charming and flashing, enjoying life to the full, finding it full of successes and excitement.

I suppose it is only the insanely egotistical or the very lonely who keep diaries. Didn't Proust explain one of his aristocratic woman characters by saying that she, who had become famous as a writer of memoirs of the great world, would never have written them—if she had not really because of some indiscretions been carefully kept out of the society she wrote about?

Refugees. One meets them everywhere. People who claim that they have been famous doctors, artists, writers, etc. in Central Europe before the final madness hit Germany. Other exiles who take you aside and tell you that they (the famous ones) were really nobody in Germany or Austria. Many of them fearfully unpleasant and arrogant about German culture, patronizing about "American culture" in the old European way. If it were not for the fact that they were Jewish they might very well have made excellent Nazis. And then those who break our heart—the gentle, the lost, the bewildered, the crushed.

W. H. Auden the English poet is in town and I hear that he is trying to get a job at Yale. If he can get the job, he wants to live here and become an American citizen. We will certainly be deluged by European "culture" now, whether for better or for worse God knows. The "culture" of Central Europe has, however, proved its feebleness.

Auden, who is here with Isherwood, has we hear at last worn out his loyal public in England because [almost two lines scribbled out] who were willing to ignore it could endure it no longer. He feels he will have more personal liberty here. Klaus Mann* in speaking of his (Auden's) marriage to Erica says, "That marriage was never what you would call intense."

March 10, Friday

A bill collector. One of those old doctor bills that have been hanging over from last year. They are our burden and dread. Horace wrote out a check at once—but I felt upset all morning—the feeling that I haven't been cured—that it was all wasted money. And I need a doctor even now—a good one, a kind doctor, a friend.

"God as the kind physician," said H. grinning.

Reading Baudelaire as if for the first time. There are poets one discovers late. But then they hit us with their full force. We see them in their full glory. When young and only half-aware one gets only glimpses, half-shaded views of their splendor.

The Millay-Dillon Baudelaire—a sacriligious job (an incredibly coy preface by Millay), inept translations by Dillon who I suspect didn't understand half of what he translated. The Enid Starkie life of Baudelaire a touching and beautiful job. She at least made an attempt to read the center of his poetry— the full meaning and value of his art.

Christopher Isherwood's *Goodbye to Berlin* extremely intelligent and charming. It should be more and isn't.

Rilke, Kafka and Baudelaire are the three writers who mean most to me today.

Horace bought a fine new radio today—with an attachment for Victrola records—thus satisfying an old ambition of ours. Now we can have all the music we want. I feel it will help me with my new poems—keep me from growing tired and stale.

Dinner with Sarah Lawrence people. Very nice people—nicer than we've ever known before—nicer than the dreadful "literary" crowds we've known. Yet Horace, though I know he's an excellent teacher, feels as I do. "They don't really speak our language." Why do we feel more at home with people interested in writing good poetry or prose (though as *people* we may dislike them) than with *these* people, intelligent, decent, kind?

A dull dinner at Columbia where I sat next to old Charles Hanson Towne, fat, silly and drunk, who kept reciting Bliss Carman to me. Bliss Carman was evidently the promising young poet of his day. A dreadful quotation about "a tune, a croon, a moon, and a bunch of lilacs." Horace suddenly jumped over a small bench and disappeared while the recitation was going on, so I made an effort to be doubly polite. Besides I had never met anyone who thought Carman a great poet, and I was curious. I wanted, as the slang goes, to find how Towne "got that way." He is giving a course in poetry and his ignorance of the subject is amazing. He says he tells funny stories to his students and reads all the poems he likes to them (Bliss Carman and Richard Le Gallienne, I gather). "It isn't hard work," he said—no wonder. I thought of the hardworking people at Sarah Lawrence. Why couldn't I get a job? If C. H. T. can do it, why can't I? Silly—I have no real reputation—no degrees, and I haven't the guts to get out and fight my way into these jobs. But I'd do honest work.

"We learn resignation not by our own sufferings but by the suffering of others," says Somerset Maugham. This is clever but not true. We never really learn anything except through our own suffering—no not even resignation.

March 15

Horace's continual exhaustion. The postman who never brings any letters. The continuing pain in my left cheek and eye. The drawing in—the exhaustion of solitude—the sense of guilt engendered by isolation. Pray to Kafka! He died in time. Hitler has entered Prague today.

Hitler as the Anti-Christ. The new Pope's eloquent and graceful gestures as seen in the news reel. The age-old power and authority of the Church flowing from his thin ascetic presence and giving him a momentary appearance of supernatural authority and grandeur.

The amiable, lovable publisher on whom I am dependent for my life, for I cannot live if I am not allowed to print my books. He never reads them—and I am not smart and fashionable enough to impress him. He has no real interest in my work.

The worst thing of all is to feel the power run out of my veins. Can't write—feel as if I can't ever write again.

> There is a desert in my brain
> Where nettles, weeds, through dry sands blow.

The inner drouth. Is it better to be burned away by a slow, low heat, or to be consumed by a swift, violent fire?

March 30, Thursday

Richard Eberhart* the poet visited us last night. He's so foolish as to be delightful. It's that naïve, boastful, childish part of him that accounts for his poetry. Otherwise he looks like a successful corset salesman. With him was Via Agee, Jim Agee's ex-wife, chastened and sad since her divorce. Eberhart walked up to us the minute he entered the room and said, "I've written a swell poem. Read it and tell me what is your favorite stanza in it. Auden told me he liked this one." And he pointed out one of the passages. Talked of all the important people he had known and knows, and traced his family tree back for us to the Kings of Württemberg.

Saw Eisenstein's *Alexander Nevsky* movie, a sort of superior D. W. Griffith spectacle—very beautiful. But how nationalistic Russia has become now—the Czars would have approved of the picture.

Saw Greta Garbo and Charles Boyer in *Conquest*. Boyer as Napoleon was splendid and revealing. The clear, slick Hollywood photography still the best in the world. For sheer technical brilliance there is nothing like it. Garbo's beauty is so superior to anyone else's in Hollywood. That long, beautiful figure, the face of a great actress. One is always surprised to see that she can't act. But her beauty is like genius—it overcomes all her faults.

Rereading Philip Horton's clever and tactful Hart Crane book. I still think Crane was one of our most important poets, though lately it has been the fashion to disparage him. But what a difficult and unpleasant person he must have been in his last years especially. And yet he had so many friends. It couldn't have been his "genius," for I know most of his "set" and many of them don't know a good poem from a bad. Tate* and Winters,* whom he revered, are now busy depreciating him—and they were at one time very close to him as friends and critics.

April 4, Wednesday

Returned yesterday from a trip to Boston. I left on April 1, on a beautiful spring morning, very much excited because it was the first trip I had taken by myself for years. I went at the invitation of M. B., a young woman on the *Atlantic Monthly* who had praised my last book warmly and who seemed anxious to have me visit her. Arrived in Boston and it rained and rained. Felt that I

talked too much and too excitedly and that Miss B. was not particularly finding me to her liking. I was modest and humble about my work when I should
have been impressive and arrogant. But honestly I can't put up great claims
for my work—yet. Yes it's good—but it will be better if I can keep on writing
and printing. As a great treat (and it was) M. B. took me to visit Robert Frost.
We had dinner with him and then we went to his apartment near Louisburg
Square where he lives alone. Frost still shows the remains of great physical
charm, but he is potbellied now, pale, looks ill and old.

He was charming, warm, and friendly, and in response to his tactful ques-
tioning I opened up and talked a great deal. Miss B. sat overcome with awe
and reverence, looking horrified when I disagreed with him from time to
time. We talked "shop," which seemed to be annoying M. B., but Frost evidently enjoyed it for he went on and on. Some good malicious stories about E.
A. Robinson, his stinginess, his sponging, his drunkenness, the awfulness of
his disciples. All this with a deprecating smile and a rather disarming "Of
course I was jealous of him. And he of me. But we were good friends." More
stories about Ezra Pound. "The poor devil hasn't a friend on earth. No one
but a group of young disciples whom he changes from year to year and eventually antagonizes. He is so lonely he even ran into Louis Untermeyer's arms
when he met him at Rapallo. He abused him afterwards of course." Also comments on Kreymborg* and J. G. Fletcher. Of the last: "He behaved so badly
while in England that all I had to do was to be mild-mannered and quiet and
everyone took me to their bosom saying, 'You see there are Americans who
are decent fellows.' " Of his beautiful, luxuriously furnished apartment: "Oh
friends got it and fixed it up for me. I never bother about such things."

In speaking of Frost I should emphasize his remarkable and indescribable
charm, which made me forget some of the small petty things I knew he had
done to people who hadn't praised him as he felt he had a right to be praised.
One forgets his malice; I only felt that air of warmth, naïveté and kindliness
which he contradicts by his own words. No intellect but a lot of worldly wisdom and shrewdness. He knows literary politics as no one else does, but the
air of naïveté half disguises it. I think I know his faults very well—and yet I
could see that one could grow so fond of him that his faults would be forgotten. And he is not incapable of using the love he inspires for his own ends—if
it were usable. His literary taste is bad—but he instinctively knows what to do
with his own work and is really interested in no one's work but his own. But

no one blames any artist for that. A great critic is as rare as a great poet and he is rarely both. Self-criticism is all we can expect.

A German woman at Miss B.'s who upset me. Here on an exchange scholarship from Germany. Violent attacks on the Jews, "the enemy nation," sneers at the exiles here. "What will you do with the trash? The newspapers in the U.S. are all controlled by Jews except those owned by William Randolph Hearst." All these sentiments expressed by a large placid young woman knitting very swiftly and looking very domestic. I shrank from her as much as possible and said nothing out of courtesy to M. B. But I wanted to run and run.

Visited Robert Hillyer* for the first time after corresponding with him for nineteen years. Beautiful house. H. handsome, ruddy and portly. A handsome portly wife. Sweet and courteous. I felt sad, for I felt I was no longer young and pretty and felt that he had romantic illusions about me.

Glad, glad, glad to run away from Boston. Felt I had flopped and hadn't made new friends which I wanted very purely and sincerely.

April 13

Horace went to a dinner at the Oxford University Press for Auden, Isherwood and MacNeice. He had a very good time, the crowd, as is usual in these things, was diverse and curious. Freddy Prokosch,* who H. says has gotten very fat in the behind, was a sort of social hostess or master of ceremonies. Auden, says Horace, was very gay and witty and Isherwood, utterly delightful. He thought that Auden bore the most amazing resemblance to the portraits of Oscar Wilde. The Boys were surrounded by fawning satellites so Horace, his curiosity satisfied, left early, having had a pleasant enough time. This must have impressed the Boys, for the next day Isherwood phoned and said they all wanted to see him again. Would he come this Sunday to a small party at Selden Rodman's?* Selden, who had been chilly for a long time, phoned too to tell Horace how much the Boys liked him and would I come to the party too. Horace said that no doubt he may have pleased them by talking lightly and cheerfully about nothing in particular and avoiding "shop" and "politics."

A young poet from Detroit, John M. Brinnin,* came around with an excellent manuscript. Some really fine poems. Horace promised to write a letter to a publisher—but his influence I know is so slight.

On April tenth H.'s birthday Jack Sweeney touched us to tears by calling up and taking us out to dinner. We had a few drinks at a strange old bar called the Marson Hotel Bar, an 1890s atmosphere, very soothing. I went extravagant and bought a pretty navy-blue suit, a rose-colored blouse, and a light spring coat. We have so many bills that I feel guilty buying anything. But I did feel properly dressed for H.'s birthday. Got ill after dinner and we came back to our house. Jack and Horace talked till midnight and I went to bed.

Visited my father and stepmother Saturday night. The hopeless poverty, the loneliness of old age, the dreadful neighborhood, a desert full of the ugly barracks of the respectable poor. Felt like wringing my hands. The only way I can help is with money, and the more one gives the more they demand.

April 22
Trouble with my eye continues. Obviously the thing, if not serious, is at least almost impossible to cure. But the pain and discomfort is wearing.

Joanna and I saw the *Wuthering Heights* movie with Merle Oberon [as Catherine] and Laurence Olivier as a dark and brooding and quite sympathetic Heathcliff. A fine atmospheric movie having a concentrated passion and unity that the book (which I've always found rather rambling) didn't have. It moved swiftly and intensely to the final love-death tragedy which is usually the best scene of the romantic tragedy.

Went last Sunday to a party given by Seldon Rodman for Louis MacNeice who was leaving for England on the *Queen Mary*. MacNeice a tall, dark, handsome, serious young man, suave and graceful in manner. Very quiet and discreet. Party consisted of Ken Fearing* and Rachel, Frederick Prokosch, Delmore Schwartz,* William Saroyan and a few others whose names I could not catch. The customary literary party atmosphere full of suppressed malice and hate, and large egos let loose. Saroyan looking like a prosperous Greek fruit peddler blowing his horn and indulging in a mutual admiration party with Delmore Schwartz. Schwartz a blond Jewish boy, very awkward in full dress, obviously *arriviste,* walking around flattering everyone. Schwartz approached Horace saying, "I have wanted so much to meet you. I am writing a piece on your poetry and wish especially to comment on your metropolitan imagery. Can you explain your imagery to me?" Horace looked at him and said, "Read my books and find out for yourself." Something in Horace's voice and manner seemed to frighten him for he gave him a scared look and ran away quickly into the next room. It was a foolish question. Ken Fearing, complaining of how badly the critics had treated him—how Horace should have defended him—absent-mindedly putting his hand under my skirt. Rachel illiterate, kindly and tactless trying to be literary. As usual I felt blue and lonely and had a weird yearning to be happy, friendly, gay. But looking around at all the faces I knew that we had no friends there. My front tooth had fallen out, I had a toothache and I felt unattractive and out of place.

Feel blue too at what looks like the failure of my Boston trip.

Zabel* is the only old friend who still writes frequently to us. Sometimes Muriel does—but most of her time is spent these days in pursuing Auden. Besides I can't get over a mistrust of her.

Read Katherine Ann Porter's *Pale Horse, Pale Rider*. Why didn't I think of that marvelous title first? Yes she's very fine, sensitive, without the occasional gaiety and girlish charm of Katherine Mansfield. A sort of delicate dignity of style. But it's all in the feminine poet tradition. Whenever it is put in prose, it always receives a large acclaim. And yet exactly the same quality is found in the best work of Ruth Pitter,* Leonie Adams,* myself, Edith Sitwell!

May 13, Saturday
A rainy Saturday—closing a difficult week. Work on my book, overcome with dissatisfaction at it—do not dare to lean too heavily on Horace for criticism on it, since I feel he resents my taking his time. When he drinks nowadays I prepare for torment. He is not unjustified. I have become a complete parasite on him and my looks are going. He is nerve-wracked, overworked—no time for his own writing—isolated (and as a good wife I should build some social life around him—and I don't seem to be able to do it). My only excuse is that I too am far from well—but my ill health has lasted so long that I may as well learn to adapt myself to it. Have had more infected teeth pulled recently. An ordeal.

I should like to get a job—but in these times it's difficult for more efficient people than myself. I depend on my writing in moments of optimism,
but common sense warns me that my poetry will never even bring in enough
for pin money. When I attempt to do some journalism for money, I find myself paralyzed. Horace has taught me his strict values—and it has made me a
better poet—but I've lost my gift for writing bright, salable little articles.

Blank saying to me, "The reason that Helen Lynd, Helen McMaster,
Anita Lerner, and Muriel Rukeyser treat you with contempt is that you are out
of date—old-fashioned, foolish, romantic." No, I say to myself—the reason is
that these women have good jobs—and have a gift of getting them. They can
repeat the latest ideas and find friends and admirers. But what if in my heart of
hearts I find Y's liberalism flabby, sentimental, and leading nowhere; X's
championship of the proletariat narrow, dogmatic and at times leading to doc-
trines that revolt me to the heart—that she knows nothing of real workers, she
with her wealthy family and expensive education; Anita Lerner's chief ability is
to talk glibly of things she doesn't understand—but she is lively, attractive, can
teach. But no, the fact remains that I'm a parasite—and they aren't. If my poetry were more successful—if I got a big acclaim from the liberal-radical press,
or if I gained a big audience—these women (Helen McMaster excepted)
would admire me. Helen McMaster's snobbery is justified. She is genuinely
cultured, capable, efficient—healthy, strong. In her eyes I'm a weakling and a
helpless little fool. The fact remains I'm a parasite. That's worse than being a
romantic, isn't it? Remember little Dora had to be killed off by Dickens at an
early age—he knew that if she grew older she would no longer be an object of
amused concern, but a real problem—a difficult and uncharming one. The little Doras are produced by the very very irresponsible rich—and by the very
very ignorant hopeless poor.

I stay awake saying, perhaps I ought to write a novel and make a great deal
of money. But I'm just beginning to learn to write good poetry. And when I
begin to think of these things my poetry dries up. And I shall end up by writing bad poetry and bad prose—or so I feel.

Excessive Humility. A form of rotted and perverted self-love—an invitation to defeat, a symptom of mental illness.

May 24

Sinus pain, causing terrific exhaustion. Have to fight hard to keep from staying in bed.

The shadowy loves touching her life and troubling its clear waters—never going deep enough, but disturbing, corrupting, blotting out light, creating false light.

The great pleasure we have in our new radio Victrola. The hunger—the real starvation we've had for good music—now half-satisfied. I got a Schubert symphony from the *New York Evening Post* by clipping twenty-four coupons. Now I need nine more coupons—for a Beethoven. Records cost more than books. And this is the only way I can obtain records. Music is my new world. It says more to me than books. I can't talk technical language. I feel humble, but also feel grateful to have a door of understanding open at last.

Collecting notes for a long poem on Dorothy Wordsworth. It's dear to my heart. I see it shaping up. All I need now is some of Muriel Rukeyser's physical energy—and the country. My inspiration dries up in the city. I want to walk out in the woods and think things out—for this particular poem anyway. This house has become the worst prison of all!

Morton Zabel hit the bull's eye when referring to Ezra Pound's foolish statement to the press. He spoke of Ezra's "dotty datedness."

We had a charming evening with Norman Pearson who had just returned from a year spent in a Chicago hospital. He is one of those rare young men whose charm is as subtle and beguiling as that of the most fascinating woman, and added to it the male strength and force of intellect. And I know he has cultivated and learned this charm—through mental suffering and through overcoming physical handicaps. Horace (when he allows himself to relax) has this quality too.

July 4, Tuesday

Horace and I had a few days' vacation at the house of Dr. Henry Ladd, a colleague of his at Sarah Lawrence. Ladd's house is in Kent, Connecticut.

Years ago when very young I stayed at Kent with the Frederick Waughs, the marine painter and his family. I was ill and almost homeless and his daughter Gwinyth, whose acquaintance I made, arranged for me to stay there. The first time I had been in the country for any length of time in the U.S.A. I remembered the overwhelming impression of the Berkshires in full autumnal coloring, the beauty and simplicity of the white house, the green doorway, the lyric landscape.

Finished my Dorothy Wordsworth poem, or rather the first draft of the poem at Kent. Not satisfied with it, but can work with it. I don't dare to think what would happen if I didn't have the Book to work with, struggle with, live with. It keeps me alive, sensitive, alert. When it goes out of my hands I shall be lost indeed. Nor am I satisfied with it, though I have written about seventy-five poems out of which I have discarded all but thirty-four for a start toward the Book. Afterwards I may discard most of these. No—it is not wasted effort—it is the practice work that leads to the finished achievement.

Joanna bobbed her hair recently. I grieved to see her long beautiful braids go, but she looks enchanting and grown up with her short hair. She's growing into such a pretty, clever, graceful girl. I hope God will be very good to her.

The feeling of obstruction. Fear of bumping into chairs, tables, people, railings. Something in the way. Want to push it aside—then can't discover just what it is. I know what the psychiatrists would say—but they would all be wrong. The whole thing is due originally to a physical not mental condition. When I straighten up, lift up my head, take a deep breath it is apt to disappear.

July 13, Thursday

The excruciating, tormenting, exasperating sweetness of an organ-grinder and his music outside my window.

Premonitions. To feel, to scent an evil, an unnamed dread, never to mention it—and yet to know it there. Then to have it confirmed by accident. This happened today. It would have been pleasanter to have clutched at the ray of hope. Yet so many of my presentiments are confirmed that I try to deny them, crush them before they rise. And though it is sometimes valuable to learn the truth, it seldom does me any good for I can rarely grasp the roots, the cause of the fatal error—

Went to a lecture at Columbia. Oliver La Farge, a smooth, graceful, dark-eyed, white-teethed young man, talked of "literature and how to market it." Had to attend because of H.'s writing class. We both sat feeling wide-eyed, depressed. How can knowledge of that kind help us? In our terms La Farge is not exactly a success. It's nice to sell—to be widely read, to be admired. We want all that, but if we tried to work that way, to think in such terms, our type-writer (we have only one) would crumble or refuse to move, our pens would drop from our hands. It isn't feeling superior, it's simply that it bewilders us to think that way. Success and marketing. Are the two words really the same? Sometimes—not always.

I daresay La Farge really (as he says) "loves to write" and is doing the best he can. Only our goal seems so much darker, deeper, stronger, wider. We don't quite understand it with such simplicity, sureness, confidence.

July 19, Wednesday

I've been frightfully ill the last few days. Pains in my head and face, spots in my eyes very bad. Plucked up courage—went to Dr. Atkinson, a nose and throat man, who insisted that I haven't sinus at all but some kind of facial neu-ralgia—and a longstanding infection due to infected teeth. Sounds sensible but the expensive treatments he prescribed are almost beyond my means. My father ill—we sent him what for us was a large check. Poor dad. He's a weight on my conscience—if I could do more for him. Horace hopes that his contract at Columbia summer school will be renewed. The work is dull but not diffi-cult. Meanwhile our debts (mainly doctor bills) drive us nuts.

Horace says that Coleridge's illness sounds like mine—the same symp-toms. If that is true his difficulties in working are more than explained. Also his laudanum-taking. Aspirin can easily become a vice with me. And there are moments when I feel I'd take to drink—if it would help.

Hot heavy days. Horace talks of the trip to Europe and it brings no pleas-ure for I get panicky about this damn illness. It kills enjoyment and excite-ment. Still, when one is actually on a boat it becomes fun.

Terribly displeased with my work—flat and mediocre, it seems. Can't work. Don't feel like working. Incredible laziness. Haven't heard from X for ages—and don't care a great deal now. That friendship has caused more torment than pleasure. No doubt some of it is my fault—but not all. X is something of a sadist.

July 31, Monday

Hot, damp days. No mail from anyone. No diversion except an occasional movie, attacks of nausea, depression. We sail on the *American Banker* U.S. Lines for England on August 11th. Half excited, half frightened. We wait too long for these things. And worn out by planning and anticipation we become exhausted when at last—the dream comes true.

Received a visit from a charming English girl, Mary Goodyear, a friend of John Hampson.* She told us she too was returning to England on the *American Banker*. Such a pleasant coincidence!

Last Thursday I gave a reading of my poems at Columbia—one of my first appearances before a very large audience. I was fearfully nervous but did the best I could. Everybody said I did very well and about twelve people came over with copies of my book which they had just bought. They wanted my autograph. Suddenly realized why people like Millay concentrate so hard on the lecture platform. It's not only the lecture fee but the sale of books! I should like to earn a little bit on my books every year—perhaps a small income for the children. (M. Z. G., you see how corrupting a "success" of this sort is. It puts the darkest thoughts in your head.)

Norman Pearson surprised me by rushing up to me after the lecture and embracing me. He had just arrived in town and Helen McMaster told him of the reading so he came along with her. We had such a pleasant evening! Horace, Helen, Norman and I.

Feelings of persecution, of being ostracized, of loss. No reason for it. A good letter, a piece of good news would relieve me of this gloom.

August 6, Saturday

A pleasant visit with Mary Goodyear, the English woman who is to sail with us on the *American Banker*. She reminds me of Helen "Middletown"

Lynd, a more restrained English version rather. She teaches economics at the U. of London I think, and listening to her soft, clipped, English voice, I thought of H. G. Wells and Bernard Shaw, the Fabians, etc. and realized that this was the kind of young woman they helped to develop.

Mrs. G. had visited an American labor court and was shocked and astonished at the fact that, after a bitter trial and dispute between labor and anti-labor forces, both sides had after the trial all got together on the most intimate terms imaginable and left arm in arm to see the World's Fair. She thought (Horace agreed) that it certainly showed a lack of integrity on the part of the labor defenders—that it may very well lead to a "selling out."

I don't know whether it has any significance whatsoever. It may only prove that violent class hatred, political violence, can't take deep hold here.

Highbrow. The person who simply can't find fun in anything but *Finnegan's Wake*. "No, I haven't been able to get a laugh out of anything but Joyce." Why do people limit their capacities for happiness—the little things by which we find laughter and consolation? Save me from intellectual aridity. Dear God. Life is sad and difficult enough.

The only typewriter in the house now taken from me. It takes H. about six hours to type one page. How can a book be written with such limited time at his disposal? He'll have to get a secretary. My typing is good enough for my needs, but not enough for his needs. We need a swift, professional typist.

O for money of my own.

The *New Yorker* took the two poems H. sent them—the first "break" for H.'s poetry in ages. It buoyed us up for a long time.

Quite excited about the trip to Europe. Dreams about it. Not happiness exactly but a feeling of half-awakening from a torpor and going into energy and awareness.

H. says that my *Cold Morning Sky* has gone into a third printing. If I could only earn a little, a very little, income from my poetry, say, $500 a year at the most. I can go off by myself to Key West—Maine—Taos—Kent, Connecticut—and make friends of my own. And—no I don't want to write just now. I want to live, to be part of a crowd, to feel useful, to give and receive love—not thin poems spinning in a sick dry brain.

There are days when the Devil Himself seems at one's elbow. My long awaited Wagner records arrived. The Prelude to *Die Meistersinger* and *Parsifal.* Terribly excited and pleased. Played them, but found the children had confused the used and unused Victrola needles. Record sounded wrong and scratchy—tone all off. Then I got up, the record album fell down and three of them smashed to pieces. Went into hysterical weeping. It seemed too tragic and it had taken me so long to save the *New York Post* tickets for them. And I had hardly heard them. Then took out my pen and ink and started some writing. Ink spilled all over my new stockings. The children particularly noisy. Joanna nagging all day, my eye bad, discovered a skin irritation on my arm.

Well the sun is shining. It's a lovely summer day full of transparent clear light, and Horace has just finished his preface to William Carlos Williams' *In the American Grain* (New Directions edition) and it's a fine piece of writing— one of Horace's best critical pieces. This does cheer me up.

August 16, Wednesday, aboard U.S.S. American Banker

Left for Europe on the eleventh—a hot day. Helen McMaster and my brother Max seeing us off. Excited and trembling with joy. Even Horace worn out with last-minute work at Columbia lightened up as the boat came in view. We shall never get over the delight, the joy of traveling.

A pleasant crowd on boat—mostly older people of moderate means, a South African missionary, a number of English people coming home after a holiday in the states. Mary Goodyear very sweet and serious. Find it difficult to mix—would like to but feel an invisible wall rising—think it due to physical cause, pressure in my head, nausea. Besides, one of my nightmares happened, one of those things one has bad dreams about. My front teeth loosened again and I shall have to see a dentist the moment I arrive. I feel so self-conscious. Little Pat and Jo are having a grand time, Joanna joining in the deck sports of the younger set, and little Pat, who has become a bosom pal of the head steward, serves the tea in the social room at four every afternoon, very gay, jaunty and smiling, a small sailor hat tipped over his ear.

The weather the first few days was magnificent. In the evening thick dark clouds studded with stars. The North Star and the Great Dipper. Then wild flashes of pale light running up into the sky, slowly fading out in a rainbow iridescence. The Northern Lights.

Reading Frazer's *The Golden Bough*, which is a delight—one of the few books that should be boxed in gold and iron and preserved forever against another dark ages. When all is lost this book may well be rediscovered to bring real wisdom, tolerance and true religion again in a new Renaissance. Grateful to dear Jim Putnam of Macmillan for sending this book to me as a gift just when we boarded the ship. It suddenly dawned on me that he is really a friend of mine, that he has a real kindness for me, that he wishes me well. I had begun to think that I had no friends at all.

This is one of the great experiences of my life. Europe again! And yet I feel jumpy—an inner lack of harmony—far away from that source of simplicity and tranquillity in which I can think and write.

August 17, Thursday

The deck steward rosy cheeked, brown eyed, squat, solid looking. Works from morning to night. Humorous and tender with the children, gives them little gifts. Something of that deep pathos of the poor who work endlessly for so little pay, and yet seem contented and keep the springs of human dignity and warmth and natural kindness running. That quality is a gift like poetry, music, religion, physical strength, great beauty.

The stewardess sitting pensively in her little cubby hole of a room. Not the reading sort, nor the sewing sort either. Seems to have little to do. She's a large, white-haired elderly woman in the late fifties or early sixties. Childish rosy face. Can't get chummy with passengers and there are no other women working on the boat. It must be a dull life.

Comiseration overheard at the bar. "And so he got a cablegram to Paris saying, "Come home to New York at once. You're pissing a fortune away." Loud laughter! The teller of the story a pretty, young, dark-eyed Jewish girl, very exotically dressed, her listeners two young Englishmen and an effeminate Italian boy who says he writes plays and lives in London.

September 30, Saturday (returned September 24th Sunday, a week ago, on the American Farmer)

Beginning of Account of Trip to England

The whole world has changed since we came back from the European nightmare.

Warnings before we arrived in England. The German radio stations that seemed to overpower all the other broadcasts just before we reached land. Mary Goodyear frightened, saying, "This is what happened just before the Spanish war began." The young Scotch poet Stuart Ian Jack, moody, silent, sensitive, who sat in a corner forever reading Tolstoi. The wealthy American woman bridge playing, kittenish, fortyish, who made continual advances to him. Her set, who resented his aloofness. Here was a much needed extra man, young, attractive, obviously wealthy, well-educated, avoiding their set— mooning by himself. Their sadistic teasing of him. His wincing whenever war was mentioned, his obvious fear of returning to England. Kept throwing things overboard, books, underwear, boxes. His saying to Horace, "I write poetry but am a very very obscure poet. I have published nothing." Played shuffleboard with Joanna (whom everybody, even this shy young man, admired). Joanna won, and his expression as he left the game. In the bar the next evening the predatory female who suddenly called to him as he came into the bar. "O Mr. Auden have you been out looking at the moonshine." His look of bewilderment and desperation. No one saw him again. He must have jumped overboard right then—when he left the bar. They found $1,000 in American money on his bed which he had refused to change into pounds. Scotland Yard met us all at the boat—much to little Pat's delight. "Oh boy, oh boy, oh boy. I've always wanted to shake hands with Scotland Yard." We arrived in England, dear Maud Stevens [children's nanny on previous trip in 1934] meeting us at the boat station in London.

The descent into the Inferno

We went to our old lodgings on Primrose Hill, 138 King Henry's Road, where Bertha Hawkins [the landlady], looking not older but thinner, frailer, met us. The street seemed dingier, an atmosphere of trouble and unrest everywhere. We hadn't realized the tension and fear that the people had lived in since the Munich pact. Nothing but gloomy talk of war. No one felt that war could be avoided. People seemed shabbier and the atmosphere at the local pub (the Prince Consort) tense. A girl (always at the pub) in a red jacket (accompanied by a dog) who played an accordion to which the dog danced. People watching solemnly. Great poverty everywhere as compared to 1934. Shops empty, people said, due to the war scare and uncertainty. Went to a dentist in an odd district called the Crown and Crecklewood. The dentist a young Scotchman, quick and intelligent, asking us wistful questions about America. The bright soft skies, fine weather and sense of something hanging over us, dim and threatening. Loneliness—no letters from the States—English friends away in the country. Frantic letters from Dorothy Richardson,* saying she didn't dare leave Cornwall. Rumors of Louis MacNeice trying desperately to get a job in the U.S., of Edith Sitwell hiding all her manuscripts in a vault in Cornwall, of publishers stopping all contracts. The soldiers everywhere, drilling on Primrose Hill, the largest anti-aircraft guns imaginable there, dugouts and air-raid shelters everywhere. Overheard: "We were unprepared last year but we're ready now."

Beautiful, really remarkably beautiful clothes for men and boys in the windows of shops. Horace said, "Tailoring is the last English art." Shopkeepers saying to us, "You Americans are really reckless to have come over this year." We hadn't realized this before. We went to a restaurant in Bloomsbury with the Goodyears and then attempted to go into the British Museum. Policemen at the door stopped us, and large vans were at the door collecting the art treasures and moving them away. A group of school children standing open-mouthed, looking at the vans. Joanna very disappointed because she had wanted to see the Egyptian room. I bought her a small bust of Nefertiti as a consolation prize, and when I came home I found the children playing "British Museum." Pat aimed his Woolworth camera at Nefertiti and Jo would hide the statuette in a small wagon saying, "The art treasures must be protected."

Dined a number of times at the Café Royale, the best restaurant I've ever been in. Marvelous food. Horrified at the small children employed there.

A pleasant visit with J. Hampson who arranged a breakfast date with Horace, himself and E. M. Forster! Alas, it was never kept. One of our big disappointments. We had a very pleasant visit with Robert Herring of *Life and Letters,* who has one of the attractive little houses in Cheyne Row, Chelsea. Herring a male beauty, about thirty-five, witty and warmhearted and graceful. He said he had put up a lot of German refugees in his place but had grown disillusioned with them and was now keeping a number of Welsh miners—sim-

ple, uneducated, nice. Hampson also warned us not to be surprised if at
Forster's house we would run into Forster's closest friend—a policeman! Uneducated but simple and nice! Such a sophisticated passion for nice simplicity.
Another pleasant meeting with Ruth Pitter, a poet I admire very much, in her
home on old Church St. near Cheyne Row.

A lovely old eighteenth-century house, one of the few houses I've been in
of English intellectuals where the personality and quality of the writer is reflected in the surroundings. A lovely drawing room full of warm old furniture.
Predominating in the room a life-size portrait of a child—late seventeenth-
century, artist unknown—a little girl dressed in rose-satin lilyish draperies, a
wreath of roses in her dark hair, a lamb at her side, a golf stick in one hand, a
fine landscape in the background. Pitter said she picked it up in a secondhand
shop in London for eight shillings—in bad condition. [She] varnished, re-
paired and framed the canvas and says that Sir William Rothenstein and others
have made her large offers for it. She showed us her garden and her workshop
in the basement where she employs twelve girls from the Slade School in her
shop where she paints trays, china bowls, boxes, etc., supplying gift shops in
England and the colonies. I admired one tray which pleased her and she insisted on giving it to me. It happened to be her own work. Her business part-
ner, a pleasant red-haired Irish woman named Miss O'Hara or O'Mara, was
nice to know. I felt blue realizing that here were friends I could have learned
to love—and we lived so far apart! Horace and I made a dinner appointment
with Miss O'Mara and Pitter. We were to go to Bath for a short weekend and
then return and visit with them, but then—Satan broke loose. Pitter is a tall
handsome woman, witty and graceful, chestnut hair cut in a fringe on her
forehead, smartly dressed.

Bath

We arrived in Bath on a Thursday with the children and were enchanted
with it. We spent an idyllic day just sightseeing—the Roman Baths, the lovely
architecture, the discreetly elegant shops, the eighteenth-century houses on
the Circus (magnificent), a mixture of classic grandeur and simplicity, and full
of historical associations. Before returning to our hotel (the Fernley) a nice
old-fashioned hotel, we admired the Pump Room, the assembly rooms where
Beau Nash and the eighteenth century still seem to be alive, and had the most
delicious tea and scones at Forts', the historic confectionery shop. The next

day we decided to visit the little town of Bathampton to see the old churchyard where members of Major André's family are buried and to view the countryside which I've heard was very beautiful.

Bathampton Idyll and World Nightmare

We walked out into the beautiful Somerset countryside on a Saturday.
Lovely clear weather, the grass rolling with the softest greenness, the fat rich
luxuriant trees with centuries of vigor and ripeness in them—trees that had
been loved, watched, tended by human beings for thousands of years, not like
our trees that look as if they had sprung up raw, thin, sharp green, in lonely
wildness. Lambs grazing in the pasture. Some pink and white little English
children on bicycles. The old Bathampton churchyard where the dead seem
almost as peaceful and reserved and quiet as they must have been in the old
eighteenth-century houses on the Circus or the Crescent in Bath or the old
houses near the Somerset Hills. The eighteenth-century and the twentieth-
century graves melting onto one. Saw the tomb, or rather tombs, I had
wanted to see—the three André sisters and mother who lived into an incredible old age, one of them far into the 1840s. Also the brother, Sir William
Lewis André, who died comparatively young. So did the father. One of those
families where the men die young, the women live on forever. Tombs in a se-
cluded corner in two adjoining vaults, amazingly well kept, the lettering fresh
and sharp. The two sisters who died last in another large brown vault (white
once?) in a very shady corner. I pushed some weeds aside to read the names—
Louisa Catherine who died in the late 1830s, Mary Hannah who lived into
the 1840s.

The strange reticent lovely house on the Circus, elegant, reserved. Tradition says the windows were always darkened. The money probably a result of
their brother's death. They carried their eighteenth-century culture into the
nineteenth and their reticence shines from their tombs. The Trevalyan family
have letters and some secrets—pictures, miniatures, etc. have occasionally
shown up in auction rooms, one in Tunbridge Wells. But there was a letter
they had which I would have given worlds to see—and a picture of the mother
by Hogarth was known to be in existence and may still show up in an art
gallery marked "subject unknown." I had once wanted to do a book on André
but couldn't. For all his romance and tragedy he was too slight a figure.

We found a tea garden at Bathampton near a weir where a black swan and a small fat white one sailed, and we ordered tea and jam and scones while the children ordered Coca-Colas. The radio was going on the porch and we fought off wasps and looked at the weir and the swans and the Constable landscape and tried to listen.

News of Chamberlain's ultimatum to Germany, and the proprietor said to us, "You Americans ought to get in touch with your consul at once. This looks like war." And we agreed with him and felt very troubled.

We found out that there was an American consul at Bristol and made up our minds to go to him the next day. Meanwhile Horace decided that the children and I ought to stay at Bath and he would run down to London first and get our trunks. We walked through the fresh smelling lane to get our bus. On the way we caught a glimpse of an Elizabethan manor house with the greenest smoothest lawns and the highest warmest flowers—a garden that seems to blend in with the soft skies, the rich trees, the old churchyard. My respect for Constable as a landscape painter went up tremendously. If he is a minor painter, it's because the English landscape has the quality of Greek or English minor lyric poetry—minor if you wish, but perfect—finished—wonderful of its kind. Perhaps the French landscape has some of the grandeur and classical beauty of Claude Lorrain and Nicholas Poussin.

We caught the train back to Bath and found everyone listening to the radio with troubled tense faces. Horace made an appointment with the American consul at Bristol by phone. For the children's sake we felt we ought to go home as soon as possible.

The American Consul and Bristol

The next morning we went down by bus to Bristol, one of the ugliest cities we had ever seen. The American Consulate is in a large business building. When I saw the American flag large as life waving outside the window I felt a wave of patriotism. Little Pat gave a smart salute as we walked in and the lift boy looked at us and said, "American Consulate—third floor," as we stepped in. "Gosh how did he know we were Americans?" said Joanna.

The American consul, Roy P. Baker, a large fat Tammany Hall Babbitt, greeted us curtly. He knew nothing about ships. When we told him how much money we had with us he said, "That's too little money. What are you going to do?" All he could advise us to do was to go to a place called Weston-Super-

Mare, where an American evacuation committee was in session. He told us to leave all baggage behind but a suitcase or two, to carry tinned food with us (as there was likely to be a food shortage) and not to appear before him again. When Horace told him that he had to go to London to get our clothes, pack his trunks and pay our landlady, he said, "I won't be responsible for your life if you go to London. War is war." We said gloomily that we knew it was and left. As we left we saw a number of fat prosperous Americans of the consul's type enter the room, and he greeted them effusively and started talking about boats. H. wondered if he had expected a bribe from us, especially as Thomas Cook told us that [there] were a number of American ships sailing that week, but that one couldn't leave without a permit from the American consul. We felt very blue on our trip back to Bath and H. said, "I must go back to London and get our things." This he prepared to do and he set out that afternoon. I felt very worried as he went out from Bath; train schedules were disrupted, everything seemed in disorder, a terrific gloom and strain on all faces.

I went back to the hotel and listened to the radio. Chamberlain's speech—war declared—then the King's speech. I became frantic with fear for Horace in London. We knew no other Americans and our landlady told us that all aliens would have to report to the police. That evening waiting for Horace we discovered a stranded American girl who had been sent on by the American Consulate in London to Bath because it was a safe place. We greeted her, the children and I with joy, since we could join our bewilderment together. Meanwhile little Pat and I went down to meet the trains coming in from London at the Bath station and found crowds there waiting for women and children who were being evacuated from London. The evacuees came in by truckloads—truck after truck of women with very small children in their arms, then group after group of school children led by teachers—the children marching out hand in hand, gas masks slung across their shoulders, and little tickets pinned on their coats. It was a sorrowful sight and I couldn't keep from crying. The crowds sad and silent watching them. Evidently the children were being led to destinations known only to their leaders and the military.

(Note: The beauty of the English children. Decadent and delicate like the Chinese.)

Again and again little Pat and I went to the station growing more and more troubled as it became later and darker. Joanna stayed at the hotel playing cards with a family of Dutch children. They and their parents had come to England for a holiday and were now petrified because they didn't know how to get back. Their return boat had canceled sailing.

First signs of war hysteria. People taking me aside and saying, "Beware of the Dutch family. They're spies." Who knows—perhaps they thought it of us. But there was such a strong American feeling in Bath—as our landlord said, "Of course, we don't consider Americans as foreigners at all"—and the old sexton at Bathampton who said he enjoyed Americans ever so much. He had a tomb in the churchyard that he knew interested all people from the colonies—that of the first governor general of New Zealand!

After dinner Jo and I took a walk over the Pultney Bridge and found an enchanting little canal street lined with Georgian houses. Two black baby swans floating on the water and the houses surrounded by brilliant flowers, especially the plump cabbage-y looking English roses, white and red. Joanna made a pretty sketch of the scene and we returned and then I went over to the station again. This time it was quite dark but train after train was coming in with refugees from London, mostly old people and the sick. Went back to the hotel again as it started to rain and had much relief in talking to the stranded American girl [Miss Purnell], whose experience with the Bristol consul was as bad as ours. She had planned to go to Germany and had loaded up with German marks. The hotel became more crowded and I more and more troubled till suddenly at about ten in the evening (I had let the children stay up as late as they wished) I heard Joanna call "Daddy" and then I heard Pat shout "O Daddy" and everybody looked up and brightened for a while and forgot the radio at the sight of the children, their daddy and their joy at seeing him!

The next morning was a lovely fresh day. We fed the pigeons at the exquisite carved door of the old Bath Abbey and then walked to the police station and had the children and ourselves fitted with gas masks. The officer in charge a civilized charming person who had been through the last war (and an intelligent, sensitive humane Englishman is as fine a creature as anyone can wish to meet). He begged us to return the gas masks—and not bring them home as souvenirs as so many Americans had done, and I blushed for shame and said we weren't that kind of people.

Walked into the hotel again. The streets alive with soldiers on the quaint streets near the old church, marching in little groups, silent, watched by silent uncheering crowds. Horace said, "This is not a people's war."

Then in the hotel, growing more and more crowded with refugees from London, we sat down to listen to the radio again. There was never any news, or so it seemed. And there for the first time we heard about the *Athenia!* I looked at the children running around so gaily and my heart went weak and sick. Why had I exposed them to such dangers! D. P., the American girl, said, "Oh how can we get back?" And the sea (I have always feared the sea) seemed vast—endless, armed with teeth, millions of miles away from home—and America an oasis, a dream Paradise that we might never see again. We sat down in the lounge and wrote impassioned letters to Ambassador Kennedy, the consul at Bristol, and Commander Bailey who was in charge of the evacuations of Americans at Weston-Super-Mare. Weston-Super-Mare we had heard was a nightmare of a place and we decided to stay on till we heard from our letters.

We paid another visit to Bathampton with Purnell, our gas masks slung over our shoulders. The sun was shining on the very green grass and the little crooked lanes seemed bathed in liquid gold and gave an airy brightness to the old houses. The churchyard was gay with flowers. We had tea again at the tea garden near the weir. But we were too worried to enjoy anything. And when we came back to Bath our landlord met us and told us that the hotel had been commandeered by the admiralty as had all the hotels and large private houses. When we told him that we were unable to cash our travelers' check he said, "Well nothing matters now. This hotel has been my home for the last thirty-five years and I don't know where to go myself." And he insisted on lending us a pound.

We held a consultation and decided to go to Weston-Super-Mare late that afternoon since it seemed the only way and the only place where we could get information about ships sailing for home—and where there was a chance of getting back to the U.S. Again we packed our two suitcases (and we were beginning to get the shabby look of people who travel incessantly) and started at noon, an endless long ride, for the trains went slowly and uncertainly. It grew darker and darker and due to the blackout we soon found ourselves riding through pitch-dark landscapes. The children grew tired, dusty and sleepy and we felt as if we had been caught in a nightmare, and that we had nothing but the American passports between us and utter negation. At last a faint blue light and the conductor called "Weston-Super-Mare"—surely one of the ugliest towns in the world. Smelling of drains, an English version of Atlantic City plus Coney Island, but squalid, a huge beach front where the tide came up in long waves of mud. Streets crowded with evacuated women and children from the London slums. One large rococo hotel where the American Evacuation Committee had its headquarters. A large America flag flying at the entrance like a message of hope to us as we entered at once and prepared to register.

Into a long darkened room—once the ballroom of the Grand Atlantic Hotel—we entered and were met by Commander Bailey, U.S.N. retired, who turned out to be a very youthful looking person with gray hair, tall, erect, courteous and really kind—the first kind official we met. He filled us with hope and confidence, assured us that we would get a boat soon, and got us in touch with the U.S. Lines—and our boat, the *American Banker.*

Americans were coming in very slowly. We met a few—a group of stranded vaudeville actors including a midget struck my attention. I talked to one of them, a very Broadway-Jewish type with a shrill effeminate voice who was in a state of hysteria and kept referring to himself and the midget as "us artists."

"The American government is letting us die like rats in a hole. Why don't they convoy us?" (The announcement had just come out that American ships would not be convoyed.) "Everyone knows the Germans hate us and wouldn't mind sinking our ships." The midget—about the size of a five-year-old, peroxide-blonde marcelled hair, heavily rouged, dressed in an imitation fur cape, very high heels—kept chewing gum (where she got it in England I don't know) and shaking her head vigorously. Joanna took my arm and said, "Get away from that horrible crowd or people will think you belong to them." And I could see that Miss P. was beginning to look upon me as an undesirable social acquaintance since I didn't know that these were people to be snubbed at once. A crowd of wealthy (obviously wealthy) Southerners came in, two smartly dressed girls with a very well-turned-out mama, the pretty-pretty faded face and the vacuous clear blue eyes of one who has always had a high opinion of herself and is used to being deferred to. She swept by and ignored the stranded vaudevillians with such an ostentatious ignoring that I felt a little frightened myself and found myself moving away—after all there were the children—I wanted to get home—Horace—and I became conscious of my high cheek bones, my obviously foreign and un-American appearance, my shabby clothes. "They sure treat us as if we were dirt," wailed the midget—and I felt angry at everybody, including the Southerners, Miss Purnell, Joanna, myself.

We then started to look for rooms—row after row of hideous lodging houses—and O such smells! Found one hotel that was clean but expensive, a flashy crowd of people there. We had an unpleasant experience in another hotel and found a foul lodging house, dark, dirty, smelling everywhere—even the soap smelled of carbolic; the sheets were gray—and since we were the only lodgers except for a funny looking little old man (who turned out to be pathetic and decent, but looked like a Hitchcock villain), I found myself unable to sleep—or to keep the children clean—especially as they would run to the beach and would get their socks covered with mud.

We discovered that Weston was the headquarters for the R.A.F.—and an evacuation place for troops to France and other places.

Noted the poor physique of the soldiers. Whether the English are actually smaller than the Americans or whether generations of slum life is beginning to be felt I don't know. But Americans of the same class that comprises the rank and file of the British army are taller and healthier looking.

We explored the town—growing gloomier and gloomier. It was I heard a favorite resort of the Welsh. But I suppose the Welsh don't know any better. Shoddy shops—no charm—or architecture or attractive prospect.

We discovered at last a pleasant enough hotel run by a nephew of Sir Arthur Quiller Couch who was courteous and kind and didn't rob us. And we resigned ourselves to waiting till our ship came in. No one knew anything of ship sailings. Every sailing schedule was confused and we were told that all ship sailings were kept secret anyway, which sounded sinister to say the least.

Meanwhile, Pat was very happy. He had picked up a darling little American girl about his age, Joan Powers, the daughter of an Irish American engineer who had a job in London and a very attractive Italian American mother, very smart and Mrs. Simpsonish, who shocked the Victorian dowagers who seemed to live in our hotel lounge. There they knitted, gossiped and listened gloomily to such war news as the radio gave them. (Overheard one day a discussion on the recall of the Duke and Duchess of Windsor.) Said one of the dowagers—wife of a clergyman I discovered—"If her (the D. of W.) own country won't have her, I see no reason why we should put up with her." The censorship, the lack of news, was driving us all into nervous panic and the blackouts seemed to have a dreadful effect on the morale of the people. The gloomy faces hovering around the radio.

One fine formal garden near the post office at Weston—the only beauty spot in town. The roses seemed thicker. They had a sort of human homemade look that our roses don't have. The American roses appear to have slipped down from the skies—finished, perfect. They seem to have nothing to do with anything on earth. They are inhuman in their beauty.

A waxwork museum in Weston that announced the following new attractions: the Right Honorable Neville Chamberlain, Hitler, Mussolini, Snow White and the Seven Dwarfs.

Spent our time at the American Committee asking for ship news. Little Pat very restless, would run up and down the grand ballroom turning somersaults and singing, much to some people's annoyance. Joanna very helpful and efficient.

I decided since we were running short of money to wire the Macmillan Company for money. We were told that cables to America were running slowly and inefficiently and Miss Purnell who had wired for money to Paris had waited two weeks and had had no answer.

We went to a cable office and were carefully inspected and interviewed by two Scotland Yard men, who were nice and friendly when we showed our American passports. They helped us frame the cable which we addressed to our friend Jim Putnam. "Ship delayed. Please forward $100 of royalties due me." The man who sent the cable said I could have one word more, so I wrote, "Cheerio." I addressed the letter to James Putnam, 60 Fifth Ave. To save words I didn't mention the Macmillan Co.

Three days later I went to Floyd's Bank and asked (rather hopelessly) if any answer had been received to my cable. The bank clerk assured me that three days were now insufficient to get a reply from the states. He said, "There are thousands of Americans who have waited for answers from their cables for weeks." However, he decided to look anyway, and came back waving a long envelope. He was fearfully surprised and I was an object of envy to all the waiting Americans. There was my check! I showed my identification papers, signed my name and H. and I left in triumph! We got back to the American Committee at the Grand Hotel. Commander Bailey met us with excitement and said that our boat, the *American Banker* had been delayed again but another U.S.S. line boat had just come in, the *American Farmer,* and would sail the next day. He thought he could get us on it in time. We asked if he could take care of Miss Purnell too—and he found a place for her. We embraced the children, ran home quickly, packed, and shipped our passports with a consular attaché who was to rush to Bristol and get our exit permit. We were to meet him at the railroad station at 6:00 P.M., grab a taxi, rush to the railroad station, which had a train leaving for London at 6:35, ride almost all night to London, get a hotel near the Paddington Station, and catch our boat train to Tilbury Docks in the morning. This we did, marking time with the nervous speed of a Hitchcock movie. We got into London at 11:30 at night through the dark, nightmarish, pitch-dark blackout. No signs of a city. We seemed to be living in an insane world. Nothing visible. Our taxi (how I admired the cabman!) seemed to drive on a black cloud. We stumbled out at last and a porter with a small flashlight came and directed us to the Hotel Royal in Bloomsbury—a large gloomy establishment that once must have had an air of genial dignity and conservative comfort.

Oh, I must tell the aftermath of our cable story. When we returned to New York City we telephoned and thanked Jim Putnam. He acted strangely and said he wished to see us at once. He called on us and said, "Do you know we never got that cable!" No trace of it anywhere—though he made an investigation throughout the firm. Nobody had seen a cable and my royalties were untouched! So far we haven't found out a thing about the mysterious $100! It gives me sleepless nights. Whom have I to thank? [Note added later: "Received letter two months later from S. Brett, president of Macmillan, saying he sent it."]

U.S.S. American Farmer. *Took boat September 15, 1939, Friday.*

On the day we were to catch the boat we walked out of our hotel into the Bloomsbury shopping center to buy a few warm clothes for ourselves to wear on the boat. Sometime in the blackout someone must have gone around with poster-stickers, for we found placards placed on walls, shop windows, doors, "Moseley will bring you peace." "Vote for Moseley." A few people walking to work. The air gray and cool. An early autumnal sadness over all. Shops all sandbagged. We bought some warm jerseys and stockings for the children, and the shopkeepers seemed to be surprised that we were still there. "I thought all Americans had gone." They all effusively wished us a safe voyage and I got to feeling jittery.

It cheered me up when we got to the boat and saw so many women with small children. Somehow I felt I wasn't alone in my worries which isn't I suppose the noblest way to gain comfort, but is I think human nature. "Misery loves company" is folk wisdom. Horace said his only fear was that of air raids, of destruction suddenly coming out of the air, dismembering or crippling you. My fear was of going on the water, of being torpedoed, of exposing the children to the horrors endured on the *Athenia*.

The boat which could have held only eighty passengers with comfort carried before the voyage was over almost two hundred passengers—almost all Americans—a few English and Canadian, who insisted on going on American boats for safety; some *Athenia* survivors consisting of two German refugees (men) who looked haunted, and a Canadian woman who spent much of the time on the boat in a state of hysteria.

When we came on the boat at Tilbury and saw the large American flag painted on the side we almost cheered for joy, a lightness came over my spirit. It seemed almost impossible to believe that this boat was carrying us away from terror, nightmare—continual nervous strain! In the harbor I saw a large boat carrying the Soviet flag. And H. said it proved that Russia was still friendly to England. The dock was crowded with ships of all nations. And it gave me a feeling of confidence for it proved (or so it seemed) that England was still the guardian of the waters and would keep our route clear from mines and submarines. The two English ships convoyed us out of the harbor, sailing with us till night time. Then our ship became suddenly all ablaze with lights, while the English boats as suddenly darkened and turned back quickly—a weird sight. Somebody said that the English had taken us out of the danger zone, and everybody on the boat became gay, excited, a little hysterical.

A young man (a returning Rhodes scholar) rushed into the bar shouting, "California here I come—maybe." Everybody laughed and cheered as another of the Rhodes scholars groups (there were fourteen) ordered American cigarettes, received some free matches and shouted, "Free matches! Three cheers for the U.S.A." An amazing gush of patriotism everywhere. Discomfort and Excitement and Rumors.

Our cabin was so small that only one of us could dress with comfort. But thanks to our reservation (a partial transfer from the *American Banker*) we had more conveniences than most. Two days of tension when we all reported for life belt drills and slept with our life belts under our pillows. The social hall was turned into a dormitory for the Rhodes scholars. The stables formerly used for transporting horses to and from Europe were converted to space for bunks. Even the deck space was used for sleeping. There was hardly a place to turn around. I described it to Horace afterwards like being locked up in a crowded New York subway for ten days.

A few days of storm when the boat rocked like a tub and we sat crowded together in a little hall near the dining room. When we were three days out at sea a rumor spread around the boat that (1) a submarine had been sighted, (2) that the captain of our boat, Pedersen, had received a message from a submarine, (3) that our boat had received an S.O.S.! requesting us to go to the rescue of a torpedoed English ship. All three rumors strangely enough were true. About 1:30 our ship began to turn from its course and about 2:30 we sighted the submarine, flat and gray, standing still. It drew up to our boat and, though I couldn't see for the crowd on the lower deck, I understood that the U-boat commander, an elderly man with a beard, told us in perfect English that there were lifeboats containing British sailors coming towards us and indicated the directions. Soon we saw the lifeboats drifting toward us. And our ship drew close to them and took in the survivors of the English boats—very young most of them seemed and partially dressed. One of them had a coat tied around his middle. Another kid who didn't look a day over sixteen had one shoe on. The captain and five officers of the boat had been killed in the first shelling of the ship—a freighter carrying sugar from Cuba to England, called the *Kafirstan*. While we were watching the rescue, the submarine turned to go when suddenly we heard a whirring sound and a plane appeared. For a while, I grabbed the children terrified when somebody shouted, "It's a British plane!" And we all found ourselves cheering frantically. The pilot flew to the submarine, which turned and fired, but the plane dropped one bomb after another, a dull, muffled heavy sound. We saw smoke come up after each shot, and the water seemed to be covered with wreckage, floating in from the shattered *Kafirstan* we were told. Then we saw the plane fly again, pointing toward something, and we saw another lifeboat filled with men. Meanwhile the submarine seemed to pitch and submerge. We saw a cloud of pitch and oil and smoke, and that was all! Whether the submarine was sunk or not I don't know. Joanna, who had borrowed binoculars, insisted that it had! We saw the pilot of the British plane wave to us—and disappear—and again we all found ourselves cheering. The sentiment on the boat was overwhelmingly pro-Ally—as American sentiment usually is. One of the Rhodes scholars said gloomily that he felt sorry for the poor fellows trapped on the submarine—on which a tall gray-haired man, a judge from Utah who looked like William Jennings Bryan, turned on him and said, "You talk like a German spy"—a remark which led to a feud between the old judge and the Rhodes scholars that lasted for the rest of the trip.

The story of the *Kafirstan* survivors.

They said that for about three days they had felt that they were being pursued and so had taken a changed route. On the third day (in the morning) a submarine suddenly appeared and first fired a shot against the *Kafirstan's* sides and killed six men. The ship then stopped. The submarine commander drew close to them and said in perfect English, "I'm sorry to do this gentlemen, but this is war. I have no quarrel with the English sailor." He then gave them forty minutes to get to the lifeboats and waited till our ship came close! Then the British plane must have surprised them. As soon as the men went into the lifeboats the sub commander torpedoed the *Kafirstan*. The crew of the *Kafirstan* became a great addition to our boat. When the *American Farmer* cook collapsed from overwork, the *Kafirstan* cook took over (awful English cooking!) but we were grateful. The captain of the *Kafirstan,* a Captain Busby (a charming Conradish sailor), had once served on the American lines and relieved our captain from time to time. The crew helped our overworked crew. When another American ship on the way to England offered to take them back, Captain Busby refused, saying his men had suffered a shock and he wanted them to have a little holiday and rest in New York before they returned.

Note: a young officer of the *Kafirstan*, about nineteen, whose seriousness, dignity and responsible attitude to his men impressed me—he made the Rhodes scholars (many of whom were older than he) seem like silly, immature children.

The fear of submarines somehow went after this episode. I understand that the real danger to American ships were not submarines but mines, and that the English had been instructing our captain by wireless how to avoid them.

Wild rumors all over the boat. The *Mauritania* and *Aquitaine* had been sunk, the Poles had driven out the Germans, South America was overrun by German spies, and at last a rumor that I couldn't bear to believe—that the Russians had invaded poor stricken Poland! This seemed like the end of the world. The war took on a new aspect. The English on the boat sat with their heads in their hands. Well, I decided, this is only what I've suspected and feared for a long time. Everything that I heard of Russia seemed strangely like the things I had heard of the Czarist regime—as a child. I remembered how mad and foolish the patriots of the last war sounded in retrospect. Yet try as I would, I couldn't feel myself neutral. It seems to me that it is a war between two ways of life—and that I can't think of the Nazi-Communist combination without fear, dread—a one-party system is fatal to the human spirit. I feel too partisan to go on. I shall give myself a chance to let prejudices subside. Otherwise I can't judge clearly.

Heard a mad German broadcast on the boat eulogizing Stalin, saying that the Germans need not fear the U.S. because the Latin American republics had taken advantage of industrial unrest in the U.S. and had started marching into Florida. A wild appeal to the Irish asking them never to forget Roger Casement, "a great English Baron, who loved Ireland and was (poisoned!!) by the British government." I asked the German refugee who was getting us the German stations whether all German news was like that—and he said yes. No person with any education or intelligence listens to them. They (the radio people) depend on the prejudices, ignorance and confusion of the ordinary person.

An English engineer said that the Romanian premier was shot by a British agent and as an excuse to round up the Romanian fascists. Later (twelve hours later) I heard a German broadcast that said the same thing.

A Romanian on board ship went wild with joy at a rumor that King Carol had been killed! At this news of the iron guard executions he said, "All my friends are killed." Wonder what he was doing or going to do in the U.S.A.? Certainly there was something strange about many people on the boat. But then war breeds fear, distrust, suspicion.

Home!!!!

At last on a Sunday, bright with sunshine, we arrived. The hard, sharp American sunlight, the navy-blue waters, turning in the light to the color of steel.

Reporters flocking on board our boat and the rush for publicity by the unlikeliest people. The judge from Utah posing in a gas mask! The young couple with the five-months baby posing against a lifesaving belt, the baby enveloped in a life belt. The Rhodes scholars rushing forward with snapshots of the submarine and a confidential account of what really happened! Horace and I ducked, took the children by the hand, feeling sad and lonely—no one knew we were arriving—and after the customs rushed home. A wave of nostalgia for the sadness, tension, smallness of England—a feeling that this hard, bright, rich beautiful city had no place for me. We talked to our taxi driver. He said that everybody was pro-Ally here but nobody wants war! This I found quite correct.

No letters of any importance, but found a few friends were concerned over our absence—X not one of them.

Discovered that a Sunnyside neighbor of ours, Dr. Wilkes, had lost his wife and eight-year-old boy on the *Athenia!*

End of Section on Trip to England

October [?]

Sick and mounting terror now that it was all over. Saw Robert and Eleanor Fitzgerald, Helen McMaster, Norman Pearson, who talked eagerly about the war. All sympathetic to the Allies. But the war seems remote to them.

Our trunks are being sent on from Europe and, though nearly a month and a half has passed, we've heard nothing of them. All our winter clothes. It makes me angry because we let our trunks be sent on because of the American consul at Bristol. The devil take him!

October 26, Thursday

Going over my manuscript—with dissatisfaction and worry. It's not good enough. It must be stronger and better or I'm lost.

Dinner at the new apartment of the James Putnams. I had on a pretty new dress and was gay and vivacious. Jim kept exclaiming over and over again how attractive and charming I'd been, the life of the party, etc.—it made me angry. I think he had made up his mind that I wouldn't be good for a conventional dinner party! He doesn't know that I really like people. And besides what honor is it in having charmed his stupid guests. I've met better and cleverer people—and they liked me too. (This is a childish entry but Jim P. did get me quite mad, though of course I didn't let him know it.)

November 4

Clear, cool day when the air seems swept by the winds into a crystalline purity. The thin trees half withered, half dry gold and fading crimson. Grant's Tomb recently whitewashed, a little pavilion near it facing the river and on the other side the white porch of the Claremont Inn. Shining, winding off, the street and, like a bright whip, the swift curve of river, a small but precious and beautiful glimpse of something mobile and alive in the dreamy air.

Grateful for Craven's beautiful book of reproductions of famous paintings. Of course his choice of modern Americans leaves much to be desired. Grant Wood seems so static and journalistic and shallow. Thomas Hart Benton's *Persephone* and the leering old man has something obscene and meretricious. Charles Ephraim Burchfield's landscapes miss the ultimate something. John Stuart Curry's landscapes seem to miss a final poetry. John Sloan alone moved me with his vision of life, the dark bar, the white-coated waiter, the transfiguration of an ordinary scene. He has given it an air of surrealism but of super-reality, truth magnified and made very clear. But there are some things that I look on over and over again—a Carlo Crivelli madonna with an amazing background of meticulously painted fruit; two peaches in one corner seem almost to burst with ripeness and fall before your eyes. The pretty, wry face of the madonna very curious. The whole picture has the effect of having been painted in very warm colors on a very cool metal surface.

Then among very fine things the enchanting children of Hogarth. The children seem to be about to begin the liveliest gayest conversation, and the little girl in the ruffled cap with the pink rosebuds will surely break into laughter and take up the small joke she left off 150 or so years ago. It's the gayest, the most domestic interior, Dutch and yet very English and breathing as naturally and simply as if the children are there, forever young, laughing, talking, about to begin a dance—and such honest, straight painting. But my favorite is 113, the Albert Pinkham Ryder *Forest of Arden*. It has always moved me and speaks a language that is the language of my favorite poetry. Of all American artists Ryder is the one that appeals to me the most and says the most.

November 6, Monday

A walk last night after a heavy pour of rain. The wind swept in from the water front until the very street seemed moving in a gray tumult. The sky an extraordinary color, a soft slate-colored gray interwoven with the flakiest, softest, milky-white clouds. They floated down from gray horizons over dark brown, windswept houses, the air very sharp and cold and clear.

Reading William Vaughan Moody and his set. My word, how I dislike them. His sloppy sentimental wife who had money (for a while) and went in for Californian brands of mysticism, and who kept his memory green by reading his poems out loud to young writers who, dependent on her bounty, felt they ought to like Moody. The "Ode in Time of Hesitation," the "Gloucester Moon," the one on the picture of his mother, have a sort of truncated grandeur, but it ends in rhetoric and bombast. The Percy MacKayes—the Arlington set—the nucleus of the Peterborough colony which in modern times has led to the aesthetics of H. S. Canby,* Elinor Wylie, the Benét brothers.

Funny class snobbery too—Harvard, travel, handsome houses, idealistic shallowness of the bourgeoisie and their particular conception of poverty—in spite of the vigorous lingo and "powerful" attitudes, something strangely fin-de-siècle about Moody and his poetry. I discovered that Moody, Bliss Carman, MacKaye, etc. did feed on the early Yeats. Ernest Dowson, Stephen Phillips, Frances Thompson—and I suspect [W. E.] Henley—and they all read and admired Maeterlinck. I think Moody's wife probably provided the mysticism, but I'm prejudiced against the type. Their conception of art is frightful. I remember meeting the much admired Mrs. MacDowell, whom I suspect of being the type of Mrs. M, and feeling as I did with her, as I did with Mrs. M. and the rest of the artistic, rich old ladies of her period—all friends of Peterborough habitués.

[four lines crossed out]

. . . Arlington Robinson and his awful friends—I knew some of them. But I do believe that Robinson saw through them and was not above using them for copy. But he was a first-rate poet, a really honest and profound artist. To such a man we can allow anything. Besides, like every real artist, he was frantically lonely.

"The Great Divide." "The Faith Healer." Absolute tripe and rubbish, yet a fine spirit through it all, like Harriet Monroe's *Poetry,* also of the period.

November 7, Tuesday

A bad Saturday party with Helen McMaster at the Brevoort. Such fine food, pleasant atmosphere, music. Helen and Horace talking shop. I did feel left out. Then the pain in my back and chest began (I've had it since I came back from Europe) and I couldn't see straight and though I wore my prettiest black dress—black moire with a ruffled collar and gold buttons and little paniers—and my gay red hat with the green feather—I saw myself in the mirror and I looked ill, heavy-eyed and unattractive.

Took a long walk up Fifth Avenue in a marvelous wind and then went up to Broadway and saw the most terrific theater rush we've seen since the depression. Horace says it's a sign of the new war prosperity, but like the depression these things hardly affect people in our position—except that it may make jobs more secure.

Reading Jacob Boehme's *Signature of All Things*—illuminated nonsense it seems, but full of fine, really amazing poetic images. Yeats must have read and reread this book.

Horace is going over arithmetic problems with Joanna. They seem to be having a good time, laughing and joking. She's as tall as I am now and is beginning to borrow my clothes.

My manuscript is slowly shaping up. But it's far, far from what I want it to be. And ill health and this locked-up feeling [are] beginning to shrivel me up. I can't write. How did Emily Dickinson keep going? But there were her garden walks, country walks—and no—it doesn't explain it. Still it is hard to take walks in the city—especially when I've developed a real phobia about crossing streets.

November 13, Monday

The worst bout of illness since the terrifying experience of two years ago. But then I've never really recovered from that. A good Samaritan for a few months might be a help, but there's no money for that. Of course the nervous strain of our trip to England is partially responsible, next my own foolish state of mind. By my continual depression, worry and despair I bring about the same condition that hit me so hard before. But illness causes the bad state of mind. The bad state of mind causes the illness—a vicious circle.

My temper vile. I've been brutal to poor Horace. I'm fortunate in having a friend like him, so patient, understanding, forgiving.

November 20, Monday

Sleepless nights, pain, anger and despair for it keeps me confined to the home more and more and makes of this apartment a real prison. Some kind of intestinal infection which came on me just after I left the boat.

Horace frail and preoccupied—no help.

Jim Farrell called us up after a silence of many years. Full of persecution complexes. The *New Masses* said he was an anti-Semite after he had written his book about Father Coughlin (Tommy Gallagher). The *New Republic* first denounced and then boycotted him. The *Nation* doesn't answer his letters, etc. etc. Comes to Horace as to a Father Confessor and then, when things go well, hides from the Father Confessor's stern eye. He is filled with delight at the Moscow-Berlin pact for now he can get his revenge against the Stalinists. His broad teasing does drive them mad. He has the advantage of a sense of humor. Says that Van Wyck Brooks* is cutting loose from the League of American Writers and is publishing a scorching resignation letter, saying he had been taken in. I can't sympathize with those who were "taken in." After all, anyone with common sense could see why they were being used.

Eleanor Clark, as beautiful as ever, in a black velvet dress, a yellow rose in her hair, dropped in after a party. Horace as usual succumbs to her.

Eleanor repeating a crack that her grandmother made about Barnard College. "It's a place where imitation pearls are thrown before real swine."

November 29, Wednesday

A delusion. To believe as I've always done that the truth when spoken out loud and clear always brings conviction and always in the long run prevails. No, this doesn't happen at all. People will always believe only what they want to believe, and a lie backed by the persuasion of force takes on an almost mystical element of truth.

One of my first literary parties in years. Depressing. Henry Seidel Canby with his face gray, sharp, wolfish. Isabel Patterson like a dried up malicious monkey. I don't care to name them anymore, the powers and personalities who make the New York literary scene. They're always there at the same parties and the atmosphere is always the same. And the same feelings of anger, fear, shyness, bravado always come over me. Lots of people whom we haven't seen for years. As usual Bill Benét was a pleasure, graceful, kindly, witty, no great intellect but somehow strangely removed from the malice, rottenness, of it all.

The wonderful whiteness and brilliance of the city, the buildings at night lit up with a million lights as if an artificial sun was shining through. The Drive with its clear sweep of water near wide white streets and the supernal American trees that seem to have no roots in the ground nor any relationship to human beings. They seem to have sprung straight out of the sky and I wouldn't be surprised if one day they spread their branches like wings and flew back into the air.

December 7

A cultural evening at the Yarmolinskys.* Sweet heavy wine, rich thick cake, lots of high-class music, when one would rather have talked. The customary German Jewish refugees also there. Babette grown very thin and gray. She's a very decent, just person, only one wishes they would relax, smile, go bawdy, go malicious—anything but this high, heavy seriousness. A lack of real taste somewhere. One sees it in her really highly respectable poetry where always the wrong word sets your teeth on edge. A little boat muzzling against the shore, or wafts of honey blowing across the air, or petal drift of stone, or rhymes where roof rhymes with opéra-bouffe. When she tries to be witty, light, and graceful, as in a poem to little Alison Mumford, she becomes embarrassing.

> Her mother's name is Truth alone
> Her dad's is iron's way with stone.
> . . . .

A turn, a book, a rune
To welcome excellent Alison.

This is from memory, but my memory is rather good and I'm not far wrong.

Literary parties: one for Oliver La Farge. Drinks give me a tummy ache, and the people frighten or make me angry. A good talk with Peter Munro Jack, critic of poetry for the *New York Times*. Horribly cynical and brilliant and corrupt. Leonora Speyer imitating Elinor Wylie but looking much more like an expensively dressed but somewhat storm beaten Valkyrie. Rather stupid and pretentious but most grande dames are. One remembers the art collection and few literary comments made by the Vanderbilt family—or for that matter by the House of Windsor. A soft sentimental streak somewhere. Said she hated Germany now and had renounced her villa in the Black Forest. Since the war, even the Black Forest was hateful to her, etc. I said, "Why quarrel with the scenery?"

Rukeyser came back from Mexico. Decided she didn't like Mexico now. Didn't say why. Was very gay, witty, lots of fun. A flashing quick intelligence that's a delight. Lovely presents for all of us. I was as pleased as a child with mine, a pretty leather cigarette case and a very nicely carved Madonna of wood, the color of ivory. I hung it up on the wall for good luck. Muriel said grimly, "I knew you'd like it," with an air of saying, "I don't know anyone else who would."

Gave a lecture on Sarah Teasdale* before Horace's class yesterday noon. Terribly frightened but I kept saying to myself, "I mustn't let Horace down. I must do my share. Opportunities to help him don't come often. I'm doing this for my husband and the kiddies as they say in the police courts." Everybody says I did well. Horace was pleased and he's my severest critic. But then Teasdale is a delight. She's a born poet, that limpid music, always the right, the exquisite word, the unstudied charm that no one can learn or imitate, the quiet gradual growth of her style till in the "Fountainbleau" poem she achieved a little masterpiece. I'm sure she'll be read long after many more ambitious poets are forgotten. And she's so limited too—so narrow—and yet it is always a pleasure to read her. Her taste and tact are amazing. She can relieve a poem sometimes from banalities or foolishness by a miracle. We say, "Now, now, now—we are going to laugh." But she keeps us from it by a quick flash, a sudden turn.

1 9 4 0

To be famous and successful when one is very young is indeed the rarest, pleasantest and most dangerous gift of the Gods. Edna St. Vincent Millay a good example. I know that it would have been bad for me. But I need praise badly now and yet I feel I've gotten all I deserve—perhaps more.

Dreamed that I was watching Leslie Powell working on his portrait of the children. Pat and Jo kept laughing and fidgeting and the portrait kept growing more and more unsatisfactory. Then I saw a shadowy little boy standing in a corner. Evidently he had dressed himself in his best clothes but he had been too young to do it properly. His hair was combed down carefully but the side part was not straight. His tie was crooked. I smoothed down his hair, rearranged his tie and said, "Leslie, you must put him in the picture too." The little boy seemed more and more shadowy. He smiled shyly and eagerly. But Pat and Jo went on talking and laughing and Leslie didn't seem to notice him or hear me. "Leslie," I said, "You *must* put him in the picture." But no one heard me. As the little boy dimmed away I realized that he had never existed.

Yes, I would like to have more children. Pat and Jo are growing up so fast.

Leonie Adams and Bill Troy* had dinner with us this Tuesday. Leonie is as attractive as ever, but her hair is streaked with gray. Bill looked ill, less erect, less arrogant. He has had trouble with his eyes. Leonie is afraid to publish her book, feeling that the popular criticism of the day would be against it. (The fact is that her reception would I think be a good one.) And she has written her name among the American poets. What more can a writer ask? All Keats dared to hope was that he too would be listed among the real poets. I wish I was in a position as good as Leonie's. But I have made more enemies. I sometimes feel that if I wrote a masterpiece, no one would look at it.

Self-criticism on my manuscript. Too much softness and vagueness. More concrete images. Less music. More force. A little more ruggedness even—to relieve smoothness. Fresher subject matter (very careful with that). I should say *bolder* subject matter. Always retain purity of diction and clarity, but in retaining them avoid shallowness and facility and innocuousness. Avoid the didactic like the plague. "Take rhetoric and wring its neck." More wit. Less heavy seriousness. Less repetition of themes. Too much introversion.

January 21, Sunday

Dinner with the Selden Rodmans. Lovely and unusual apartment, modern furniture, fine view of the city from the bedroom window. Selden graceful and beautiful to look at but an insensitive heavy mind. He wore a red quilted jacket, like a British Army officer's in its color, and gold buttons, and a beaded Mexican belt. He reminded me very much of a beautiful woman who wears odd and original things that a plainer sister wouldn't dare to appear in but which in her case only displayed her beauty in novel aspect.

January 25, Thursday

A biography of Beethoven by Sullivan sent to me by Morton Zabel [*Beethoven: His Spiritual Development,* by J. W. N. Sullivan. Inscription reads: "To Horace and Marya, Companions of God, from Morton, as ever, 12–25–39"]. It looks very good. But for the first time in my life I feel as if time is too short for all the reading I want to do. So troubled about H. that I can't do my own writing. And my poems seem too smooth, too lifeless, too delicate. I want more strength, more penetration—but I must change my life. I need more love, better health, a more attractive existence. "You must change your life."

The dead, half-forgotten books of verse on the library shelves. So much labor, charm, effort *wasted* as in the collected works of Josephine Preston Peabody. She left behind a charming, foolish, exasperating journal all gush and ecstasy and sensibility of the wrong kind. There but for the grace of God was Katherine Mansfield.

January 30

H.'s day off. Either Friday or Monday we go through the art galleries for recreation, since we have so little money to spend on theater, concerts, ballets. It helps me to do my writing, sometimes clarifies or lifts or points to a poem. We saw the Ingres-David show at the Knoedler and, as always, admired and yet worried over Ingres, his firm, strong, smooth *boneless* faces and bodies. David is fine too. The danger of neoclassicism always there—the inner death. Nobody should be neoclassical while they're alive. The desire, the suggestion of perfection and clarity, yes—but not the thing itself.

Saw an exhibition of Modigliani portraits, very witty and breathtaking painting. But I felt that living in a room full of Modiglianis would drive me mad. Now one doesn't feel that way about Picasso.

Auden's new book of poems arrived. Called *Another Time*. Auden is the most talented writer of our time. Talent, cleverness, wit, ingenuity enough to make the stock in trade of a half-dozen poets. In fact one half of his brilliance, added to that unnamable something that lifts talent into no not genius (but that something real that first-rate poets have), would make a better poet than Auden. In all this display of wit, of brilliance, technical ingenuity, there is not a single finished or completely satisfactory poem. Everything is at sixes and sevens and we are left with a vague dissatisfaction, the feeling that somehow, something like a marvelous but facile *journalism* has seeped in and corrupted the poetry or rather enervated it.

February 2, Friday

L. P. came yesterday afternoon and took me to the Frick Gallery. It is not far from my home and I was astonished and ashamed that I hadn't seen this most charming and unusual collection. It has the intimate, warm air of a small provincial gallery in Europe, or as if one had made a very careful pick of some of the treasures in the London National Gallery and put them in a few rooms in a fine house. The taste in selecting these pictures is of a kind that is becoming rare indeed, not only here, but in Europe too. A conservative taste but delicate, refined, sure. There are no mistakes or so few mistakes that one hardly notices them. The portraits of Lawrence, Reynolds, Romney; the customary choices of American millionaires of the period are all there, but they are in every instance the best of their kind. I've never even in English galleries seen a better Romney than the Countess of Warwick and her two children, a better Van Dyck than the large Earl of Derby and Family. And if one has to take Lawrence seriously, his Lady Peel will do as well as any. A beautiful Hogarth portrait in a small drawing room. Some of the finest Rembrandts, that wonderful thick gold light seeping through smoky darkness—excellent examples of Vermeer and other Dutch masters. A portrait of a young man by Bronzino in olive green and gold, probably one of the finest Ingres portraits in existence. And then there are my favorite Dutch landscape painters: I would give six Van Dycks and ten Romneys for one landscape by Rysback or Hobbema or Cuyp. That rich grass and thick liquid air that seem overflowing with light, the color of honey.

Constable must have learned from them (and Constable is well represented). A few remarkable Turners and a room paneled with Fragonards as delicate and gay and fragrant as flowers, the childlike faces, the light bodies clothed in silks the color of rose petals, tea rose, yellow, pale pink, ivory-tinted with rose. It is only when one sees the Fragonards or Bouchers in their right setting, a fine eighteenth-century room with appropriate furniture, that one can realize how perfectly of their time they are, the overcivilized elegance, the beauty refined to decadence, the joyous half-sad grace of a culture that has reached its zenith.

L. P. a pleasant young man to go out with, graceful, simple, intelligent to talk to. I had the feeling of poise and assurance that I always have when out with a congenial woman friend. None of the nervous tension that a woman still young must always feel when out with a sexually attractive man who is still a stranger to her. I can understand now why intelligent wealthy women buy the type as gigolos.

February 4, Sunday

H., Joanna and I visited the Frick Gallery this afternoon. I insisted that they both see the collection with me. Horace was delighted with the magnificent Ingres, the woman in the heliotrope satin dress, and the small but brilliant David portrait near it. "You see, he said, "why people become impatient with the English portrait painters, after this." The Fragonard panels upset him. He insisted that they exuded a particular kind of corruption, and he felt that same way about the gay little room with the Boucher panels, of children. It was true that the children had something of the ageless and perverse look of midgets, but that air of corruption with the background of roses, soft sunlight and summer, that gaiety which was fixed, unforced, graceful and almost despairing was what I liked in the pictures. Another series of Boucher paintings, *The Seasons,* attracted me. H. insisted that they were on the same aesthetic level as Currier and Ives prints.

Read an article by our friend M. on contemporary poetry in which he traced a great deal of E. St. Vincent Millay's failure as a poet to her continual appearance on the lecture platforms and before the women's clubs. The sources of failure like the secret of success are not easy to discover. It is perfectly true that the lecture platforms and the clubs have not done Miss Millay any good, but then old Yeats, surely the greatest poet of our time, became the darling of the women's club and one of the most popular lecturers who ever came to this country, so I was told. Even at the end he spent his time being pampered and petted by rich old ladies, and people in London told me that Lady Dorothy Wellesley's poems gained a heightened interest in his eyes, because of her connection with the Duchy of Wellington. Sir William Rothenstein's latest book of memoirs half-confirms this. In fact Yeats broke a great many rules which we are told make for strict integrity and yet somehow remained a great poet. It was the triumph of real genius over human weakness and vanity, and yet, isn't there something a little stagey, a little posed about even the wonderful later poems of Yeats? Just when we are about to say that we have caught him, just as we are ready to expose him, just as we have put our finger on the fraud, he suddenly lifts us up and the poem carries us away into that world where only great and genuine poetry can exist.

Who was it who said of Ingres that "he was a smoldering voluptuary burdened by a stern conscience"? The same could be said of Milton, and in another way of Landor, whom Ingres so much resembles.

"That which you love with the greatest power and passion becomes the ideal of beauty which you impose on others." This was said by the painter Jean-François Millet.

I was talking to L. the English poet at a party given for him by Miss S. "Of course," he said, "Whitman is your greatest poet, perhaps your *only* poet." This infuriated me. The air of gentle condescension, combined with that complete blithe ignorance of American literature found so often in the most cultivated of Englishmen, is no longer justified. If he had attacked Whitman I would have defended him, but this irritated me. "Whitman may be our most remarkable poet," I said, "But isn't it a fact that the American and English public has always preferred Longfellow?" "Oh, no," he said. "That's impossible. Why in England Whitman has had the greatest, the most remarkable influence etc." I said that I didn't doubt it, but I had noticed a bust of Longfellow in the Abbey and I hadn't seen one of Whitman. I also insisted that he give me a list of important English poets in whom the Whitman influence was very apparent. He said he couldn't think of one at the moment—but—and then we got up quickly with a look of clear, cold dislike, and parted. I felt ashamed of myself afterward, for bad manners are never excusable. But that my irritation was justified I have no doubt.

Paul Elmer More has a good comment on one of Oscar Wilde's sonnets, one of the embarrassing confessional poems where he speaks of himself as a reed on which every passion blows. He mentions the fact that it is for those windy passions that he has given up "his ancient wisdom, and austere control." (Did he ever have them?) Commenting on the poem, More says, "This has the pathos of conscious insincerity"—a penetrating and truly witty remark.

February 12, Monday

My father called and was very touching and wistful. He spoke of his five years' service in the Russian army, which he said convinced him (we had been talking of the war with Finland) that Russia could never win a war. To explain, he offered us an anecdote. He had been on guard duty on the night Alexander III had died, and at five in the morning had received the news. He went to a higher officer and said, "Have you heard? The Tsar has just died." The officer spat on the floor and said, "Well, I won't grieve for him. May his soul go to hell." Now, said my father, "The Tsar meant nothing to me, but if officers behave like that, you can't have a good army." And, he said, "I suppose things are still the same in the Russian army." He had also served with the Russian expedition to China during the Boxer uprising.

I must go today to see a school play in which Joanna will have, as she told me, "a pretty big part." This being fathers' day at the Lincoln School, even the small children put on a play and Pat is taking part in one too. But he says, "I've got only a little part. I'm one of four mouses." His class play is called "The Meddlesome Mouse." If fathers can't come the mothers are invited to take their place. H. is at work on an essay on A. E. Housman and can't spare the time. I envy the parents who sit through those things with rapture and passionate interest. Nothing bores me as much as these juvenile performances. After my own child goes through his role, I feel like getting up and leaving. The rest is politeness and half-irritation.

February 15

Read Vernon Louis Parrington's rather sketchy book [*The Beginnings of Critical Realism in America,* 1930], and I began to feel that I was sick and tired of it all. No doubt criticism of this sort elucidates many facts, but it can't explain the real freak that genius or even talent is. So far Parrington's theories lead to a kind of high-class journalism—and to a Granville Hicks. Certainly the arts he writes about are forgotten in the heat of his argument. His attack against poor old Thomas Bailey Aldrich is so ferocious, so full of venom and hatred that one begins to wonder if perhaps there isn't something to be said in defense of him. Was Whitman a more lovable and attractive character—as a human being I mean? One reads Bailey's poems—some of them are lovely, well made—but it wasn't the ivory tower that ruined him, but a lack of real talent. He was a pallid imitation of Tennyson and the lesser romantics. No amount of the right subject matter could have helped him. He could never have overcome his fundamental deficiencies. After the poetry renaissance it was found that E. A. Robinson, who wrote in strict, almost conventional, meters, somehow survived and endured. So did Robert Frost, who wrote about the New England countryside (his narratives don't hold up), and Wallace Stevens, whom I dare to prophecy will outlast Sandburg as he has outlasted the Amy Lowells and Edgar Lee Masters! An individual speech, a unique way of looking at the world, the power to set it down so that others can perceive a form that holds the contents and feel with you—that is more important than work based on a million finespun theories. A burning conviction, a guiding philosophy is often necessary and can be a help—but it's not essential. Mozart's political and literary ideas were I suspect naïve, but he had an unerring critical instinct about his own work. Parrington's misunderstanding of Henry James is to be expected. I doubt if he had the patience to read him, and for James' particular profundities and subtleties he had no affinity! Parrington says that he prefers Sherwood Anderson to Henry James. Well time has answered this comment. James' reputation keeps growing and growing. And Anderson's————?

February 17, Saturday

I am still thinking of Parrington's ferocious attack on poor Thomas Bailey Aldrich. It is a superb piece of writing, for hatred like love gives a rhythm, an inner fire, a style. One is reminded of Alexander Pope's terrific invective against Lord Hervey in the character of Sporvus. But even Pope hesitates and in the middle of his fury stops and asks, "Who breaks a butterfly upon a wheel?" The fact is that (what dreadful heresy!) between the aesthetic opinions of Henry James and that of T. B. Aldrich there was little difference or so I think. Their tastes in poetry were similar (one has to read James' letters to see this), though he may have had a more intelligent understanding of the continental mood. But essentially these two men might have gotten along very well agreeing on art, literature, politics. Then why isn't Aldrich as vital a writer as James? But I have explained it all before. James had *genius*. Aldrich had a small fine little talent but it never developed. But the aesthetic principles of either man can't be blamed either for their success or failure. We write from what we are.

March 6, Wednesday

A fine dinner party with the Donald Clarks of Columbia, given for Wyndham Lewis* the novelist and artist. I expected a wild, colorful person, someone like Ezra Pound perhaps, and met this sad, quiet, shy, fattish Englishman—or is he an American? A sad, dowdy English wife, quiet and worried.

Had a pleasant talk with L. S. about Byron whom she adores. "I'm afraid I'm going to die if I write about him. Elinor Wylie died writing about Shelley, and look what happened to Amy Lowell when she finished the life of Keats." Old Charles Hanson Towne simply shocked and horrified at the revelations about Augusta and Byron. "Now look here Mrs. S. Even if a man is dead for a long time one shouldn't say such things unless they have been proved." A number of people assured him it had been proved, naming the Lovelace book and others. He put his head to his hand. "O this is awful. To think I've admired him all my life."

Horace home with bad cold. I have a frightful constriction in my throat. Hysteria or sore throat? I no longer know. It's annoying and frightening.

Early spring feeling in the air today. A gleam of sunlight on damp streets dirty with melted snow, slippery sidewalks, damp air.

March 11

My father and stepmother visited us yesterday. Father looks frail, thin, and as usual is sad and inarticulate. He has a real feeling for music and when we put on our records or turn on the symphonic concerts on the radio his face lightens and he goes into a long, sad, dreamy trance. A feeling of sadness and irritation comes over me too as I watch him, of hopeless affection. All I can do to help him is to give him money, which at present he needs more than anything else in the world, and that is impossible.

A tea at Mrs. L. S. L.'s. She has lost most of her money which at one time ran into millions. But the depression and the Hitler regime in Germany reduced her to what by her standards must be comparative slavery. She lives in a modern apartment house in Gramercy Square. The walls of her apartment covered with valuable paintings, all crowded together, till the walls seem to gasp for breath.

Her social functions and even her literary reputation (which was always an artificial one) have fallen off since her income dwindled. Still handsome, exuberant, rather noisy—a Wagnerian opera style of beauty. Ignorant, indiscreet, worldly, shrewd—a manner reminiscent of the days when she had an English title and was with her husband a favorite of the Edward VII circle—a manner that must have been both aristocratic and charming in that set. But without money, with her beauty tarnished by age (she's a grandma now), with no particular prestige, it becomes a little dangerous (for her) and a little impertinent. I always avoided her because of her diamond lorgnette, insensitive noisy writing and arrogance, but recently, perhaps because time and misfortune have toned her down, I've gotten rather to like her. I see the charm that was hidden behind the wealth and arrogance, and she's not vicious, ugly, time-serving like so many of her former friends who now avoid her.

Ran into H. S. C., probably the most detestable figure in my literary life. H. and I call him the "Wolf" and whenever I look at him I begin to think of the really dreadful caricature with which Thomas Wolfe immortalized him in his "Portrait of a Literary Critic." An Edmond Gosse without E. G.'s charm and catty wit. We can't meet each other without my feeling the flood of hatred (for he did us a great wrong once) that flows from him towards us. "We are always most brutal to those we have wronged," as someone once said. A woman sitting near him asked me how it felt to have received a Pulitzer award and I said, "It's a terrifying experience." I saw in the Wolf's eye that I had made a faux pas of the first order, for how can one so insensitive realize what it meant? No, it would all be charged to flippancy, ingratitude, etc.

A very warm friendly letter from Malcolm Cowley* accepting one of my poems and saying kind things about them. It was exactly what I needed. I went around the house in a cloud of happiness. When I looked in the mirror, I seemed prettier that I'd been for years. I began to work on my book with renewed zest and confidence. One needs such "lifts" now and then or one can't go on living. Even the greatest genius withers under perpetual indifference.

March 23, Saturday

Saw Kenneth Fearing yesterday. We had dinner with him and Rachel. He says he is going to give up poetry and turn to novel writing. His slow, lazy, half-sleepy drawl is an amusing as ever. He never grows older. He still looks like a little boy. Of course I didn't believe him about giving up poetry, but he did seem gloomy and depressed.

Bad fever, heat flashes in the head, unable to work and I have so much to do. I beg and implore God for at least one year of good health. The prose book is getting along so well, though slowly. And my best poetry is yet to come. But I'm unable to summon strength and energy. No money for doctors. Afraid of expense of illness.

Good letter from Mrs. MacDowell. Fills me with hope for a good summer. H. and I want to write poetry—and drop everything else—but I must get well.

From Sainte-Beuve

"For a man of letters there is nothing so consoling as production. Nothing reconciles him better with others and himself. Thought alone, solitary meditation, demands in an ardent nature a sort of virtue, in order that it should not turn into bitterness and envy when it measures itself with others. Active labor . . . translated into works, distracts us from the perpetual comparisons we are tempted to make between ourselves and others less worthy, though perhaps often more favored. And it better fulfills the aim of life, which is to believe oneself useful and not to cut oneself off in an abnegation painful to sustain and not readily sincere."

Speaking of Madame du Deffand's love for Horace Walpole:

"She loved Walpole as the tenderest of mothers would have loved a son, long lost and suddenly found again. Thus many . . . singular and bizarre passions in which there appears an abuse of sensibility are only the revenge of nature punishing us for not having done simple things at the right time."

May 3, Friday

Very soft tender spring day. My heart and spirit go out with pleasure and hope into this fine air so full of lightness and renewal. But then my body feels ill, heavy, tired. It is in the spring weather that I feel most keenly that my youth is gone. One can only follow spring now with the eyes and with the mind.

A number of visitors, some interesting, some foolish. But I want a friend badly—a contemporary preferably. In all these people I can hardly find a friend. Let me be grateful for the short hours of companionship and light talk that while away that deep loneliness that grows deeper every year.

May 6, Monday

The cherry tree in the International House park has come out with creamy, soft flowers, lighting the thin, faint-gold air of May. I watched it in fascination yesterday afternoon, with mingled pain and delight. Usually at this time I would have longed for the country passionately, deeply. But now the tree seems enough. It did not even stir me to poetry. I kept thinking of spring after spring wasted in futile endeavors, in enervating longings—and wanted something more solid, more earthly, something harder and sharper to stir me not with delight but into some kind of action—not reverie.

Dreamed of Sunnyside for two or three nights in succession. Why does my heart and mind return there so often? Perhaps because we found some roots there as we have found them nowhere else. Eight of one's most creative years, one's most hopeful years, take a deep hold on one's after-life. I saw the little house, with its tiny airless but pretty rooms, the little garden with its lilac bush in front of the door, the box hedges carefully clipped by the Scotch gardener who lived next door, and myself sitting on the doorstep with a baby in my arms, always restless, wistful, worried and unhappy. Horace very frail and abstracted, working on his poetry or criticism in the damp basement study and the click-click-click of his typewriter as it came up to me when I sat in the back garden.

And always the babies—toddling, talking, running to me—very little and sweet—and my heart going out to them in anxious love.

The news from Europe a source of nightmare to me. The possibility of a Nazi victory seems like some unmistakable proof of the anger of God. With all my heart I believe that only an Allied victory can save us from future horror. Again and again I remember lovely eighteenth-century Bath with its sad, restrained people listening, silent, to the declaration of war, or watching the soldiers with their poor physiques and sloppy uniforms marching off, the beautiful, decadent, overdelicate faces of the little English boys. The gentry as formal and ritual-bound, as overcivilized as the Chinese—the cowardice, frank homosexuality, charm and futility of the intellectuals. I felt a feeling of foreboding even then for I wanted them to win, and their way of life offered some hope for the human spirit. The other—the Nazi—way offered nothing but the most terrible barbarism. And my childhood fear of the Russian soul has never abated. I dread it even in myself when I find it working in my worst moments.

Looking forward to the MacDowell Colony rather eagerly. Both Horace and I received fellowships. So grateful. Afraid to talk of it because I fear the Evil Eye. "Never boast," my mother used to say. "Never arouse envy or it will bring the Evil Eye upon you."

Horace Gregory

William Ellery Leonard: *"As usual L.'s conversation very good when off from his phobias but as I have a few phobias of my own these days I don't mind."*

Kenneth Fearing: *"Age cannot wither nor custom stale his infinite juvenility."*

T. C. Wilson: *"His unhappiness penetrates us."*

Bryher: *"What a loyal, sweet friend she is."*

Beatrice Shedlovsky: *"I like Beatrice more and more. Her restful common sense, her delicacy of feature and constitution and her loneliness as great as mine."*

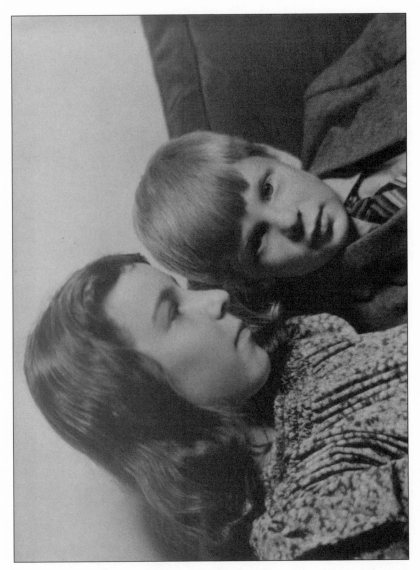

Joanna and Patrick

James T. Farrell: *"A birthday party at Jim Farrell's. J. affectionate . . . the crowd fantastic."*

Eleanor Clark: *"As beautiful as ever, in a black velvet dress, a yellow rose in her hair. . . . Horace as usual succumbs."*

Dunstan Thompson: *"Dunstan Thompson called . . . bringing me a beautiful bunch of red roses."*

Morton Zabel: *"Difficult to talk to, as usual, but we love him very much."*

Muriel Rukeyser: *"Impossible not to like her, difficult and disappointing as our friendship has been."*

Klaus Mann: *"Such a charming, ineffectual, scatter-brained person."*

Joanna by Marcia Silvette: *"Marcia is working on a portrait of Joanna. . . . She borrowed my precious Victorian locket . . . to use for the portrait."*

Norman Holmes Pearson: *"[His] charm is as subtle and beguiling as that of the most fascinating woman."*

The house in Palisades: *"Full of charm, and with repainting, cleaning and a few repairs will be lovely."*

May 13, Monday

Pleasant evening with Jack and his sister Ann Sweeney. Jack makes me feel gay and witty which is fun. Ann's luxurious place near the Plaza is beautifully furnished, fine original paintings of Matisse, Picasso, Rousseau. A marvelous crystal chandelier hanging in a luminous cluster from the ceiling. But the windows are never open and a thick nervous air permeates the room after awhile. A very fine modern library there, especially on modern art.

Horace and I working on our poetry history book, and I've just finished a piece on Lizette Reese and am almost through with a piece on Adelaide Crapsey. Though Horace's critical pieces are sounder than mine, yet I do think my little essays are well written and with a fine narrative sense and a real feeling for the form of the thing. I'm enjoying doing prose very much. And if only Horace had more time for collaboration our book would be going along at a great rate.

I wince a little as H., with a dreary editorial eye, goes through my copy and strikes out a favorite purple passage and unwinds a long Jamesian sentence of which I've been rather proud, or points to my favorite image and says, "Heavens I must straighten out this mixed metaphor." But when once I get started I write with delight, with ease my mind joins in, my spirit rises in gentle harmony. I feel good. But H. works very slowly, painfully, sometimes with torture.

The news from Europe is so dreadful that I find myself dreaming of it and wake up from my sleep expecting bombs to fall, the house to crash. Worst of all are the dreams in which I find myself on foot with a large crowd of refugees, weary, hopeless, the children at my side and I keep saying, "But I must find a home for *them*."

Wyndham Lewis (with whom we had dinner the other day) telling us of an experience in the last war where he served in the ranks and was afterward advanced (I think) to the rank of sergeant. His commanding officer called him up at parade and while he stood at attention said, "By the way Lewis what is this Vorticism business of yours that I've been reading about?" Lewis rather nervous said, "Oh it's nothing sir." "I thought so Lewis. I thought so. You may step back," said the officer moving on.

Went shopping at Macy's with little Pat and bought him a pair of new shoes. He was delighted with them and sat gazing with rapture at his feet during the long subway ride home. I saw more anxious faces in the subway reading the war news than I had seen since the war began. One large blonde woman kept looking at the headlines, tears running down her cheek. She may have been Dutch, Belgian, or merely a German refugee. The unreality of the war has now at least in New York been wiped away. H. says that it still seems remote and unreal in the Middle West. Troubled about dear Bryher* in Switzerland—which will, I suppose, be the next scene of horror. Will anything stop that monster Hitler? Or is he in a pact with the Evil One? The news is bad, look at it as one will, and we feel shock after nervous shock on listening to it over the radio or seeing the morning's headlines.

Read Dr. Johnson's *Lives of the Poets* for recreation, a beautiful job. It's true as Strachey says that he summons up his poets as if they were criminals to be tried before the dock, but how eloquent his summing up of his cases, how witty and trenchant. His mind is a fine one but his moral sensibilities are of such a high order that he takes on the qualities of an aesthete. He makes truth appear to be beauty. He does incite us to virtue; one feels that one would like to have had the esteem of such a man. But of course he had no conception of what poetry really is—or rather his conception of poetry leads invariably to excellent prose—rather than verse.

We cheered ourselves also with César Franck's Symphony in D Minor, a work whose deep feeling and understanding of human suffering lifted us into a world of resignation and consolation.

May 24

Today was Poppy Day and wounded war veterans were selling poppies on the street. In front of the public library a veteran with one leg, on crutches and in uniform, kept holding out his poppies and saying, "Buy these poppies. Red as the blood we shed for you in France." People were buying like mad, yet in previous days we had always watched the poppy sellers with annoyance and stopped only to say, "Oh those dreadful legionaries are here again." In fact in the circles frequented by the "intelligentsia" the term legionnaire was something of a reproach. One said the word as one said Babbitt. But today all this was changed. We saw the fighting fields of Flanders and France, we felt the suffering and horror, especially as all these names are in the papers recently and war is no longer something that happened ages ago and may not come again. Its shadow is at our door.

We're working on our poetry history book. Horace slow and exhausted. It takes our mind off world events anyway. H. had a fine poem in the *New Yorker* and a review in the *New Republic*. I had a longish poem in the *New Republic*. It seemed like a blossoming out of the Gregory family in literature— for one week! But in fact the poems etc. were written and taken a long time ago and it's only by accident that they all appeared at once.

May 28, Tuesday night
Continual sleepiness. I sit at my desk and fall asleep. I try to read and fall asleep. At present I am working on my E. A. Robinson chapter which seems the most difficult, the most impossible of all tasks. H. exhausted with last minute work at the college. My poetry manuscript in the light of the war and world events seems soft, weak, thin—all wrong. I'm fearfully upset over the news. Today the treachery of the King of Belgium was announced. Will the French, torn by inner dissension, be next? These are the dreadful things we brought so close to us. We all became tools of these agents of bloodshed, treachery and destruction, who used foolish liberals for their schemes. And aside from H. I have no outside friend to whom I can talk freely and frankly and be assured of sympathetic attention to my views, which have proved not so wrong after all. All these years I have allowed myself to be surrounded by people who despised and ignored and sneered at everything I cared for and now I find in a moment of crisis no one to talk to with frankness and ease.

The M.s here last night. It always surprises me to find out over and over again that these people are exactly as they appear to be. They are so charmless, so unimaginative, so petty, so envious, so mean and unpleasant to look at too, that I always feel that there must be a tender soul, a heart of gold, a secret virtue hidden under so many obvious disadvantages. But the more one looks the more one sees that there's nothing—nothing—there but what appears.

June 6, Thursday
Watching little Pat outdoors from the window, wearing a large, green embroidered Mexican sombrero that Muriel brought him. It looks charming on

his red-gold head. He walks around with his hands in his pocket whistling loud and clear.

Joanna skipping rope, looking very handsome and dashing. She is wearing the jet and gold Victorian earrings she inherited from her grandmother. It makes her look very grown up.

The news from Europe still unbearable. I feel the war like a deep wound for which there seems no remedy, no healing.

June 10, Monday

Early this afternoon while dressing to go out, heard a shouting and screaming on the radio that seemed to come from some bestial subhuman voice, a sound as if all the damned in inferno were preparing to climb out of the bottomless darkness and storm the upper world. Shuddering, half-weeping with fear I turned to Horace and Joanna who had run to the radio. They said, "Mussolini has declared war and these are the mobs cheering him." I had planned to work on our poetry history book in the library today but felt paralyzed—unable to think or to go on. Longed for a friend—our loneliness is too great.

June 17, Monday

France capitulated today.

Muriel Rukeyser told me an amusing story of running into Phillip Rahv of the *Partisan Review* in the public library. He stopped after a brief conversation, looked around wearily at the long shelves and said, "I can't find anything to read."

Peterborough, New Hampshire, July 3, MacDowell Colony

Arrived here on the 1st of July at noon. Lovely wild (but a classical wildness!) country. . . . Everything white, immaculate and *ideal* in our room and in the atmosphere of the country around me. What is there in New England that reminds me of an exquisite graveyard, but a graveyard from which the disembodied spirits still speak, in a sharp, pure idiom?

Thornton Wilder very nice. Nervous, intense, morbidly shy. Very much like his poet-sister Charlotte. Large visionary near-sighted blue eyes. Reads a great many eighteenth-century French memoirs (a weakness of my own), has marvelous anecdotes of Gertrude Stein whom he admires and whose literary executor he is. He gives his verbal portraits of G. S. a glow of such enthusiasm, such subtle shadings that she becomes a glamorous, a legendary figure. H. has always admired her and as a person she *must* be very remarkable.

Wilder has the E. A. Robinson studio. This place is full of Robinson anecdotes; one has a feeling that the exorbitant reverence with which he was treated here (especially by fatuous elderly ladies) must have bored him. It *should* have bored him.

July 4

Wilder's large visionary blue eyes are like a sign that I never fail to perceive now. The few that have them are the *elect*, the chosen, fanatics, idiots and children.

Everything incredibly neat, orderly and white, a *classical* quality to the place. It may produce a Robinson. It *can't* produce a Sandburg. I believe that the greatest American poet of all when he comes may (in spite of prophesies) very well come again from New England. For though the guts, the belly, the blood, the impulses may come from elsewhere, the *spirit* of the country is here in New England—perhaps not only its spirit, but its deepest conscience.

H. interrupted this writing by a visit. He is enchanted with Peterborough and my studio though his is very pleasant too. He fell in love with my sunporch and is now on the hammock reading the small volume of Kierkegaard, *Fear and Trembling.*

Carl Carmer* told another Robinson anecdote. One of the elderly lady admirers (a spinster of virginal spirit) began to tell Robinson one of her dreams at the dinner table. The dream became more and more horrific; more and more was it apparent to the other people at the table that it was full of the simplest Freudian symbols. Robinson grew dreamier and dreamier, more and more abstracted, and as at last the dream reached its embarrassing climax, Robinson touched the dinner bell and began ringing it softly. The waitress ran up to him and asked him what he wanted. "I just thought," said Robinson shyly, "I just thought I ought to ring the bell."

July 10

How instant the recognition of spirit for spirit. How swift, how penetrating and after a certain age (and with certain people) how irritating, unnecessary, disturbing. Peace after all is a good substitute for joy.

July 17

Visited with John Gould Fletcher and his wife, a nice motherly woman who smothers J. G. F. with endearments and attentions. F. full of interesting anecdotes. He seems to have everything but the divine spark. He was wearing a five-gallon hat of which he was boyishly proud.

A violent rain outside my window. Magnificent effect, the trees and the grass bowing under the force of the storm.

I have collected enough Robinson anecdotes to fill a book—the worship and reverence and love which he incited here is unbelievable. Even F., who rarely has a good word for anyone, said nothing unkind.

The Wylie anecdotes are floating around here too and one gets them in furtive whispers, for Bill Benét is here, and no one is better liked than he. In her case the anecdotes are decidedly unfavorable. Never it seems was so much exhibitionism, vanity, selfishness rewarded by such affection and admiration on a husband's side. J. G. F. has a story of a studio party here where she suddenly turned on everyone and demanded they leave at once, saying in shrill hysterics, "I can feel your hatred everywhere. It *exudes* from the walls."

The ghost of Elinor Wylie is supposed to haunt the woman's quarter, The Eaves. Innumerable anecdotes by women who say they have seen or heard strange sounds from what used to be her room. Someone asked why Robinson's ghost didn't return. H. said, "R. was a good poet and so he sleeps in peace."

Mr. Benét speaking of a visit to Edith Sitwell. "She was wearing a gold dress of stiff heavy material, brocade perhaps. Her manner was stiff and formal, her face was made up beyond belief. There was something inhuman about her. She looked like a Manchu princess—or rather say she looked like an

Englishwoman who had assumed a clever Manchu mask. She was terrifying. In fact she frightened me so I couldn't talk."

Illness cutting into my work. Benét, the Carmers and others have left today; a new crowd coming. Pain and the extremely hot weather make me cross and irritable. I try to hide it. How well I succeed I don't know. I'm not a good dissembler. Sooner or later all my secrets are out.

Jim Putnam visited us and we had a pleasant convivial evening. Chard Smith drove us to a picturesque inn at the top of Mount Monadnock. The location delightful, the inn seemed parked on top of the world and had real atmosphere. The food was vile. Horace, Chard and Jim then returned to our cottage where they drank till midnight. J. confidential which is always a torment now, for I wish to know nothing of the private lives of my friends. This is not an affectation. I have no interest. I can do nothing. My sensations are only that of pain, irritation, responsibility. I do not feel buoyant enough, strong enough to learn more than I need learn.

An automobile trip to Temple, New Hampshire, a beautiful village that looked like an eighteenth-century print. Nothing lovelier since I saw Bathampton. A churchyard dating from the early eighteenth to the beginning the nineteenth century, slate tombstones with engraved carvings, simply magnificent art. Some of the mystery, firmness, sharpness of the Egyptian bas-reliefs. I must photograph these stones. They gave the cemetery a curious atmosphere, as if a strong, disembodied spirit, inhuman and indifferent, were talking or wandering between earth and air.

August 14, Wednesday

Drove out to Keene, N.H., with the Fletchers and a Miss Esther Bates (one of the Robinson set) to see the movie production of *Pride and Prejudice*. Badly overacted, a Hollywoodish and showy Elizabeth Bennett and the play of course overcostumed. Only as if heard in a dream, in stray bits of dialogue did, we get flashes, glimpses, undertones of that delightful, sparkling book. As a Janeite I found the performance depressing. H. said gloomily that, judging from the antics of the Bennet sisters and the costuming, Hollywood had evidently confused *Pride and Prejudice* with *Little Women*.

A curious story about Van Wyck Brooks and Mary Colum. Well one never recognizes a femme fatale these days when one sees her!

August 22, Thursday

Little Pat and Jo paid us a surprise visit again. I heard their voices as if in a dream coming down the walk that leads to my studio. I ran down and there they were looking very well and sunburnt! What a joy and relief, for we had been so homesick for them. Horace played the records of his favorite poems (made at Harvard) for the children and Jo listened with an approving critical air. But little Pat's expression was marvelous, a mingled combination of embarrassment, emotion (because it was Daddy saying something intimate and deep) and the shyness of the little American boy who feels that poetry is something for girls. Added to this an air of great politeness.

H. had a poem returned from the *New Yorker.* As one grows older these things become more and more difficult or rather one never gets over the pang of a rejection slip. Though this slip came from an editor who is a friend, it made the morning gray. H. is better at such things than I. A rejection even from a person I don't particularly respect makes me for a moment or two lose self-confidence and in some cases I find that I can't do anything new. There is a time in all our lives when praise, encouragement, love must come. Before and afterwards we can do without these things, but that moment of encouragement, no matter how brief, how small, must arrive or we shrivel and die and let our talents dry up or decay at their source.

August 27, Tuesday

I count the days now rather wistfully for we must leave this place soon and it is so beautiful and restful. Jack Sweeney visited us. He was very gay and pleasant. He came in a magnificent car, a chauffeur in a uniform at the wheel, much to the dazzlement of the colony. Alfred Kreymborg, dying with curiosity to know who Jack was, kept teasing us to tell him and we enjoyed keeping him mystified.

The lawns in front of Horace's studio were beautiful, the failing summer light on the green-golden grass. Jack was delighted with the place and we began to talk eagerly of buying a summer house in New England, Jack saying that he would rent the attic or barn from us. These things are pleasant to talk about, though the thought of burdening ourselves with property is frightening.

I've built a roaring, lively fire in my studio fireplace. It's so pleasant to watch. There are two ways of experiencing The Vanity of Human Wishes. One is by finding that the thing one has so long desired is within our reach—and is no longer desirable. The other one is of course simply to attain it.

When I see R. and S., I realize that there is nothing so depressing as the spectacle of an old age or middle age without reserve or dignity.

August 30, Friday

Many people leaving, cold settling on the air and I sit and shiver in my studio because I've forgotten to bring matches and so cannot build up my fire. We leave tomorrow. Irritating and discouraging news from friends, a bad attack of neuralgia affecting my left eye and cheek again. H.'s subject matter in poetry irritates me. There is no catharsis in so much gloom. Had a dreadful afternoon tea with Jean Starr Untermeyer when Horace, John Gould Fletcher and I, suddenly hit by a common frenzy, tore into her when she began her customary bleating about Robert Frost and her depreciation of Robinson. Curiously enough this took place in the Robinson studio. She is an irritating person, selfish, pretentious. But all of us suffered from remorse afterwards. Fletcher going off in a fine fit of temperament on all of us afterwards for having made him come along. Frightfully depressed, full of that self-contempt which is more dreadful than the disdain of others.

September 14, Saturday

We returned from New Hampshire about two weeks ago. That beautiful wild exhausted country now remains in my mind as something incredibly clear and high and remote, like the disembodied spirit of America, the America I used to see in my dreams as a child when I looked out of tenement windows with a book on my lap, Whittier's *Snowbound* or Louisa Alcott's *Little Women*. Trying to reconcile these books with my environment was very difficult. They seemed so near and so very remote.

Read Van Wyck's book *Indian Summer*. After my visit to New England it was particularly revealing. N. tore it to pieces, the clever little academic politician flying at the touch of real poetry—real literary skill. I don't agree with Brooks' provincialism. I can't see why an American literary tradition can't arise that is worldwide in its significance. If Howells isn't read while Henry

James is, it isn't because Howells used the American theme and James didn't, but because James was a better, keener, more exciting writer. The fact that the American theme is all the rage now and that Thoreau, Melville, Hawthorne, etc. are read as never before proves that Howells is not read because he is more difficult to read than even Henry James. Dullness is an insurmountable obstacle.

But the essay on Parkman the historian is superb, the Amy Lowell very revealing. So are the other portraits, vignettes, little bits of penetration and poetry. It pays too much attention to Frost, too little sympathy and understanding is shown to Robinson, a finer (to me) more significant figure—nor can I think of Edna Millay as a fine flower of New England culture. But in spite of this, Van Wyck Brooks comes very close to being our American Sainte-Beuve—the same faults, almost the same virtues.

I am rapidly becoming convinced that our finest, most humane critic, the possessor of the richest, cleanest prose style, the greatest learning, the sanest mind, was Paul Elmer More. But to possess these qualities is enough to keep one from being read by the average reader, even the average reader of literary essays. The fireworks, the display, the still fashionable moral anarchy, the hatred of distinction, which some people consider a democratic duty, make these virtues a dangerous and lovely gift to possess. For even the intellectual snobs prefer something less genuine and profound, a little more pretentious, showy, a fine outward display, pedantry rather than a real learning, which is worn so simply and naturally.

A large dinner at the Waldorf (over a thousand people) for Irving Berlin by the Society for Music Appreciation. One of those dull dinners full of strangers. But to hear Irving Berlin standing on his tiptoes singing "Gold Bless America," his face aglow with awe and wonder, was an experience. Then Hendrick Van Loon made a fascinating rambling speech about Bach and the war—"I come from a country that is no more, from a city that is no more"—and then again tried to talk of Bach and music but always returned to the same theme. "The guns from the other side are getting me. There is too much smoke in my eyes." Sat next to Gillett Burgess, he of the "Purple Cow" fame, who kept insisting that there would be no more Art—no such thing as "genius" in the future.

September 16, Monday

Horace's school started today. The vacation never seemed so short, or his going back so difficult. He needs a year's leave for his writing and I know such a year would give our country, our time, some of the finest and richest poems it has ever had. But the Santa Claus awards go to the Willy the Weepers, the brisk men on the inside, the mediocre who make people feel safe and comfortable.

A young librarian poet from Colorado, a Mr. Kees,* visited us also, with a pretty, young, new wife. He was full of interesting details on the terrific drive on the universities by Allan Tate and the *Southern Review.*

Upset this morning by reading a newspaper account of John Wheelwright's* death in a useless automobile accident. He was killed by a drunken driver. We had missed him in Boston this summer and had planned to get in touch with him again. He was the most original and talented of men, his poems if carefully edited and collected would prove him one of the most brilliant poets of his generation. I can see his aristocratic profile, hear his clipped Bostonian voice and watch the half-crazy look in his eyes come and go, witty, humorous, half-fanatic. He was too great an aristocrat to be interested in the banalities of his own class. His heart and his energies went to the poor, the disinherited, the outcasts. If he defended Trotsky against Stalin, I always felt it was because his sympathies were always with the persecuted, or the man out of power. One remembers stories of how he led unemployment parades in winter, wearing a magnificent fur overcoat, or made soap box speeches for the Socialist Party, beautifully dressed, a flower in his buttonhole.

September 21, Saturday

Was it ten or a hundred years ago that we were at Peterborough? The place has faded. I remember the clean white atmosphere, the legend of E. A. R. haunting the place, the stony road that lead to my studio, the overwhelming sense of emptiness, hope, failure and then hope again.

Decided to hand in the manuscript of my poems, *The Listening Landscape.* It's not a good time to send out the poems but I can't work over them any longer. The strain, the tension, is too great.

October 3, Thursday

The beautiful lucid red-gold charm of Indian summer. My favorite season. It has the same effect on me that spring has on others, melancholy, yearning, aspiration and a sort of exhilaration.

Feeling of great depression since I've handed in my manuscript of poems. I feel lost and frightened without it and can't think of any poem of which I'm completely confident.

Reading Ignatius Donnelly's fascinatingly absurd book on Atlantis [*Atlantis: the Antediluvian World*]. Donnelly was a quaint character, a friend of Horace's grandfather, and in this book he has left a monument to his talents and eccentric charm. An amazingly well-written book, and at first one is carried away by the author's enthusiasm, his amazing amount of wide and indiscriminate reading and a real poetic imagination. Then one slows up and begins to grow a little uneasy, though the interest is still keen, the trail still exciting. But it has all been too fascinating, too glib. Still I know of no subject so interesting as the Lost Atlantis legend, and can understand why it has driven some people mad.

October 7, Monday

A dinner party at Jim Putnam's last Friday. The John Gould Fletchers, Norman Pearson, Helen McMaster, Marianne Moore, Donald Adams of the *Times*. Marianne Moore as always a disconcerting delight, her clothes as usual in the smartest mode of twenty years ago. This gives her a very odd distinguished Queen Mary look. Her conversation clear, crisp and somewhat oblique too. Everything she has to say has the same flavor that one finds in her poetry. Very fresh skin like a little girl's, very large blue eyes, erect somewhat boyish walk.

Lunch the next day with the Fletchers and the children, a pleasant time though F. has a fearful habit of repeating all the unpleasant things other people have told him about you. At least it is not done with unction. He does not pretend that it is good for you to know and that he is doing you a service. It is sheer, childlike, innocent fun, simple pure-hearted mischievous malice. But he can be gay and affectionate and Charley May is angelic, and we laughed and gossiped a great deal.

Long endless monotonous obsessive days when I can't do a thing, can't even read. Since I've handed in *The Listening Landscape* manuscript I feel lost, worried and frightened.

October 23

Poems returned from magazines. I never overcome that feeling of frustration that comes over me when this happens. I always begin to agree with the editors and find myself wondering if I am any good at all. A gallantly polite, exasperating letter. A rejection from John Crowe Ransom. I am not a feminist but certain male attitudes make me angry.

Klaus Mann visited us with plans for a new magazine. Has some of his father's charm and quickness of movement. Frightfully anti-German and Nazi and very sensitive about being German at all. He had just run into H. G. Wells with whom he had quarreled. Wells had argued that there was nothing to German culture at all. The literature was second-rate, the poetry not as good as the English, the philosophy was all poisonous, etc. As for the music—well he didn't know much about music. But of course the two personalities were antipathetic. K. M. said that one of his sisters had been on the *Benares,* the children's ship that had been bombed. Her husband, a Hungarian, was drowned. She was rescued after drifting in an open boat for hours. Erica has been playing the heroine in London, making fiery speeches against Hitler, addressing the German people and no doubt enjoying herself.

Read a life of Chopin. Realized again how with the exception of Berlioz all musicians seem to be helpless when attempting the written word. Atrocious clumsy letters for a genius so sensitive and delicate. Still toward the end human experience and suffering touched his pen and made him eloquent. The letters take on dignity and pathos.

November 4, Monday

Saw Chaplin's *The Great Dictator* yesterday with Pat and Horace. Chaplin's fine sensitive acting—really great acting. But the picture is a few years late. Somehow it is impossible to laugh at Hitler or Mussolini at present. I have never been one of those who believed that Hitler was a megalomaniac avid for personal power and private glory. I believe that his fanaticism is pure and terrifyingly impersonal. Nothing is more dangerous than to underestimate the adversary.

Quarreled with H. on the way to the show over the subject matter of one of his poems. I can no longer endure a certain type of unmitigated flat realism especially in poetry. Farrell, Caldwell, Dahlberg* in prose, Fearing in poetry—I am not mentioning the less talented Communists—are more than enough for one generation to endure.

Hemingway's book *For Whom the Bell Tolls* has received the wildest press of the season. It is I daresay the best of his books, but even his best irritates and depresses me. He always seems to me the bright romantic newspaper man's highest dream of a *literateur.* The style is good but faintly arty, the sex makes me squirm because it seems rather soft, sentimental and flabby in spite of its heralded virility. And always that sentimental, adolescent, schoolboyish, pretentious mind. Something morally corrupt too which cannot be said of Dos Passos.

Wildest election fervor within my memory. For the first time I registered and took the literacy test so as to be able to vote; feeling that the privilege of the vote is a rare and beautiful one now as the democracies go down, one by one.

Hysterical crowds in front of the public libraries. In the buses, subways and streets one hears nothing but political discussion. The doorbell rings incessantly, usually with people electioneering for Wilkie. I shall vote for Roosevelt, but I daresay it will not matter too much if Wilkie wins.

November 14

Frightfully unpleasant experience with S., one of the very few people I've always liked and trusted. Again and again I remember the painfully cynical adage that one must always treat our friends as potential enemies. This does not mean quarreling, suspicion, anger at all but it means keeping a perpetual watch over too generous impulses, a tendency to unguarded confidences or too great intimacy. Discretion has never been one of my virtues. It's not the most amiable of the virtues, but surely, the most necessary. Only the most painful experiences drive me to it.

Two drinking literary parties. One leaves a little ill, confused, worried. I always feel I've said too much, and I haven't been to so many of these parties as to feel at ease in them. Malcolm Cowley, Donald Adams very amiable to me. Horace looked ill and tired. Poor old Scudder Middleton, a poet I used to hear of in my youth, bitter, foolish, speaking of how as an American of colonial descent he hated England and loved Germany. Ugly drunkenness a feature of these parties. Drunken women peculiarly repulsive.

A foolish talk with Mary Colum at another party. I rather liked her large voluble cynical expansiveness but I was much too indiscreet.

November 28, Wednesday

Dinner with Frank Morley of Harcourt Brace at the Chatham Hotel. Like most Americans who have lived for a long time in England he has become more English than the English and he seems very English indeed in his New York setting, slow, ponderous, correct. He talks of American publishing always in terms of Faber & Faber. One gets rather fond of him and his slow humor, his passion for Pepys, his quotations from the classics, the withdrawn inward look, which makes one feel that no matter what he tells you, it is not the thing he really wants to tell you.

H. ran into Matthew Josephson* in the library recently, another ghost from the past. Full of complaints, his income had dwindled, his books did not sell, his friends had deserted him. He has begun to hate the country (like Millay) and wants to be in the city again. He has no money to educate his children now, etc., etc. I think he said something about writing poetry again. Curious how poetry seems to be the last desperate gesture of so many a disgruntled journalist.

December 15

Horace turned in the manuscript of his selected book of verse, *Poems, 1930–1940*. Have much hope and fear for it. It's a beautiful and powerful book.

December 23

The children have just decorated the Christmas tree and are full of chatter and excitement. H. and I have come back from a weary shopping tour. I can never get over the feeling of awe, gratitude, wonder at having money to spend on gifts.

H. sold a poem to the *New Yorker,* one of his best, which filled us with pleasure. There is hope of selling two more at present. H. and I need places to publish poems very badly.

Scott Fitzgerald's death filled us with sadness though we never met him. Many years ago John Farrar, then a young editor on the *Bookman,* offered to take me over to the Fitzgeralds for a visit but something happened and we never went. Perhaps F. was as the papers say a failure, yet he has *The Great Gatsby* to his name. Nor did he ever decline into the voluble vulgarity, silliness, the undignified literary decline of—let us say—Edna Millay—or the blank foolishness of a MacLeish—and I can mention other contemporaries of his who are never talked of as a "failure" who have failed as greatly. What strange stories there were about him and his Zelda in the '20s. Like Millay he caught the fancy and mood of a generation and the personality overshadowed the work. I suppose Hemingway stepped into his boots.

T. C. Wilson* sent us Mozart's Concerto in B-flat Major, which gave us days of real pleasure. No gift could have pleased us more.

One usually hears from everyone but the people one wants to hear from most, or so it seems every Christmas.

The shops and streets brilliant and glowing with luxury. Never have I seen so many mink coats, so many expensive women wearing them, the high-priced shops so crowded. Riverside Drive draped in gray light, the Tomb whitewashed and cool like clear Reality rising above a dingy Dream.

My chief Christmas dream, and New Year's wish is for a brilliant, favorable reception for Horace's new book, *Poems, 1930–1940.* My *Listening Landscape* ought to appear about the same time too. I think it is better than my last book. I feel that if I can have enough encouragement I will do better and better with each book.

December 25, Christmas Day

Dudley Fitts and his lovely Cornelia visited us on Christmas eve. A strange slow friendship has grown up between H. and Dudley. One hardly knows when or how it began or why. Only I seem to feel that it may grow into some-thing deep and warm or blow away in evanescent air.

Have been reading Lord David Cecil's book on Cowper, *The Stricken Deer*. Beautifully written, I thought, in an intelligent rich poetic style. (H. says however that the style is too soft, too full of falling cadences and clichés.) But Cowper's life—Cowper himself and his friends, his background—fascinates me, the tranquil, pure sacred accents of his poetry arising from that tormented life, that twisted soul. He might have written Kierkegaard's books, or been a character in a Kafka novel.

1 9 4 1

Spent a strange quiet New Year's yesterday. There was no reason or heart anymore for our customary attempt at a New Year's party, so I got a fine young turkey to roast for the children. Helen McMaster telephoned and she dined with us. It was a pleasant surprise and a joy to spend the holiday with her. After dinner we took her and little Pat to see *Night Express,* an exciting new English spy movie. Jo had seen a movie in the afternoon and decided to stay home.

Such crowds on Times Square and Broadway. One could barely move or breathe. It was gay and good and I felt dizzy like a prisoner who has lived in a dark room and encounters too much light all at once. Drums, noisemakers of all kinds, drunks in front of restaurants and subways, the army and navy particularly in evidence in all this merrymaking. All these uniforms brought back vague disturbing memories of my teens and the last war. Little Pat grew silent with excitement as he always does. We bought him a horn and he blew on it for a while, but he seemed relieved when we got a cab and went to Helen's apartment. Gramercy Park very elegant, very much like a street in old London (before the bombs came down), full of Christmas lights and a full yellow moonlight streaming down, the weather unusually clear and warm for January. Longed for some human contact. Wished to make talk, afraid desperately of being indiscreet. H. tired and dullish. I looked over some of Helen's magazines. Saw some poetry reviews and began to feel frightened for our two forthcoming books. Oh well if one must run the gauntlet—we must!

Little Pat fell asleep on Helen's couch.

Morton Zabel called a few days ago. His mother was dying, he said, but he had had to come east to read a paper before the Modern Language Association. Reading papers and listening to lectures during holiday seems like a businessman's holiday to me. M. was difficult to talk to, as usual, but we love him very much. I'm humbly grateful for his loyalty and kindness to me—to us.

Aimless days full of fear, loneliness, self-reproach. If I made any New Year's resolutions it is to work harder, to regulate my scattered days.

January 13, Monday

Thin shrill biting winds blowing in from the river. From my window I see the American flag on a long flagpole in front of General Grant's Tomb waving wildly in the air. It arouses strange fears, childhood memories, something that must have come from my parents, from old Russia, perhaps a fear of the Official, the established authority.

Went to a party given by Klaus Mann for his new magazine, *Decision: A Review of Free Culture*. Such a crowd —everyone from Wystan Auden to Robert Nathan.* The strange little girl who wrote *The Heart Is a Lonely Hunter* there, a pale touching juvenile face marked by a sort of innocent corruption like a child who knew and had experienced more than was good for her. A small-boy carriage and stride, and a petulant assumed manner. Millay had it in her palmy days. I suppose it comes from being too much praised at too early an age!

Have met the incredible Oscar Williams;* as Louis Untermeyer says, he is not real. He is Max Beerbohm's Enoch Soames. His hair looks like a wig. His teeth seem unreal. His face looks as if were made of cardboard or papier-mâché. His conversation, shrewd, naïve and foolishly bright, is unbelievable. He is full of wild plans, great projects, grandiose schemes for organizing poets and poetry into a vast force—for something—he's not sure what. But one may be sure he will figure in it—and largely. A sort of horrid fascination makes him far from unlikeable.

Saw the proofs of my book and my heart sank. It seemed so mild, so colorless, so———I thought of Rukeyser's electric energy and brilliance, of Marianne Moore's solid distinction, of Bogan's pretentious but impressive airs, and my depression grew. But the book may be better than I think.

Auden I had always heard described as incredibly ugly. This is I think a mistake. He has a fine physique, a vivid blondness and a face that, if not regularly attractive, does possess an interesting and disturbing charm. One *feels* the personality in a room; people who do not know him look up. The feeling one gets is not entirely a pleasant one. It is as if some extraordinarily rare and fascinating form of illness and death had projected itself on the atmosphere.

Speaking I & D (Illness and Death), James Joyce's death announced today in a catty and malicious obituary in the *Times*. His in its way was an amazingly strenuous life and he was still far from being an old man. In the quarrels over his obituaries we see the ambiguity and unresolved feeling about his status as a writer. H. who is a great admirer felt very much upset at the death—at the stupid, misinformed notices.

January 15

H.'s health a source of worry to me. If only there was some way of earning money for him. I should like to take him to Florida for a month at least and then arrange for at least six more months so as to give him leisure to write and rest. The proofs of his new book arrived, the new poems extraordinarily powerful, but painful reading to me sometimes, knowing how they were written. A good reception would do wonders for his morale and health—and mine too. For what affects him affects me too.

Decision, Klaus Mann's magazine, took one of my poems, "Woman at the Piano," for the March number. It's nice to have a poem accepted. I do so hope this magazine will go on. So many new magazines fold up quickly.

Frightful cold, the streets damp and slippery. The days pass in reverie, silence, fear, brooding. Put Purcell's *Golden* Sonata on the Victrola yesterday and then a fugue of Bach, the *Dorean,* and felt alive, warm, and close to real tears again. But an hour later the panic began once more.

January 17, Friday

Snow, sleet, slippery pavements and that damp cold that eats into nerves and spirits. Slept late today out of sheer depression, the feeling that it was too difficult to face another day. H.'s health troubling. He is so nervous, taut, exhausted and I suspect—discouraged.

George Barker* the English poet and Dunstan Thompson* visited us last night, but H. was too tired to make conversation. Barker a charmer, graceful, rosy-cheeked, very blue-eyed, simple and easy in his manners, with a nice, broad, almost American sense of humor. T. S. Eliot, who had once described him as looking like pictures of Keats, was perfectly right.

January 21

Joanna's fourteenth birthday. She looked very beautiful and touching and tall for her age. May God bless her!

Last night a visit from Horace's old friend Joseph Freeman,* once a power in the Communist Party. He is now disgruntled, bitter, angry. As I told H., nothing has come of his youthful talents because he had put them too early in a bad school. It is hard for him to make a readjustment. A spoiled Communist is like a spoiled priest. We agreed with F. that anyone who had carefully studied Russian books, papers, and Stalin's statements at least a year before the present war need not have been surprised at the German-Soviet Pact.

We also agreed that the reason for the great hold the C.P. had on the "intellectuals" in the '30s was in its "moral force." F. gave an account of his adventures in Hollywood where he raised $20,000 for the *New Masses.* High-salaried stars and writers and producers would take him aside and tell him of their disgust with their jobs, their self-contempt, their longings to be pure, to do real, honest work. "They then gave me money," said F., "in the same spirit that the great sinners of the Middle Ages built cathedrals or paid huge sums to the Church as an expiation for their sins that they would never renounce." But when the C.P. stood unveiled, exposed, they were relieved and are now almost free from the need for self-justification.

Macmillan offered me a contract for another book of verse, thanks, I suspect, being due to my old friend J. P. [Jim Putnam]. Felt moved to tears, especially when I feel no impulse to write poetry lately and I take the Macmillan gesture as an act of faith towards me. Looking over my proofs depresses me. My book is so quiet, so unsensational—a little too placid and correct. It has *finesse,* delicacy, intensity. But it needs more flash, more excitement, perhaps more life to live on.

January 24, Friday

Stopped at the Washington Square bookshop and H. showed me an attack on my work—the first one—by a Clement Greenberg. Felt both flattered (because I'm not usually noticed) and annoyed. His language exactly the same as that violent hysterical and sudden attack on me that an old friend launched—when I first began to attract attention. It comes from the same circle I'm sure and I must I suppose summon up strength, courage, and faith to endure it.

January 28, Tuesday

Dunstan Thompson called last night bringing me a beautiful bunch of red roses. I'm so unaccustomed to such gestures that I feel a little awkward when they happen. The roses fill the air, large, rich, scattering a rich perfume over the living room. It's almost too much, and I long for the simpler grace of other flowers. I prefer the Japanese custom in a way, two roses in a small vase, a flower at a time. But this I think may very well lead to a niggardliness of emotion, a thin-ness of soul, too great a contraction and withdrawal. No, let the roses spill over, opulent, profuse, over-rich, filling the air, coloring the room: I have overcome the other thing.

Jim Putnam and Helen McMaster dropped in later. I was quarrelsome and rude and felt sorry, for they are two of the best friends I have in the world. We were left alone with D. T., who was charming, clever, very bright—what the eighteenth century would call "a pleasing, accomplished, sprightly, and amiable young man."

Visited the nineteenth-century French art exhibit at the Metropolitan Museum. Large crowds, so dense that it was almost impossible to see the paintings. But what a great period! I left with a renewed feeling for the greatness of Delacroix and a new feeling of respect for Manet. A little gem of a picture by the forgotten 1890 man Gustave Moreau, small and delicate, shedding a jewel-like light, and another warm and intimate sketch of Corot by Daumier. Walked into another exhibition and saw a black and white portrait of some Frenchmen by Whistler, extraordinarily brilliant—a Sargent beside it looked cheap, flashy and tawdry. Horace pointed out to me how close some aspects of Whistler's work were to the earlier (and better) poems of Ezra Pound.

I must record the marvelous gray-gold light that flooded the museum rooms and touched up the pictures in the late February afternoon. A mellow winter light that began to come from above and slowly saturated the atmosphere. The pictures seemed alive and yet melancholy as if a thousand dead hands and voices were still working on them and talking through them.

February 22, Saturday

H. and I saw the Preston Sturges movie *The Great McGinty,* heartily recommended to us. It has freshness of dialogue, of characterization and acting. But when we left the dingy little theater on East Sixty-eighth Street and Third Ave., my heart sank at the implications of the picture. One felt that racketeering, corruption, was inevitable, that it was inherent in so-called democracy. One thought of the abasement of democracy, the contempt for distinction, finesse, depth, form that makes the poems of Carl Sandburg so much admired, and his Lincoln book praised for its more slovenly aspects. Something faintly 1920ish, Menckenish, about the moral attitudes in this picture. I can't quite put my finger on it but it is there I'm sure.

Rode in the Third Ave. el for the first time in years. H. reminded me that the els would all go down soon. I remember the discomfort and feeling of fear, the difficulty in breathing, the longing for clear air that I had when riding on these els as a child or hardly more than a child on the way to my jobs in too-hot summers or gray winters. Too many of these inventions have long outlived their usefulness, and it is now time to realize that the harm they did far outbalanced their practical value. The blotting out of the skies, the darkening of the street, the unbearable noise overhead, the brutal ugliness—did these things leave no psychic horror behind?

Gave two poetry readings, one for dear Horace's class, and another for Norman MacLeod's class at the Y.M.C.A. I did the best I could. The last reading netted me $20, which I couldn't afford to turn down. Difficult and nerve-wracking but I felt pleased at earning some money for the family and in turning in the $20 to the family purse. But I know nothing that can dry up the springs of poetic creation more thoroughly than these public appearances.

March 3, Monday

Muriel telephoned. Has wild stories of persecution by a former friend who really seems to have gone mad. In spite of everything M.'s friendship seems to go on as always. I feel grateful and a little surprised. One is so unaccustomed to such loyalty. I hardly dare to believe in it.

News from Europe rather worrying. Two refugees, a Mr. and Mrs. Uzedil from Prague, visited us on a letter of recommendation from Bryher. We felt sad and depressed at their story of wandering, persecution and distress. The woman is a poet, the man an art-historian—middle-aged, speaks English fairly well. But what *we* would have done in their place makes us shudder. They both knew Kafka well. Uzedil says he delivered the funeral oration, and they say they have letters, pictures and interesting anecdotes concerning Kafka.

March 6, Thursday

Rather discouraging silent days in which I find myself so low in spirits that I can't work or think. A constant panic which in spite of all efforts to overcome it seems to get loose again and again.

However, H.'s book arrived on Tuesday (the first copy) from Harcourt Brace. We read it over and over again. It looks fine and beautiful. I put it carefully away in the old glass bookcase among the ancestral books we're keeping for the children.

Muriel arrived for dinner that day. We had a fine talk, though all the uneasy edges are not yet smoothed over. But time, good will and patience will overcome them I suppose. She had on a beautiful new tailored dress of English cloth—peacock blue in color—and looked very smart and handsome. We were all gay and full of wit and gossip when for no reason at all I began to feel cold and ill.

I *must* mix more, meet more people, learn to converse with all kinds of people. I'm becoming frightfully narrow and absentminded through sheer isolation.

Empty cold, yellowish-gray streets when I look out of the window. A thick foamy smoke rising up from the tugboats on the river. One can almost *see* the wind, and the dry black trees standing sturdy and stripped, their black branches graceful and delicate as if made out of a fine strip of wavy black air.

March 7, Friday

Christopher Lazare* and Dunstan Thompson visited us last night. I felt sad and unwell and Lazare always makes me a bit uneasy, though with all his violence and malice and gossip I always feel that there is something fundamentally decent about him. But with people like L. one has to delude oneself or we would go mad. Some bitter and not unamusing comments delivered in that fearfully unconvincing accent full of French phrases. Of B. the French refugee: "There he is bewailing his poverty and Nazi persecution. Robbed of his possessions, bitter with privation, he staggers with grief daily into his suite at the Ritz Carlton." Or describing a young poet: "He's not a bad sort. Just the kind of sweet dear boy who likes nice warm luxurious apartments full of rich warm influential people who can help him!"

Thompson polished, sensitive, charming, equally bitter and sad and a little dazed by L. After L. left he—with more subtlety than L.—told us of his difficulties and fears. But this was done with understatement and good taste and, if it was not as momentarily amusing, was equally depressing in the long run. Very ill in the morning. In the afternoon I went down to Wall Street with Joanna to collect an English check [from Bryher] at the First National City Bank. The city beautiful under gray, cold skies, the sky scrapers are beginning to acquire an air of almost classical antiquity. Trinity Church spires in the background like the remains of a remote pastoral world—which of course it is.

Joanna's powerful dominating personality full of vigor and charm overwhelming me. I bought her a pretty new dress later at Lord & Taylor and she became a little girl again.

March 17, Monday

The attitudes of the refugees toward Thomas Mann is interesting. Rukeyser, who knows more refugees than we do, told me more about it. One would wish that he showed more humanity and less pomposity, but Mann has his own interests to look after and cannot, even if he wished, do all these people expect of him. As Muriel said, "Suppose we are all refugees in, say, Russia, and our chief of refugees is—he would be—Archibald MacLeish!" How would you approach him for help? How would you expect him to explain what your literary status is—or was—back home?" But I notice also a curious fear among the refugees in approaching Mann. He is their last hope, their last court of appeal—and if he fails them, repulses them—all is lost.

I think of these new emigrants from Europe with all their pretensions and think of the other kind that came in my parents' day. Their humble hopefulness, their simple wish to start from the bottom, to learn the language, to give their children (perhaps) a better break than they ever had. The great majority never rose from the morass. A few of their children did, but scarred to the soul. What these new people will do I don't know. The intellectual corruption of old Europe clings to so many of them. Their hearts, minds and souls are defiled.

A catty letter from Marianne Moore saying she had received my book. Her letter full of double meanings, an effort to evade saying anything—full of little feminine pin thrusts. The thing that hurt me most was the feeling I had that after she wrote the letter she obviously had said to herself, "Now I have had the fun of writing a letter in two meanings, and of course poor. M. Z. is too obtuse to get all but the surface meaning."

Still I have a great deal of admiration for M. Moore's work—which makes it all the worse. I also know her small, strange, tight little soul, that sharp, small, penetrating birdlike mind.

H. got another letter from William Carlos Williams, saying he had received Horace's book, that he liked it, etc.

March 21, Friday

Horace's Easter holiday begins now. Both our books are being sent out. So far very little response. Feel rather blue yet know that this means little. I did get a very long, carefully written, very understanding letter from John G. Fletcher, and a rather vague, puzzled one from my old friend Hillyer. With each book one loses an old friend and finds a new one.

Finding it difficult to get down to my essay on Hilda Doolittle. And yet I'm quite interested.

Corroding loneliness, made deeper by guests.

One guest we enjoyed was Klaus Mann. Much sensibility, beautiful manners, some perceptions but no brains, and very weak. Eleanor Clark was with him, very charming, gay and irresponsible.

March 27, Thursday

Visited Norman Pearson and his bride Susan last night in New Haven. As usual in these old Connecticut towns one is touched by vestiges of some old, vague charm. One sees the place as it must have been in the pastoral period of the eighteenth century—the small university, the pure white architecture, the poverty, the rich, sharp, clear, sophisticated and yet innocent spirit of pre-Revolutionary War New England.

Dudley Fitts and Cornelia were visitors. Norman charming, his two little stepdaughters delightful, Susan very nice. Went home on a late train and overheard a drunken soldier on leave reciting *Barrack-Room Ballads* of Kipling to his comrades. All were listening with awe and admiration, and again I wondered at that quality in Kipling that survives and keeps on surviving while so many more finished writers hardly live beyond a season's fame. He is not profound or witty, or even clever. All is on a school-boy level (spiritually and emotionally and intellectually), but his poetry has that force of life that nothing or nobody can simulate—one has it or one doesn't. He writes a language which for all the lack of the graces has something—*life*—again I think of the word—and I suppose one says too the other word, *genius*. But I don't like him. I don't like him, his mind, his imagination, his universe.

Have heard good news from Donald Adams about my book. Have hopes of three good reviews anyway. Hope and pray for H.'s too. We have not received many letters.

First days of early spring weather. Mellow, sleepy sunshine, thin, treacle-colored gold light appearing with a shy slowness. It falls on the cold street in a pale half-tone, draws back into the gray skies, lightens them for a while, and then falls on the street again.

April 10

Dear Horace's birthday and the first day of real spring weather. The gold, the brightness of the green utterly astonishing. One is taken by surprise every year.

Muriel is giving a birthday party for Horace today. Dread facing people. Wish only to be with Horace. The rest of the world is full of horror, murder, poisonous spirits; the air drips blood, the ground is wet with it and the streets smell like a jungle.

April 22

Saw Ted Wilson on Saturday. He rushed into the Forty-second Street library where I was checking some heavy tomes and embraced me before the startled librarians and onlookers. I felt charmed and pleased.

Dinner at Ken Fearing's—gloomy household. K. drinking long and without pause, his conversation coming up from some profound stupor. Told Horace how much he admired and loved him and how he wanted to answer B.'s filthy review on his book. H. and I told him he had always been a moral coward but that we loved him anyway. If he wished to do a review in answer OK— but it wouldn't matter. He won't do anything—I'm fairly sure. We left him at a bar still drinking at five in the morning.

Reviews of my book so far extremely favorable. If they keep on, I shall be established at last as a real poet.

H. got a warm letter of praise from Elizabeth Drew—one clutches these things.

Another headline: "British make stand at Thermopolae." And so we return to the ancient sources of Western civilization—and this time, who knows, the Persian hordes may finish us all.

April 28, Monday

Heavenly spring days. Through my newly washed windows the thin fine green of the trees and grass startle one with their sudden freshness. If one could only be well enough, strong enough to *give* oneself to all this beauty.

The news from Europe the most unbearable since the fall of France. Perhaps only a person with Jewish blood can feel the full terror, the dreadful feeling of a great tide of evil drawing nearer and nearer. It may be unreasonable, but all my dreams are nightmares and I tremble for my dear beautiful children. H. teases me, saying, "The British lose all the battles and win all the wars."

Another story of Klaus Mann whom C. said insisted on cutting articles sent to him for his magazine. "But Klaus, you can't do that. Nobody will stand for it." "Oh," said Klaus, "but my father allows me to cut his articles."

At which C. said despairingly, "But he is your father," at which Klaus stared in bewilderment.

H. and I were touched and surprised at his receiving a comparatively empathetic, decent review of *Poems, 1930–1940* from Allen Tate of all people. It is always the unexpected hand held out that saves the day.

May 12, Monday

A frightful torpor in which I find myself hiding in my dark bedroom, unable to read, to work, overcome by a dreadful drive to sleep and sleep and sleep. H. and I on one of our rare holidays together took a walk near Broadway. It was full noon, the air fresh and full of May. Everyone who passed us seemed to swim by in a pale gold light.

Had tea with Muriel Rukeyser or rather a cocktail at a place near her apartment on Thirty-eighth St. A very dark little bar, made to resemble a ship, the waiters dressed as sailors. Had to fight off the torpor so as to carry on a pleasant conversation. Her half-resentment and competitive attitude to me so obvious that I can't do anything but feel—feel my way out like a person stumbling through a dark place trying to avoid pitfalls and dangers. Left her in depression, for I am fond of her, but knowing again that aside from H. (who has difficulties of his own) I have no friends. Thought of X whom I have loved so much and realize that he has not been too considerate, or kind, that we have given him more than we have ever received.

Joanna growing up very fast and full of adolescent vagaries. I do not perceive them fast enough, and scold her, do not show enough sympathy and tenderness. Afterwards I lie awake with remorse and worry. She has a maddening habit of arguing every point, disagreeing with everything I say.

Harper's Bazaar accepted a poem of mine and I plan to buy some pretty clothes for Joanna and myself when I get the check. I am frightened at the way my desires have narrowed down, how few are the things I really want. It's not only a physical but spiritual torpor that seems falling down on me. When one ceases to desire one almost stops the full flood of life.

Went to a party given by the George Morrises who subsidize the *Partisan Review*. I was introduced to Allen Tate and his wife. He has a charming personality. One understands the hold he has on people. He spoke with warmth and admiration of Horace, saying, "You know I've always identified myself with Horace Gregory," which was strange. The Tates, Horace and I, and Eleanor Clark with Denis de Rougemont,* the French-Swiss who has written a book on love [*Love in the Western World*] much admired by Auden, all dined at the Princeton Club. I suddenly became desperately, violently ill, and H. took me home. I *can't* endure these things. Yet why should I evade them?

May 15, Thursday

A few more parties where one goes looking for what one knows we shall never find. Always the same—hostile, curious eyes, each person hoping for something unnamable, something that may happen but never happens. One party at the home of a Mrs. Winthrop Palmer, where the guest of honor, a visiting foreign poet, and some of the guests kept walking around stuffing their pockets with the cigarettes lavishly laid on the table! I should prefer thieving on a less petty scale. Felt frightfully tired, and a few drinks excite me and make me talk incessantly.

May 29, Thursday

The children's school is over now. It's delightful having them home and yet I long and yearn for and need a change, a place where I can get down to work. After all I am not much good for anything else.

Continual psychopathic sleepiness.

Frequent visits from Dunstan Thompson of whom we're becoming very fond. Elizabeth Johnson may become a friend but she's as mad as a March hare. Still she is on my side—and has made advances of friendship. A silence on my book. One becomes avid for reviews. Dinner with Constance Warren, president of Sarah Lawrence College. She seemed a handsome, intelligent shrewd woman. I liked her. Dinner with André Spire, the French poet. Very charming, delightful to hear beautiful, pure French. He's over eighty (I think) and has just become a father. Felt depressed at the thought of what exile must mean to a man of his age. How does one start all over again at that age with a new language? I've heard that his poetry is very lush and florid and his attacks on Paul Valéry annoyed me for I admire Valéry.

The President's speech. Dunston Thompson, Horace and I and three Sarah Lawrence girls (all beautiful and rich) listening in on our radio. The girls decidedly anti-Roosevelt (all have boyfriends of war age), frightfully upset. Horace and Thompson (who is the son of a naval officer) thought the speech a good one. I would have been upset if the President had not said what he said—but the thought of war fills me with anguish. When has war ever settled anything? And when have the great mass of people ever gained anything by it? Still I'm glad that we're not cringing to Hitler.

Last Saturday a long bus ride, noticing again and again how beautiful the city has become. Stopped at a record shop and listened to a beautiful Mass by Buxtehude and then H. and I went to a Viennese restaurant. Excellent but rich food and a fearfully gloomy atmosphere. A melancholy violinist played sorrowful tunes. People in various attitudes of gloom sat with heads in their hands or moped in majestical pathos, bad murals of Vienna on the wall, and German mottoes. We were glad to leave. We had dear little Pat with us. He refused to eat but stuffed his pockets with cookies.

July 2

Dinner at Petipas with Helen McMaster, a young Mr. McAdam (who is editing Dr. Samuel Johnson's poems for Oxford University Press), Christopher Lazare and T. C. Wilson. Lazare witty, brilliant, malicious. Helen McMaster took a great shine to him and we went to her apartment and drank a great deal and had a wild merry time. I drank less than anybody but got fearfully ill the next day.

Reflections on reading a life of Clara Schuman: "No matter how long it may be delayed the time comes when one can no longer hide the fact that a difference of technique, a change of feeling towards life and art must come and separate friends who have worked together—and fought together. Suddenly we see that our roads are divergent—that we have different friends and different enemies." This has happened to every one of my very few literary friends, except H. G. But this is because the personal love and understanding is great, his own rare and wide learning and tastes—and the fact that as far as my poetry is concerned we were not working together in a final sense. If I were to name the two women I admire most I would name Madame Curie and Clara Schuman—women who never lost their feminine instincts and who managed to give their valuable best without whines of self-pity or aggressive shrill attitudes.

Thick extraordinary heat fell over the city . . . difficult to endure.

I've bought some adorable coral red beach shoes which I wear without stockings. It's a delight to be so cool—and not to hide my really nice-looking legs.

An elaborate tea at the James J. Sweeneys'* apartment on the East River. Given for André Breton,* the French poet-painter, an interesting looking person wearing the strange clothes that Frenchmen think look very sporting and smart—loud checks, funny tie. His wife once beautiful but now looking harassed and frightened. With them a fearful French infant aged four, female, in very short skirts, who went from table to table talking brightly in a squeeky voice and helping herself to drinks. But the poor parents may have been too unsettled in a new country to have fully disciplined her. French refugees of all refugees make me the most uneasy. Note: the wonderful river view and terrace in the apartment!

Peterborough—MacDowell Colony, July 4

A long hot uncomfortable trip with the Edwin Stringhams by automobile to the Colony. Frightful heat wave, the children who were with us uncomfortable but very lively. With difficulty I found a place for them in town where they seem contented. I have Horace's old studio, full of pallid, pale-blue and pink watercolors, a luxurious and uncomfortable room. To begin work at once is difficult, the new faces, the high clear air so different from the city, all affect me. K. A. and his wife here. I dislike and distrust him as much as ever, though he is gossipy and amiable. There are some people who keep all conversation down to the pettiest level, draw out the pettiest and most disagreeable qualities in others. He is one of them. However, it will be a lesson in social tact, decorum, discretion for me—qualities that I need badly.

An unbelievable Miss H. from California, fat, florid, middle-aged, who writes detective stories and speaks of the "inspiration" she receives from music in composing her works. Amazingly self-centered, self-absorbed conversation which would have been embarrassing even in a young girl of great beauty, talent and charm. At the dinner table at the Colony Inn she began about herself again, and feeling tired, worried, overwrought, I did something I hadn't done since I was an adolescent school girl. I burst into an uncontrollable fit of schoolgirl giggles, hysterical laughter which I couldn't stop. Everyone at the table was embarrassed. I felt ashamed, shocked, angry at myself too. Controlled myself with difficulty but made an effort to be attentive and polite to Miss H.

A few days before starting for Peterborough we returned from a six-day trip from Milwaukee. The family kind, attentive, more at ease than on previous visits. H.'s little nephew Tom Goadby Gregory a vigorous and delightful child. The beautiful Wisconsin landscape, rich and rolling, dotted with bright blue lakes, were things I will remember. H.'s father unusually kind and generous. Uncle John and Aunt Victoria at their historic house on Jefferson Street like figures out of a Victorian past. Uncle J. remembering General Grant and G. Sherman whom he said had kissed him as a child, an incredible remark that made us all smile. It is so hard to think of him as a child. The Skeleton in the Closet, Cousin Paul, brought down to see us for awhile, his fat dead hands and yellow ageless face, his "literary" conversation and amazingly wide, curious, scattered reading. Most horrifying of all the flashes of real poetic sensibility that now and then lighted up the strange, lonely-ravenous, eager, frightening conversation. One began to wonder if perhaps under other circumstances—but no there was no hope ever I'm sure.

July 5, Saturday

Missed breakfast today but it meant that we went to town and saw the children who looked well and happy. Jo went back with us and collected her clothes and I watched her from the doors of my studio (the Lodge), trudging back to town, a handsome figure of a little girl.

Last night a concert at the library. Fine Bach fugue played by a young composer from Harvard and a young Cherokee Indian composer who played Indian songs. I don't pretend to have a feeling for Indian folk music. Some incredibly vile poetry read with club-woman graces and the brassy assurance of the stupid and insensitive. I no longer have the tolerance I had. I boil over with impatience and anger. People who have been practicing a craft for many years can at least show enough affection and respect for it to learn the bare essentials, the technical tools of their job—genius or talent cannot be acquired, but *skill,* a little taste, some knowledge of their craft *can* be learned—and with little difficulty if one is really interested.

July 19, Saturday

Long conversations with the Richard Days, the people at whose house Joanna and Pat are staying. Descendants of old settlers in Peterborough, pure old New England stock. High level of culture and intelligence, though they are very poor—a much higher standard of thinking and feeling and refinement than among many of the people here at the Colony. The long drive by automobile home from their house in town to our studio at the Lodge. The pure high air, the quiet sound of the leaves, the great half-wild, half-cultivated air of calm in the landscape. It is, as Marianne Moore says, "a privilege."

The people here intolerably difficult and I fight hard to retain common sense, courtesy and calm. Lost my temper the other day and became indiscreet, which put me at a disadvantage at once. These people live, live their being, earn their living, have gained their little reputation, not with their work, which is of inferior merit, but through their social adaptabilities, their ability to manipulate a certain type of person, the charming elderly ladies who are sentimental about the arts and like their artists to appeal to their facile sentimentalities, and like them to appear "artistic." Ridicule, says H., is the greatest weapon. I don't think so. I can be witty but wit has a quality of intellect in it that to the average person is as hateful and frightening as straight intellect. They may laugh but it is frightening. They can't laugh with ease at it.

July 22, Tuesday
I felt dismally for a while that we had not made a single new friend here, which depressed me greatly. But I was wrong. There is a delightful young Frenchman and a composer, André Jacques, whom we like and whose work makes us respond, and a young painter called Pearson or Person, with a subtle, sensitive mind who seems to be fond of us. . . . Diamond* the composer is interesting, red-haired, as neurotic as Hart Crane. . . . This is a beginning anyway.

Troubled about not getting a letter from Dunstan Thompson. I must be fonder of the boy than I thought. A sort of warm maternal solicitude for I dreamed last night that he came to me, his face unusually transparent, dark circles under his very large speaking eyes. After a while the face faded away and the eyes, very large, clear and blue, began to speak to me and transmitted a message which said he had just died, died of dysentery. Now dysentery is not a favorite disease, nor have I any reason to associate dysentery with D. T., though he does look frail. Still I shall be glad to hear from him. The dream *was* disturbing.

The pompous Pole here, L., who plays continually on the piano. "I no longer play anything but me," he said, and he shakes his Paderewski mane and goes on playing muddy post-Rachmaninoff compositions by the hour. Then he makes an elaborate professional bow. Diamond told me he (L.) was a Polish count. "You know they're very dignified and stiff." I said, "Do all Polish counts play the piano?" and Diamond, who is after all a Copeland protegé, said quickly with an odd look in his eyes, "Why not?"

The Hysterical Sculptress with her fantastic clothes, her outbursts of emotion as she talks of African art, "the *only* sculpture. The Greeks were children beside it." Her curious eye infirmity which gives one the impression that she is always leering or winking at you.

July 25, Friday

Am reading a great deal of Henry James if only to learn to say the most subtle and simple things in the most subtle and exquisite way. His beautiful precise diction, that touch of sudden surprising sweetness and piercing penetration that one finds only in Proust or Rilke. But something odd, something sterilizing about the mind, the soul behind the books.

July 28, Monday

Went down with severe grippe, neuralgia, fever. Utterly disgusted. All our dream vacations seem to evaporate. Is it all our fault?

A surprise visit from Dunstan Thompson who brought four other Harvard boys, all gay, delightful, clever, all interested in poetry. Dunstan and I got lost walking to the lodge in the dark and he was charming, reminding me that he had a marvelous sense of direction, that at the age of five he had helped his mother find her hotel when she had taken him for a walk in Rome and had forgotten the name of her hotel and her address. When I became nervous he offered me a cigarette and we wandered on, in what seemed like black moors à la Emily Brontë, looked into houses that looked like Wuthering Heights and at last ran into Dunstan's friends looking for us. A delightful evening but the next day a frightful letup. To be happy, treated with affection and respect, after the ugly ordeal here was too much of a change.

Reading H. James' *Princess Casamassima,* while I was ill. Moved and disturbed by it. It's the kind of proletarian novel I understand, the best and most understanding pictures of the types that made up the Movements here in the 1930s. I kept identifying myself with Hyacinth Robinson.

The people here incredible and unbearable. Writers who never write, painters who cannot paint, poets who no longer care for poetry (if they ever have cared for poetry), dwindling, dead or stillborn reputations, tension, bad manners. (H. in his usual beautiful courtesy had to give up his chair to an old lady when he found that everyone was letting her stand up during a concert—yet H. is lame and frail!) The children delightful, loved, beloved, above all things, but one can face them with more pleasure if we feel that we are building up a name of which they will be proud, a home where all is well.

Blame myself. I cannot hide "black-blood" traits, nor have I H.'s exquisite taste, poise, stoicism, fine manners that come from a fine-grained mind and soul. I've learned from him slowly, but every once in a while when I see the dreadful others I wonder if he too suddenly sees similar traits in me. I look in the mirror and the ancestral taint, the horror scenes, very plain—and my fear is that I may pass the poison on to H.—perhaps to my darlings.

August 1, Friday

Saw *Charley's Aunt* with Pat and Joanna and André Jacques, the delightful little French composer who is here. The playhouse barn set in the lovely country was charming. So were the young actresses who kept running in and out, lighting candles, chattering, singing. Pat amused us by shaking hands with many of the actresses and carrying on gay conversations with them. It seems that they live at Mrs. Langley's where Pat and Joanna had their meals. He was obviously a great favorite and was given a seat in the front row. The play delightful and foolish, the stock types must of course be doubly amusing to the English because they *are* stock types, the foolish young Lord obviously a forerunner of a Wodehouse character. The play was written in 1892, the program says, and I couldn't help thinking how in the perfect state of the future, horrified historians would examine the immoralities of the thing, the pursuit of any woman, no matter what her age and appearance, who has money, the really lustful pursuit of easy money (the theme is immemorial, only in Edwardian England it had a certain stuffy hypocrisy about it), the silly antics of the Oxford undergraduates whom one was never sure could pass an examination, and one of whom was planning to become a member of Parliament. Anyway, the airy, silly nonsense did us good though I had a bad cold.

Dear God, purify, purify, purify me. Cleanse my soul, clear my mind, make me silent, wise, tolerant. Free me from vindictive feelings, fears, unreasonable jealousies, and from the Power of the Evil One. Save me from the impulsively foolish word, the impulsively histrionic act—which always betrays (in the worst sense) the "black blood."

August 6

The hectic excitement and fervor of the last weeks has died down, leaving shattered nerves and bad tempers. Marcia Silvette,* a little artist from Virginia who was here last year, greeted me with affection and I felt startled. One had become so accustomed to averted looks and downright hostility and even abuse. I have a real *rapport* with her and her work too, which is so close to many of the things that I'm doing in poetry—or rather trying to do.

Ed Stringham and his wife have been wondrous kind and they have taken us for rides in their car. To get out deep into the country is fine. It lifts the spirit up, and my imagination flowers again. I feel young and pretty and at one with the beautiful moving landscape and at home in the sun.

Norman Pearson and his wife Susan surprised us with a visit. Norman laughed when he passed through my studio and found it was called *The Pearson Memorial Room.*

August 8

Pleasant sunny day yesterday which I spent partly in a painful stupefied sleep, partly in sitting in the sun. Began a poem which seems to have nothing in it, all vagueness, pain and confusion. An abscessed tooth again brought on pain and fever and I became discouraged and angry. It means more teeth pulling. In the evening the Stringhams took us out riding to Dublin Lake. Very serene and beautiful country, but my mind was too sullied and upset to really benefit by the smooth shining lake, the heavy rolling hills, the black and purple mountains.

We went to an auction given at the town hall here, and found Pat admiring some swords and guns and Joanna, the old furniture and objets d'art. She and Marcia Silvette bid for an old candlestick, a Crystal Palace horror, a sort of Victorian-Italian monstrosity. They explained that they intended to decorate and enamel the gilded figure on the stem and give it a new coat of paint. Joanna said that she would give the figure, which was that of a little girl swathed in bronze heavy draperies, a real classic touch and call it "Iphigenia in Peterborough." The thing was bought for forty cents, Marcia paying twenty cents and Joanna twenty cents.

Marcia is working on a portrait of Joanna which from her description sounds lovely. I haven't seen it yet. She borrowed my precious Victorian locket with the heavy silver chain and the blue enamel flowers to use for the portrait.

August 11, Monday

T. sent us a copy of the *Southern Review.* A review of Horace by Blackmur again! Respectful but quibbling. A copy of *Partisan Review,* a magazine that is becoming more and more repulsive to me. Auden's poem on the grave of Henry James wordy and heavy and scattered, but touches of that wit and intelligence that serve only to show the mediocrity of his imitators.

H. throwing aside a copy of Emily Dickinson's *Collected Poems.* "I may be prejudiced. I daresay she *is* the American Sappho, but every once in a while I can't help thinking, 'What a fine foolish old maid she is.' "

August 18, Monday

Crisp windy cold spell. Nights of insomnia and nervous exhaustion. A loss of morale that affects my work. The only pleasant and hopeful sign a note from K. A. of *Accent* asking for some work. I sent two poems, but it's not my favorite magazine. Fears, worry, panic, difficulties with one of the servants here due to my untidiness, though not all my fault. I have been careful so long that it's like a retrogression here in all respects, in looks, self-confidence, habits.

Pleasant talks with little Marcia Silvette who is very amiable, but I don't know how to respond. Not a line or letter from a friend. Reviews of our books seem to have stopped. It's as if the hostility here has spread to the outside world. Went to church here with Silvette. Found no consolation, for the inner disturbance was too great.

A pleasant walk and talk with my dear little Pat. Felt the greatest ease and pleasure—delight in walking down the street with him and talking and listening to him. My love for him too passionate and intense, too many elements of anxiety in it.

August 20, Wednesday

Tomorrow our wedding anniversary. Had a very pleasant afternoon talking with H.—one of the nicest in this nerve-wracked vacation. The sound of rain outside, the damp cold which even the wood fire did not dispel. Did very little work. I read a detective story, *The Bucharest Ballerina Murders,* one of those nice quick international spy stories with an exotic background. Have always been fascinated by accounts of the Balkan capitals.

But far from well. I'm troubled, for how can one do live, strong, clear work if one is always languid and only half-well?

Looked over Emily Dickinson again with new respect and envy. What makes her is the freshness, the originality, the prodigality of her mind and imagination, her never-failing keen sensory perceptions. Creative energy so overwhelming that it spilled over and made her forms mold themselves into poems, created her own universe. One of the few poets who had so much to say that the thing said almost makes the complete poem, and is the technique. How, how did she do it? She saw so much in such a limited space. Her reading was narrow and excellent. Too much of the fashionable reading of the day would have marred that freshness. Of course there was Elizabeth Browning, but it seemed to be a personal identification rather than a *literary* influence. Literary *coteries* would have been fatal. One agrees again with Rilke that isolation, loneliness, even a good amount of frustration is necessary for a poet.

The love poems absolutely authentic, obviously springing from a *real* experience. No imagination no matter how much charged with gems could have invented these poems; their look of agony is too convincingly true, undeniably convincing, springing from a real source of love, frustration and pain.

August 21, Thursday

A brief attack on my book in the *Christian Science Monitor,* denying me everything. The *CSM* has always fought me and I've never taken it seriously, but at this moment everything shocks, disturbs, lowers my wavering morale. The complete silence from friends very demoralizing.

Went in the evening with Peggy Stringham, Marcia Silvette and her sister Mildred, Joanna and Pat to see *George Washington Slept Here* at the Peterborough Players. The place full of prosperous-looking people, the young actors very good. The play almost cured me of a desire to own a house in the country, one of my most ancient dreams. The something malodorous that one always finds in a George Kaufman play like the dehumanization in the Restoration dramatists. A frightful scene where the people who have learned to love the house so dearly start to destroy it with fervor when they learn that an enemy is planning to take it over. These people can destroy as easily as they can build—no, one feels that destruction pleases them more. Little Pat as usual got a front-row seat and sat starry-eyed. He is proud of knowing some of the pretty actresses.

August 24

Pleasant Sunday, very sunny. Did a little work after a long period of silence. Elizabeth Johnson is visiting us. I have never become quite intimate with her, but she's a relief after the underworld of old ladies who write foolish dialect poems and cute verses for kiddies. A disgraceful occurrence in the music room when Ed Stringham had a fine composition of his performed and Koussevitsky the famous conductor came as his guest. The old ladies went hysterical when the audience demanded an encore since they were cheated of a scheduled reading of their frightful poems and a playing of a piece by a heavy-handed spinsterish girl who had put one of their poems to music. Amateurish, appalling, the words, the music, the playing. Koussevitsky showed much enthusiasm for Stringham's piece (his first composition in ten years) and the old ladies complained that he had broken the rules by inviting a non-Colonist to come. To them a man of the conductor's distinction was nothing. They felt the distinction, the genuine passion for an art and hated it with all their vulgar, frustrated little souls.

August 27, Wednesday

Nothing can describe the pure tranquillity, the perfect beauty of this approaching autumn landscape. The trees slowly reddening, the quick wind blowing through everything, sweeping the grass and air and preparing us for cold, the half-cold, half-gold tinted light, melancholy and serene. My favorite season and I'm so enchanted with it that I rush through my work so that I can go outdoors. I like the people here less and less and love the landscape here more and more.

September 6, Riverside Drive

Returned last week, exhausted, the change of air brought on cold and grippe. Fewer and fewer the friends who welcome us on our return. Thought of the Dick Eberhart wedding we attended in Cambridge, the hundreds of friends and relatives who were standing in line at the house and in the church to wish the bride and bridegroom joy. Dudley Fitts playing the organ at the church. His wife Cornelia very charming.

On reflection the Peterborough episode this year seems like a failure. The whole thing now appears as a nightmare. Yet we have done some good work this year, a handful of real poems.

Have been reading Landor's poetry again—he is completely out of the customary English tradition which is one reason why he is one of the least known (and read!) of the great English poets.

A new maid, Ozelle Mills, never showed up, to our regret.

Jim Putnam who saw H. yesterday told us of a visit he had had from Jim Farrell. F. told how he was sick of his own writing—felt dissatisfied with his new novel and was starting to keep a journal! He felt that the journal was the very best thing he'd ever done.

Want to lie down all day. Unable to work. My hands callused and sore from my few days of housework. Shocked, distressed, angry at my inefficiency.

September 12, Friday

A clear cold autumnal light from our window. Nothing of the wildness, the exuberance of the autumn light I have seen in New England. In the city it takes on a hard sharp aspect but it is beautiful nevertheless.

Attended an academic conference at Columbia, always a difficult thing for me, for I wriggle and twist like a child and am always glad to run home when it's over, saying to myself, "School's over." Noticed the prosperous appearance of many of the well-known academic figures from eastern universities, the reverence with which Cleanth Brooks of the *Southern Review* is treated by the younger academicians, the tentative, timid, graceful discretion of Elizabeth Drew in defending modern poetry. There is no doubt that the conservatives have it here as always. Van Wyck Brooks was cheered for a half-hour in a foolish virulent attack on modern literature, Eliot, Pound, Joyce, etc. Good, bad, indifferent, all together. The attacks on Eliot always the worst. He has a genius for arousing hatred. Yet no one can take his undeniable talent away. *Murder in the Cathedral* still remains the most moving of all the poetic plays written so far in the twentieth century. "Ash Wednesday," for sheer haunting cadences and delicate music, is one of the great lyric as well as devotional poems of our day, and who can take away the historic importance of "The Wasteland"? He has the thing that Van Wyck Brooks lacks, a quality of mind. In spite of Brooks' delightful writing, all seems flabby, soft, blurred because somewhere is lacking a hard firm center—a strong intellect.

Today is (I think) my birthday, at least I always give September 12 as the date, though I have no proof of it. My father only remembers the date from some religious holiday and can't place it in our calendar, but it's vaguely around this time and somewhere I've see a passport (now lost) that gives this date. But that is only an uncertain memory. I can't remember where I saw this date.

Joanna has started at public high school. It's difficult. I'm troubled, but she's old enough now.

September 15, Monday

Found myself unable to walk—must see doctor. These endless illnesses are exhausting and the fine country air did me no good. H. says he has nightmares about Peterborough. I'm afraid it was not the place for us!

Sarah Lawrence opened again today. Hated to see my dear H. off again since I do not feel that he has had a too restful summer. My ambition is to save as much money as possible, so as to give him a year off. If I were not so lazy (or really *feeble*, that is the word), I would try for that damnable Guggenheim. And there is fear as well as laziness that holds me back.

Muriel R. coming for dinner tonight, the first time since we've arrived. Have a deep rapport with her but it's hardly a soothing or helpful friendship.

H. and I went window shopping on Fifth Ave. Overwhelmed by the luxuries, the beauty of the windows, the great amount of spending so obvious to anyone. A great deal of money is being made by the class that always makes money. As for the poor everything is going up, food, rent, clothing, the small luxuries.

Note and prayer: Teach me dear God to guard my tongue especially with my dear ones. Keep me gentle, humble, patient, uncomplaining. Have been so cross lately, nagged and scolded, and ill health is no excuse.

Troubled about my father. Give him small sums of money, but I should do more. I can't.

September 16, Tuesday
Went to the doctor yesterday, and as I paid the bill felt my old sense of panic at seeing so much of dear H.'s hard-earned money go in such ways. I must get well, must acquire more energy, well-being, strength.

Must take a vow to cut out three-quarters of my smoking.

M. R. visited us last night. As usual, H. and I too tired to be entertaining and R. is used to a pretty snappy set, smart, quick. Told me about the innumerable French refugees who sit around sneering at the U.S., wishing they were in Paris, of old Thomas Mann's difficulty in making an adjustment in this country. "He insists on being a Master and as you know we are not a reverential lot here." An amusing story of Golo Mann referring seriously to his father as the Master, and everybody bursting into laughter. We invented nice nicknames for Klaus and Erica, Roco and Coco. The split between M. and ourselves pretty deep but there are old ties now that keep things going.

The reviews of our books. If we stop to brood, to worry, to be angry, we are lost indeed. I do not know which is worse, to be praised and misunderstood or to be misunderstood and attacked, in either case by people whose work we usually despise and whose character we don't respect. To be patronized by fools!!

Too ill for normal human intercourse, no spring, no resiliency, or gaiety—and yet one longs for it.

September 20, Saturday

T. C. Wilson arrived from Columbus, Ohio, and was full of unusually good conversation. It was so pleasant and the warmth that came from greeting an old friend made me feel how little of that great pleasure we have had recently.

He repeated a comment of C. Lazare with whom he had been visiting Hollywood. L. had been invited to a popular Hollywood painter's house and, having been introduced as a New York art critic, was very well received. After the man had shown him his paintings, he turned to L. and asked for an opinion. L. said, "There is enough Picasso in them to hide the Marie Laurencin influence."

C. L. and Ted had visited the Thomas Manns and gave an attractive account of the old man who looks so much more vital, elegant, alert and youthful than his children. He was worried about Klaus and asked C. what he thought K. ought to do if the magazine is given up. L. suggested a job in Hollywood, at which Mann sighed and said, "It means having the Warners to dinner again." He then asked the young man as they left to take his son Golo out, since the boy was depressed. "What he needs is a little debauchery," he said hesitating, trying to find the right English word.

September 22, Monday

Visited the dentist, always a painful ordeal. He gave me a long lecture on relaxing, on "cutting up," on taking things easy. I need peace, love, a little encouragement and praise, but I've "relaxed" enough. I need a good steady job and the sense of work well done. I am distressed at my lack of energy.

Unable to read or write with ease. This useless journal has become a source of consolation. It is a habit I can no longer even think of relinquishing. A critical period for us. I try to console H. by saying that we have lived through critical periods before—and come through, but if he despairs I despair too. I depend so much (too much!) on his courage, brilliance and optimism.

September 27

I wake up every morning with a frightful cold that half disappears in the evening and returns again. Wearing and discouraging, uncomfortable and yet too trivial to complain about.

Ingres on Delacroix's paintings. "The complete expression of an incomplete intelligence." The Delacroix admirers can turn this epigram back on Ingres, of course. Ingres' painting is amazingly like Landor's poetry. Those who don't like it *won't* like it and find the very perfections irritating.

Long lonely bus rides when I watch the crowds go by as if watching a fiesta of light and life from which I'm left out.

Sent two poems to the *Atlantic* three months ago, perhaps four. Not a sign, not a word, not an answer. Very wounding. If they don't like it, why not throw it back at once? These little things do much to shatter my morale.

I am beginning to see why those who become preoccupied with death end up by falling in love with it.

Walked through Morningside Drive Park and admired the 1880ish charm of Morningside Drive which is taking on a period air, and the almost old-world charm of the park. Memories of my youth when I would call on Marguerite Wilkinson and her husband, who lived near there. I remember thinking their apartment heavy and stuffy and remember the Pre-Raphaelite pictures on the wall, and M. W.'s influence on the poetry I was writing must have been bad. She was a literary power of a sort in those days but I never knew it. All I wanted was someone to like me, to admire, me, to talk poetry to. No one started writing with less ambition, more ignorance, more confusion than I did. Nor did I ever have large hopes. It seems that I have only found myself in the last few years.

September 30

Let me call the last week or so "the days of the passion" and keep them from now on as days in which I can meditate on life, its ebbing away, ambition, and the strange forms it takes. Think of its penalties and rewards, the great fortune that would have changed the world if it had not eluded us by a breath, a turn of the wrist, a slip of the tongue. The mysteries and uncertainties of love, the fluctuations of friendship. There is no doubt that both H. and I are passing through a critical period of our lives, but we shall survive and conquer. Haven't we learned to see more clearly, suffer with more patience? Are we not being stripped sharply and cleanly of our last illusions? Now is the time to begin, now we can change our life. What stands in the way? Only the Two Great Obstacles, financial insecurity and bad health, but it is the body not the spirit that has ever failed us.

October 1, Wednesday

On Monday H.'s day off we went shopping at Stern's, buying some household linen. H. urged me to buy some trinkets, shoes, or a dress since these things were all going up in price, due to war taxation. H. also foresees rationing soon. But it is only easy to economize when one has money to economize with. H. says the state universities and poorer schools are falling in registration. On the way from Sterns we dropped in at the Gramophone Shop and bought an excellent recording of Handel's *Water Music* (a concession to luxury buying). The first movement delightful, fresh, gay and pure, the rest merely charming. A bad evening, illness, quarrel with H.—we said harsh things—sleepless night.

The *Southern Review* commissioned H. to do an essay on Yeats—the first good bit of news in ages. M. R. telephoned, was in her best mood, is publishing my Leopard poem in *Decision*. Heard but indirectly good news from D. T., and that his magazine *Vice-Versa* will be out soon.

Read George Barker's new book of poems, some of it very fine, glowing, full of real imagination and talent and good direct writing. The influence of Hart Crane on a new group of English poets very interesting. It's an excellent antidote to the crisp, bare journalism and spiritual sterility of such poets as MacNeice, the later Spender and Day-Lewis and even some of Auden. The later poems of Barker (especially the American ones) full of mannerisms and parodies of himself. Like Auden he seems to have lost his roots here and his real field of reference. The faults are then apparent and one sees the strained image, the facility, the lack of a firm center.

October 2, Thursday

Never have I needed more courage, more resolution to keep on going. Even H. seems to have lost any feeling for me. I think if I died tomorrow it would not affect him greatly. I feel that the reviewing of our books together has wounded him and that unconsciously perhaps he is angry with me. But it wounds me too, first to have him exposed to ridicule at my expense, and because I too can't help but feel the sneers and slurs on my own account.

Must keep on working when all the heart and impetus is going out. The four walls maddening. The locked in feeling dreadful, the isolation terrifying, the indifference of friends paralyzing. It's as if they secretly rejoice in our misfortunes and must have resented any small good fortune. It is not to them we can turn—but to whom? There is no one left but God and one doesn't do Him the discourtesy of leaving Him for the last. One comes to Him with all our richest feelings. One should not bring him nothing but our emptiness and despair.

October 11

A bus ride as usual and I watch Fifth Avenue glow in the first Indian summer weather of the season. A renewed spirit of health and I find myself looking at the clothes in the department store windows, feeling pretty again, hopeful and warm.

H. complaining of exhaustion again, his slowness, his maddening slowness, when he writes. Yet his only hope for escape from teaching lies in his writing, and his teaching keeps him from writing. Sometimes I feel as if I'm in a jail that is slowly being turned into a padded, quiet madhouse. Desperate attempts at economy but H. wants to give up nothing and yet wants all the results of economy. The few literary opportunities he has had slip away and I'm consumed by the fear that soon they won't come again.

A slow steady rain breaking in on the gnawing silence. The Weldon Kees and the Teddy Shedlovskys to dinner. It's difficult to write when one's mind is torn by a thousand hopes and fears and distractions.

October 13, Monday

Marcia Silvette's copy of Joanna's picture arrived. I had it framed in a heavy antique old-gold frame with silvery tints and a gray linen border. It looks delightful, and we've found just the right place for it over the old eighteenth-century desk that belonged to Horace's grandmother's grandmother. The picture has given me great pleasure. I look at it whenever my spirits fall too low, and my heart is lifted. It made the bad summer in Peterborough seem worthwhile.

A frightful party to which we were taken by the young poet H. M. College classmates all arrogant and young, their young wives full of social pretensions. All on the make in the arts. Conversation such as we haven't heard since the 1920s. A young Harvard man in uniform, interested in painting, talking self-consciously about army life. Ted Wilson (whom we had asked to come along) came in drunk and became a little obscene and insulting to the company, not without justification, but it was painful. I lost control only once when the young soldier (a really sweet boy) said airily, "After all the army is a very honorable profession," and I said, "Yes, it's the oldest profession in the world." It was the self-conscious "I am a soldier air," that irritated, not of course the army, and one couldn't resent the obvious shot. He stared. I think my little joke was lost.

Visit from Wilson. Confidences about his private life. I usually leave him to H. and disappear. There are some confidences I've learned it is better for *me* not to receive. T. C. is a nice boy, so much of his charm depended on extreme youth, and he feels the passing of his twenties heavily. He has real talent but his private conflicts ruin everything. A bad conversationalist, except occasionally on abstract subjects, but warm and polite.

I am beginning to feel conscious of the fact that my brief good looks are going, that I always look unwell, that my conversation is rarely what it was when it was good. But wit and gaiety desert one in ill health. H. looked very frail as he walked down the street in the brisk autumn air, and I became angry at Fate that had rewarded his warm, generous heart, his fine intellect, his great talent with so little.

"Few characters can bear the microscopic scrutiny of wit quickened by anger and perhaps the best advice to authors would be that they should keep out of the way of one another." – Samuel Johnson

October 15, Wednesday

Humility. The most deadly quality any man or woman of talent who is growing and developing can have. Let it develop after achievement. In too many cases it is an excuse for groveling, for laziness, for indifference, for lack of proper self-respect or confidence which is essential. "What have you done to be so modest?" said Ibsen to the diffident young poet. "What have you done to be so humble?" might be asked of the writer who has no body of work, no serious effort to his credit.

Monday, October 20

Visited Ted Wilson in his new apartment near the Murray Hill neighborhood. He had furnished the place in exquisite taste and received us at the door beautifully dressed, looking very handsome. We had Winfield Townley Scott* with us, who had dropped in to see us, and after a few drinks we broke into conversation.

Horace and I were much touched by seeing over T. C.'s mantelpiece three framed photographs, one of Marianne Moore, one of Horace, one of William Carlos Williams.

A letter from Dunstan Thompson who is evidently going through one of those psychological messes which now fill us with horror. Only an Auden can survive these things and keep on doing excellent work. In most promising young men, we now know it for a danger sign—one does not dare to hope for their future. What a pity for he has so much wit, capacity, charm, cleverness—and money. One hoped much from his magazine.

Oscar Williams called, full of stupendous and colossal plans. His lively, shrewd, advertising-man's imagination carries us away on wings of enthusiasm. We see millions of copies of the anthologies he is planning distributed through women's clubs, book-of-the-month clubs, government agencies, all

Big Names united to help Oscar. Everything becomes simple, easy, nothing is too incredible. Only when he leaves do we realize that we've been fed opium, that it must all be a daydream, that everything is too grandiose. He told me with great surprise and no little irritation that W. H. Auden, asked to give a select list of his favorite American and English poets, sent one in and that my name was on the list, which surprised and pleased me for I've never tried to get his approval. But it proves that my poetry does appeal to those who boast of a *modern* sensibility, that I'm not so remote, unread and airy-fairy as my critics would like to believe.

I try to keep my mind off the news from Europe which is more frightful than ever. The papers casually talk of the slain in millions. How difficult it is to give birth to children, how easy to destroy them! Nor am I one of those sentimental optimists who believe that if women would run the world all would be peace and Utopia. The fact is that women are people and are apt to be as brutal, selfish and ugly as anybody else. No, their position of slavery throughout the ages has made them narrower, harder, less generous, usually more selfish than men. For what is more terrifying than a suddenly emancipated slave rising to power? Anyone who has worked in a place where women are in authority knows the difficulties.

October 23, Thursday
Met Horace at the Museum of Modern Art at four in the afternoon to see an old German movie, *The Loves of Jeanne Ney*, a strange period piece, dull, slow-paced and yet full of some powerful fascination—a historical fascination. The costumes, the heavy, thick-set, awkward heroine with her dull strange eyes that seemed as if they belonged to a drug fiend or sleep walker, her clumsy dreamy movements, her thick ankles. Shots of Paris in about 1918–1920 (I'm not sure of the date) like some world seen in a fantasy or nightmare. A street scene in Montmarte with a darkening sky and the sight of a rain falling that fell so long ago (was it a real rain?) gave one a feeling of sadness and uncanniness. The Communist hero who is sent to France to foment strikes or insurrections in Toulon. Rather amusing if one knows the connotations put on these things today.

On the way out in the entrance hall we ran into newspaper photographers, many school children. A crowd of onlookers listening to Mayor La Guardia making a speech. La Guardia, with his short fat grotesque figure, his lively coarse clever face and raucous voice held me as he exhorted the crowd to help get rid of Hitler and so get rid of heavy taxes for defense. A very faint applause as the photographers got busy. But war still seems faint and far away though American lives are being lost on the high seas, and the clouds grow darker.

October 29, Wednesday

Horace returned from the college complaining of illness, probably due to overwork, strain and the bad food served at the luncheon table there. He had started to pitch in and complete my Elinor Wylie chapter but worked with excruciating slowness and as usual left it unfinished, undone, making it difficult for me to go on. One cannot blame him and yet it filled a world full of unfinished fragments and again I felt the sense of a great blockage before my eyes, a wall of frustration. The book *must* be done, even in spite of obstacles. If I had sat around waiting for the perfect income, the perfect respite, the right moment, when would I have ever made my poor beginning? But one must not expect the impossible. And yet only by making the effort can we find a way out.

The closed-in, shut-in world growing narrower and narrower. I walk out in the little International House park near the Cathedral, and the gray beauty, bleak and nostalgic, of the season, the long wide empty street fill me completely, but I have no desire to interpret and translate this beauty into my poems as I once did.

H. home from school today and in bed. I've never seen him so languid, so ready to give in. I live by his courage.

Reading Fielding's *Jonathan Wild,* a magnificent, virulently moral, burning, horrifying book. I agree with Saintsbury that it's one of the great English books but can easily see why it's not one of the popular or most recommended books. Even the Victorians who can approve of its moral couldn't but be horrified by its brutality, its ferocity, its freedom from sentiment and illusion. There is not a softening of the horror or tension or contempt in the whole book. Even the humor becomes too sharp and bitter and cuts like a knife. It's an unendurable book, a strong man's book, the book of a man who has looked so deeply into life that the truth has driven him into a frenzy, a book written by a magistrate of genius. It's not a book one can read without pain, disgust and uneasiness—and therefore most people prefer to praise it and let it alone. A curiously English book too, the hard morality and brutality and vigor of the English mind at its most characteristic period.

Sheridan Le Fanu. For a long time I've been fascinated by this obscure Irish writer who has written such powerful and imaginative stories of mystery and horror. One gets too from him such a clear, strong picture of eighteenth-century Ireland—full of vigor and strong poetry, still saturated in the great prose of Goldsmith, Sheridan, Swift and Burke before the Lovers and the Tom Moores and the purveyors of sap and sentiment came in to defile that peculiar mixture of strength and imaginative wit. Le Fanu's stories are full of sentiment and strong poetic touches worthy of a Joyce and a Yeats, and he can create a really extraordinary atmosphere, a Dublin street of the late eighteenth or early nineteenth century, a deserted moor, an old cemetery, a broken down manor house from whose windows we always see a vivid face, and through that manly colorful diction we get a deep romantic fervor and a really distinguished style. His ghosts and phantoms seem to come from a real world. If they are from the world of dreams, they are inhabitants of a dream world that has its origins in the living beauty and terror of the real world.

October 31, Friday

The children getting ready for a Halloween party tonight. Little Pat as a pirate, Joanna as a ghost. Great noise and excitement.

A visit from Peggy Stringham in the afternoon. Delightful to have a visitor of whom we are fond. And I've become completely unaccustomed to daytime visitors. But at a word, a sign of affection, I freeze up with fear and longing.

An American battleship sunk. Must remember the German refugee woman, fat and terrified, who leaned over my shoulder, looked at the headline and began to cry, saying, "More blood, more murder, more murder." I said that we must see to it that Hitler can no longer do such things to American ships, at which she said, "Oh no, no, Americans can't beat Hitler, nobody can beat Hitler." Her panic and fear made me wildly angry. I wanted to shake, to slap her. One remembered stories one had heard of the refugees who piled into France before it fell and infected it with fear and discouragement. And yet one can understand her fear.

November 4, Tuesday

Had one of my queer execution-cell dreams. This time I was in an incredibly dirty cell, the floors littered with newspaper and rubbish. I kept seeing myself as if looking in from an outside window, a blonde handsome girl somewhat resembling the portrait of herself by Marie Bashkirtseff, the one in the museum at Nice. Any moment I knew that I was to be taken out to a beheading block and in [an] agony of horror and despair and hopeless friendlessness I began to look around for my old black slippers. For I saw that I was barefoot. At last I found one slipper under a pile of rubbish but could not find the other. Then as I heard a sound of feet approaching I became frantic and tried to search quickly for the other slipper. But instead I found my best pair of shoes, my expensive gray suede slippers with their elegant little leather bows. I felt pleased at finding something attractive to die in and, in attempting to put them on, found that they were filled with blood. There was nothing to do but put them on!

November 11, Tuesday

This Saturday L. Untermeyer called us on the phone and we had a few drinks with him in the afternoon. He was very kind, very understanding. When we left him I felt the first wave of relief I had since we left Peterborough, the feeling that we had a friend.

A cool gray day as we returned, but the pleasant visit even made the drab approaching Sunday full of little household jobs and silence seem endurable.

I cannot recover my strength and small irritations do nothing to revive it. Find it difficult to walk up a hill, the wind leaves me breathless and exhausted. I took little Pat to Sterns and bought him a pair of sneakers. His delight in new clothes is such a pleasure. We had lunch at Woolworth's, the food amazingly good and cheap, the service excellent.

A short visit from Rukeyser. She spoke with excitement about her book on Gibbs, making it sound more like an epic poem than a biography. Dr. Einstein has written a preface for it.

Another visit last week with the Stringhams. Ed Stringham felt the bad atmosphere at Peterborough almost as deeply as I did. What a mistake it was! And yet how was I to know?

Great pleasure in rereading some of the *Shelburne Essays* by P. E. More. How he has been sneered at by the facile, the flabby journalists, the cheap "formula writers." He has such learning, such sure taste and a style clear, simple and rich. An excellent essay on Francis Thompson written at the height of the Thompson fervor, "placing" F. T. with deadly accuracy not with Herbert, Donne, Crashaw, but with the 1890 aesthetic pietists, with Dawson, Lionel Johnson. This is very true. He might have added Coventry Patmore. Another essay on a forgotten poetess, Loman Shore, both frightening and touching. There is a certain type of badness like Letitia Landon's that acquired a kind of mocking immortality (if one calls it that), a certain kind of fine but inadequate gift that received the final oblivion because it is too fine and delicate to laugh at and yet is not strong enough to survive or colorful enough to touch the popular memory. It aimed for the highest approval and when it failed nothing was left.

Went to a concert at the Museum of Modern Art with Ted Wilson and E. Johnson to hear the Negro singer Maxine Sullivan sing eighteenth-century English folk songs to the accompaniment of a swing orchestra and a harpsichord. M. S. dressed in fluffy girlish white seemed too conscious of her refined and classic music, the ultra-fashionable audience who looked like people who in the '20s had really admired Van Vechten and Wylie but took up Eliot and Joyce. An eclectic not esoteric crowd, they howled with undisguised joy at a new tap dancer called Baby Laurence. The player at the harpsichord, Sylvia Marlowe, dressed up to look like Marianne Moore, very quaint indeed. She swung some seventeenth-century music. Everyone was amused.

Carl Van Vechten in the audience looking like a stuffed lion with the tail drawn out and the fur moth-eaten.

Read H. G. Wells' *The Shape of Things to Come*. This extraordinary clear bright mind which he must wrap in cellophane when he retires for the night. His dreary sensible Utopias which always seem run by the brightest minds in secondary progressive schools. A kind of vulgarity of which G. B. S. is incapable. His appalling heroines who act like lady editors of liberal newspapers, glorified Dorothy Thompsons and Rebecca Wests, overpowering, masculine and insensitive and yet melodramatic.

November 14, Friday

Am no longer able to rest in the afternoon and so lame. Lost the ability to shake off nervous tension. No sooner do I lie down then I have a feeling of constricted breathing and a congestion in my chest. I live in fear of another breakdown like the one in 1938. What a miracle to have recovered from that without a sanitarium.

Have been reading Irving Babbitt's *Rousseau and Romanticism*. At first the clear, sharp angry style carried conviction. The wealth of brilliant quotation, the authority of the learning impressed me. But in the middle of the book I stopped with discomfort and irritation; for one only saw the blind, angry sneer of the hysterical reactionary, not the sound conservative. In his effort to demolish the romantics (and silly and unsatisfactory many of them are) he becomes violent, almost abusive, narrow. He seems to forget the very virtues he is expounding and in the long run one finds oneself sympathizing with Rousseau who, neurotic as he was, did have the perceptions of an artist and poet and insights into the mysteries of the human soul. But the trouble with J. Babbitt is of course the flaw I've heard people mention when discussing him—a complete lack of understanding of the creative process—a mistake P. E. More (the great and finer man) never makes. One feels that to Babbitt the writing of a poem, a novel, a play is nothing more than an act of well-disciplined common sense, and that in his heart of hearts he really feels that most artists are foolish fellows (which is true enough!). But their work may be something else, something better, more valuable than the man. The style has too much anger to be convincing.

What a pity that I. B. became the archetype of the humanist for he frightened too many people away from following his arguments. Yet they had a great many useful, necessary, really important things to say, true and sensible things! But Babbitt gave his antiromanticism an air of romantic wildness.

November 19

Collapsed early this week and had to go to bed. The doctor diagnosed it as the same thing H. had, a form of intestinal flu. I was put on a dreadful diet of rice and boiled milk and feel a little better but far from well.

My dark bedroom the only room in the house which I can call my own has become an obsession. I should like a pleasant, largish, airy room of my own, full of sunlight, a desk and typewriter of my own. I think I might be able to work with more ease—or would it make any difference? I've done my best work under worse conditions but in my present state of health these things are irritating.

After all who cares for my work? Now and then a stray review, a remark, comes to me that tells me all is not entirely lost and I take heart again. I should like my dear H. to get the full recognition he deserves, and a guarantee that I may be allowed to publish as many books as I wish—and the far-off hope that someday a small but sure income may come in from our books. In my case it is of special necessity for it is all I can do.

Read the Flaubert letters to Louise Colet. What a love affair! What an opportunity that foolish woman had to learn from a truly superior man. But her interest (like a great many woman writers) was not really in writing. The poetry was used as a kind of sexual come-on—as a form of sex appeal, sex-expression; naturally it was false and artificial. She had a bright journalist's mind (she returned in the end to sentimental journalism) and I kept thinking of how successful she would have been in the 1920s and 1930s writing for the liberal journals or the *New Yorker.* She had the kind of glib social jargon, the journalistic awareness of current tendencies in popular science, the most fashionable attitudes towards current events, the accurate knowledge of the best mediums of publicity. And her kind of good looks would have made her a heroine among similar minds who fill the literary tea parties. How honest, brutal and unromantic was Flaubert's relationship with her. It was he who was the keenest realist (he the great romantic) who saw through her as if she were made of glass. But people like Colet for all their insistence on current realities are fundamentally romantics in the worst sense. Flaubert being a real artist naturally pierced through the deepest reality.

November 26, Wednesday

Bad nights—illness. Little Jean Garrigue* visited us bringing some remarkable poems, full of color, vitality, charm, the best woman's poetry I've seen for a long time. She's a very pretty girl too, prettier than Millay ever was in her prime and is very much "on the make" just now—justifiably so. Felt my own poems pallid, weak, stiff after hers. I drank some sherry and smoked a great many more cigarettes than I should have because of the tension and strain of visitors, and this of course did me no good. Struck by Garrigue's astonishing slant green-blue eyes. Amused at the thought that they resembled Millay's and how shocked she would be if I told her—Millay is *not* a fashionable name now.

Went to Wall Street to the National City Bank to collect some money from England. Part of Bryher's blessed gift which means Christmas gifts for the children, especially my lovely Jo who needs clothes badly. A gray-blue day and lower New York seems beautiful and strange. Old St. Paul's and Trinity haunting as ever and full of memories of the sad difficult days I worked in that neighborhood. Ted Wilson went with me. I was grateful for I've been ill and am afraid to travel alone now. For a moment I felt that the subway would be too much for me and I would have to return. I stopped at a drugstore and was able to continue.

Yesterday thought and felt well enough to go to the library and continue my work on the poetry history book but I got ill on the bus and as I entered the reading room I fainted. Found myself in a restroom. Someone had discovered my name and phoned Horace, and old Yarmolinsky of the Slavonic languages came down and offered to take me home. I talked too much and foolishly to him. As usual when I am ill I become conscious of a mad loneliness. Then H. came and we drove home in the rain in a taxi—another expense.

December 8, Monday

Sunday afternoon while H. and I were reading the Sunday newspapers we suddenly stopped to listen to the radio which announced that Hawaii had been bombed, that Honolulu and the Philippines had been attacked by the Japanese. It seemed unbelievable at first. We spent the rest of the day listening to the wild reports and rumors that started coming in. Fearful depression and suspense and I had to stop listening and lie down. It all seemed unbelievable and yet why should it have been such a surprise? But the war has been remote for most Americans—something very far away indeed. And this in spite of newspapers and propagandists.

Complete calmness in the street, deep quiet, very little agitation. Whether it is indifference, shock, unbelief, or courage I don't know. But London on the day war was declared seemed less calm.

Today the declaration of war of the President and the news from Hawaii much worse than we had expected.

Went shopping with H. and bought a pretty and expensive dress for Joanna. Who knows whether we can buy these things next year? The large shopping crowds were much diminished. People will be afraid to buy anything—perhaps to walk the street if air raid rumors spread.

Two young poets, H. M. and J. P., visited us Sunday night. The last aggressive and brash and ignorant and insensitive but will I suspect push himself as far as he can go with not too much talent. We talked poetry and kept off the war but every once in a while I sneaked off to the radio. Both boys have been to the most expensive colleges, have made unbelievably helpful "contacts" at an age when the poet who has not gone to Yale and Harvard is still dreaming of a faint hope of publication. Talent scouts surround these boys. Distinguished older poets never forget that those boys are rich and perhaps scent the fact they will never be rivals and so are more than willing to support them. We think of our struggles and get angry at these softies. H. M. a nice personality but not fully developed yet and it's absurd to overpraise him. "The coming poets" of the 1940s are now being carefully groomed and so far most of them (as usual) are bad, exact replicas of their predecessors, or mediocre enough not to offend dull editors. Little Jean Garrigue seems to be the best. Dunstan Thompson the brightest but not the most likely to succeed. He has published too many unorthodox reviews—his last one a wild attack on Marianne Moore who is now a Sacred Cow.

A long bus ride with H. Visited the Gotham Book Mart, very dusty and dark as usual and Miss Steloff very kind. Quite lovely. I longed for a friendly call, an affectionate gesture. The war, now a close nightmare, always at the back of my mind. If I could only make myself useful.

M. the editor told H. that Saint-John Perse the French Symbolist poet so much admired by Eliot and MacLeish was in this country and was loud in complaints of Eliot. He doesn't like Eliot's translation of his work. Doesn't like Eliot's work, doesn't like Eliot, and his grievances fill the place. Yet without Eliot no one would have heard of him in English-writing countries. And *we* complain of ingratitude.

December 11

Horace is staying in late at the college today seeing a performance of E. E. Cummings' *Him* done by the drama department. Without Horace the evenings are intolerable. Dinner seems a useless ritual, even the children cannot quite compensate me. O the pleasure, the peace, the feeling of security when at last we have retired for the night and I have him for myself alone after having been separated by so many distractions in the day.

Have been doing Christmas shopping by telephone, a reckless way but a saving of precious energy. Feel my lack of money badly at this time of year. I'm so dependent on my dear H. I try to save out of my household money—almost impossible. No one seems to want my poetry this year and I wonder if my book is moving at all, if anyone is reading or buying it.

A fearful afternoon yesterday. The war a vague heavy shadow; bad news from Hawaii and the Philippines. An air raid alarm was sounded on the radio, saying that enemy planes had been sighted off New York City. The announcers kept up lurid, frightening comments. I was not afraid but I can't stand excitement. I simply took an aspirin, closed off the radio and went to my room and read myself to sleep with a volume of Sherlock Holmes stories. The alarm was probably a test warning.

At night Charles Trinkhaus of the college came in to listen to the President's speech, a speech eloquent, moving, reassuring. We are reminded of the bad days in England in Bath or Weston-Super-Mare where we sat in the gloom of the blackout and listened to the radio which grew noisier and noisier and gave out less and less news.

The *New Yorker* has taken a poem of Horace. Such good luck. It was the weakest of the three poems H. had sent, but it's a good poem.

December 13

Couldn't some of the money used so lavishly, given up so cheerfully in wartime be used in peacetime for relief funds, decent housing, intelligent employment agencies, free medical services (God knows how people of our class can afford to be ill), scholarships for bright children of the poor, subsidies for artists, more parks, etc.? Why is this so impossible? Am I going Utopian or Communist? Surely this is not so insane as the feeling that we *must* have war on war, generation after generation. But first those who have built their states on the concept that they can survive only by war and more war must be disarmed, must have a change of heart, must be converted. No not Russian Communism; that too has its horrors, its spiritual aridity, its own brutalities— but something must be learned from Russia's partially successful experiment.

What a remarkable man Rousseau was. As I reread Matthew Josephson's intelligent but lush biography [*Jean-Jacques Rousseau* (1931)], I wondered why I had never realized before that his insecure childhood, his youth of vagabondage, his social humiliations as a very young man, his sexual humiliations, his difficulty in getting and keeping jobs was the real cause of his persecution manias later? Even later fame, honor, great friends can never compensate for memories such as he had. They were the cause of his great difficulties and the source, where he fed his genius. The very charm and repulsion he exercised on almost all who met him had their root in these early years, these unforgettable experiences of humiliation and failure. People are fascinated and repelled by those who have been to hell, returned, and insist on talking about it.

December 25, Christmas Day

A quiet gray Christmas. Helen McMaster our guest and a delightful Christmas eve. The turkey was perfect, the children delighted with their gifts, opening them with great excitement and joy. H. got me a luxurious bathrobe and he liked our gifts, a beautiful recording of Stravinsky's *Le Sacre du printemps* conducted by himself and the Beecham recording of Handel's *Faithful Shephard*. Morton sent us a recording of Lotte Lehman's rendition of Schuman's German lieder. Helen's gift a large box of liquors and liqueurs. It enabled us to spend a jolly Christmas eve. Ted Wilson came looking lonely and handsome and bringing gifts. We all listened to the *Sacre* and the Handel and took a long intermission to prepare for the lieder—which was a little anticlimactic. Lehman has a clear, pure voice, very nice indeed.

Took a short walk in the International House park and then sat on a bench reading Walter de la Mare's *Collected Poems*, very unsatisfactory and shadowy to me as if the mind was watching the flight of too many iridescent, pale soap bubbles. But the wonderful *music* remains; there is I'm convinced no real poetry without music. When a poet loses his ear for sound he may as well turn to prose.

Saw two beautiful Utrillo prints at Brentanos, street scenes of course, and I realized more than ever that he is my favorite painter, that he is closer to me and my secret world than any other modern. I do not say he is the best of modern painters, but to me he means the most. I too have lived on his lonely deserted streets. I know their mystery, the sadness.

December 29

A bad party at ___ where I lost my temper. ___ suddenly out of a clear sky burst out into a wild tirade against my poetry. Full of hatred, slime, hysteria. "Why the critics don't tear you limb from limb is more than I can say." Obviously the hatred comes from a source not her own. The language sounds too much like the familiar tone I heard in Peterborough, and before then she had been favorable enough in her comments. I lost my temper instead of walking out or changing the subject, acted with ill-breeding and H. and T. C. Wilson who were there joined forces against me, all playing into ___'s hands.

December 30

Full of depression and sadness at my mistakes, my stupidity, my indiscretions. Yesterday H. and I went shopping and we bought a pretty afternoon dress and a heavy warm beautiful coat—too beautiful for me who go out so seldom.

A clear sharp cold day, one of those winter days when the air is as fresh as spring and more bracing. Felt encouragingly better. But spending money these days fills me with terror. I feel precipices under my feet as always but more so now than ever.

A letter from M. R. that cut me to the heart but perhaps I've deserved it, being too confidential and too reserved with her, too intimate and then too uncandid. With X my trouble was in complaining, in making emotional demands, in asking for sympathy and understanding instead of waiting for it to be granted freely.

1 9 4 2

January 5, 1942

Went to the doctor's today. He was encouraging which was a great relief. I have a great fear and dislike for the profession, and feel a sense of guilt when money must be spent on doctors. It's such large sums for what seems such slow results.

A sad New Year's. H. went to a gloomy refugee party to console Klaus Mann who said his magazine had gone under. Today K. phoned to say he had received funds and would go on. It will be a bad time for writers, and magazines are already folding up. Since Peterborough I feel that a trail of ill will has clouded and veiled my lucky star, but it will shine again. One is poisoned by the hatred and ill will of others even if that hatred and ill will is passive.

Kind letters from Allen Tate, John D. Fletcher, Thornton Wilder on a fine poem of Horace's that Norman Pearson sent out as a Christmas card. Norman and Susan, the William Rose Benéts, and Jim Putnam visited us Saturday night. We had a pleasant party and I know I did the honors well. Some faint consolations for past failures. Dear little Pat was a love, asking Marjorie Benét to autograph two of her children's books (which he admires) with an air of graceful shyness.

The children are so fine, so beautiful, so hopeful. I must learn to be a discreet and civilized human being for their sake.

132

Marcia Silvette brought a young Armenian artist around to see us who was telling us of his difficulties with the draft board. He was born in Tiflis, but came to this country at the age of nine. Turned down by the draft doctor, that gentleman turned to him and said, "I suppose you're glad. All you foreigners are yellow. You're a Russian, aren't you?" The young man said, "No, I'm an Armenian," to which the doctor retorted, "Well you were born in Russia weren't you?" to which the impatient reply was, "Now look here. A dove may be born in a stable but it isn't a horse."

The worst melancholy, depression for a long time. Can neither work, nor pray, nor weep and quarrel with everyone who comes near me. A great fear of hurting my dear Horace.

January 12, Monday

A new maid, Leola, which adds to our list of strange names, unwelcome necessary strangers: Ozelle, Beulah, now Leola. Beulah disappeared and with her the lovely golden coat ornament my dear H. had given me for Christmas, a small angel made of gold—and the grandmother's ring. My hands feel naked without it. I must learn to do without a maid. Such dependence is dangerous, does me harm, and fills me with shame and the sense of being useless. But I've been ill, unable to get out of bed or walk outdoors. Walked out Saturday and became violently ill. Had to take a cab home (more expenses). H. and I are talking of taking a year off. I long and pray for it and am a little frightened too, things on all colleges now being in a bad state. The reception our books have received seems a little frightening. Silences from friends, and I read innuendoes, hostilities in letters or comments I receive. Never have I been so lonely or felt so useless, morbid, friendless—so helpless.

The news from the war far from encouraging and the general atmosphere far from cheerful. Only Russia is doing well and there is a tendency to over-idealize a state that has no particular fondness for our country—that may turn and carry its stooges in this country with her. A gloomy thought—that only the totalitarian states know how to fight the totalitarian states. I should like to feel that we are fighting the Axis because we never want to hear or see a world like them again, but the *New York Times* had a delightful story recently of how little Russian children are taught that killing Nazis is their sacred duty (this was on Christmas), that hate was their sacred duty, etc. Meanwhile the old people went to the Christmas services of the church to pray for the men at the front. This was treated with hilarity and contempt. And yet something in the account of the education of the Russian children reminds me of the sort of thing the children are getting in Germany. One wants to believe and hopes that from this war a better, kinder world would arise, not a world of hateful children, intolerance, contempt for human dignity, where man's aspiration for God is sneered at—a world of efficient lovelessness and that cold humanitarianism that works like a machine, regardless of human feelings and longings, coldly, ruthlessly, brutally—a humanitarianism without money, charity, love, or pity, thinking of man only as a cheaper machine.

But I feel so humiliated, so bruised, so much of an outcast these days because of my inability to work or make friends, and that damn illness that keeps me tied down, that I feel as if I have no right to any opinions. Let the noisy, the healthy, the shrewd, the brutal, the liars, have their way. For theirs is the Kingdom. The war will be won but not by them. But they will reap the rewards of victory—they always do.

January 21, Wednesday

Joanna's birthday. We bought her a few nice gifts, a fine English gray flannel jacket, a pretty wool dress and some books that she had wanted. In the evening she went to see *Lady in the Dark* with her girlfriend Margery.

Silent nerve-sick days. My dearest H. too seems tired and depressed. O for a stroke of luck to relieve our low spirits! Difficulty in getting up in the morning and every noise, every sound is a torment. A very new baby upstairs that seems to cry all day. The sound of a carpet sweeper, the darkness of the rooms, and worst of all the odors in the long corridors—all make the world unbearable.

Vice-Versa arrived last Saturday. I was surprised for I was sure D. T. would never bring it out. Full of bright amusing schoolboy humor and wit, some of the poems rather good. Dunstan had a warm defense of H.'s poetry. It was sad to think that a man so fine and strong, gentle and generous and brilliant should need to be defended against rats like A., crawling worms like J. A review of my book full of that sort of praise which does more harm than good, especially when the person (whose name I don't know) praised me so wildly and attacked Marianne Moore with equal wildness. Knowing how strong and snobbish the Marianne M. cult is, especially among the most powerful of the old literary guard today, I shudder at the hatred I will arouse—I who feel the waves of hate, envy, anger poison[ing] my room already. It's not that I've gone so far, but that I've gotten too far even in that little. They won't give an inch. And of course they don't read me at all, and what they read they don't understand. But M. is recognizably quaint and modern. All knew her on the *Dial*. She's an established "intellect."

Kenneth Fearing and Rachel to dinner. Ken affectionate and amusing and delightful with Joanna. Rachel sour, full of grievances against Ken because of his drinking and his inability to support her and the boy. Poor girl. Her life is not an easy one. She has done wonders for Ken but I don't like her as well. At one moment I expected her to make a scene, and I'm sure she doesn't like us. They left very late. Rachel funny and complaining. He looks as slight and boyish as ever, is well dressed and has become rather attractive, a resemblance to the portrait of Kafka—a weaker, less tragic Kafka.

Every once in a while with K. I recapture some of the ease, the gaiety, the lightness I used to have with him in our college days. This sensation is so delightful, for a while the heavy torpor, the feeling of nausea, sickness, despondency leaves me.

January 23, Friday

H. came home very tired and depressed last night. Though I love him with all my heart, I could find nothing to say to him. Guilt possessed me, for I felt my fears, my secret phobias, my discouragement creeping toward him, though I never said a word. But once our Luck changes for the better it will be brighter and easier again.

January 26, Monday

Sleepy and dull all day. Aimless wasted day. Nausea in the morning, sleepiness all day. Desperately in need of work and amusement, hard work, energy to do it, and then some fun. C. L. visited us, full of lively conversation and good anecdotes. He's a scamp but a pleasant cheerful one—and a good talker.

A number of checks arrived in the mail. Thank Heavens, but I long for warm personal letters almost as much.

Saw the new Harcourt Brace catalog and was cheered by the announcement of the new Untermeyer anthology, where I am one of the few poets included for the first time! Horace's group is expanded but so is ___'s, a bad poet and Louis knows it of course, but a university job usually keeps a name in—in that anthology. I was grateful for my inclusion. It's a little sunshiny note in the wave of dislike and contempt my work is getting in certain quarters. The Pulitzer helped to place me, but I made many enemies too.

Horace told me of a conversation with Joe Campbell,* who teaches at Sarah Lawrence and whose wife comes from Hawaii. Joe said that the family wrote him that on the day of the Pearl Harbor attack they heard the sound of firing and thought it was simply army maneuvers! They telephoned the police saying, "Why does the service have to have maneuvers on Sunday?" They were then assured that the shooting was the real thing—the Japs were over Hawaii! In a short time they saw the Jap planes flying over their suburb! The small boy of the house (about Pat's age) rushed out of the house in joyful excitement and the family went frantic trying to find him. At last he returned, brought back by some soldiers who found him watching the fighting. One of them had given him a tin hat and he was in a state of self-importance and bliss.

February 5, Thursday

Nightmare days increasing, sleepless nights. A dull cocktail tea at the house of an ex-mistress of a celebrated editor. A gloomy Swiss psychiatrist whose pet theory was that the medical profession was prolonging human life too long and so introducing new diseases of old age. Anyway people lived too long these days when they didn't go to war, etc. I slipped away from this cheerful creature, and talked to Carl Carmer, the Celebrity of the Affair, who was evidently eager to leave the place as soon as possible. It is true that the party had a back-door, literary-underworld, cast-off flavor. Carmer had just published a best-selling novel and was amiable, healthy, full of benevolent feeling, telling me that he had never forgotten that Horace had given him his start by praising his first book—a book of poems. Had dinner with the hostess and the Swiss at an Armenian restaurant—the food very good and quite cheap. Then Horace and I fled into the night—back home, feeling lonely, somewhat cheated, and sad. William March the novelist there, lively, racketty, witty, down on his luck, impertinently obsequious to Carl Carmer. March is a

cleverer man and a better writer, but Carmer is the Literary Success and a social favorite.

February 7, Saturday

Dark stormy days. Rain, gray weather, damp, cold. I went to do some
shopping at Macy's yesterday and had a return of the congestion in my chest
and almost fainted. H. thinks it's nothing but a form of nervous indigestion.
The first symptoms came after Joanna was born and have cropped up again in
times of extreme nervous strain and tension. I had one attack in '33 at Yaddo
while walking in the woods and had barely strength enough to run back to the
mansion. But it's discouraging, discouraging.

Little Jean Garrigue the poet visited us and was full of excitement and enthusiasm over George Barker's poem. It's the fashion in certain places to insist
that he's better than Auden!—with which I don't quite agree.

We were too confidential with Garrigue, a mistake. Also I should have
taken Disraeli's axiom to heart, that one must not be too confidential even to
one's closest friends. Fortunate the husband or wife if they can turn to each
other and keep each other's secrets—yes. I at least am fortunate. Why ask for
more? But I think of ourselves as one—and I want the outside world. When I
am accused of living in an ivory tower, I get angry. I have lived all my life not
in an ivory tower but an insecure, rickety, air raid shelter.

February 13, Friday night

Went to the Metropolitan Museum to keep a date with Jim Putnam. I
came too early and went down to the cafeteria there to have a cup of tea and
ran into Hortense Farrell. She had a delicate, neurotic air about her and
looked lovelier than I'd seen her. The particular flash of good looks that
women have just before the looks go entirely. It's impossible to like or dislike
her. She's not a character. Nor does she have a definite personality of her own.
She's a bundle of different moods, changing rapidly from hour to hour, and
her straggling conversational flights are like that too. Perhaps this is not un-
common in an actress, and I hear that in her day she was a good one.

In the evening Jim Farrell called us up. They live near us and we saw the
baby Kevin, aged seventeen months. A healthy, lively, pretty child. Had a
vague feeling that Jim has been deserted by his fine friends and was looking

longingly and with nostalgia to us again. H. was quiet, discreet and sad with Jim. After all he had done us more harm than anyone could ever have done to friends who had been good to him in his need. But J. F. was all affection and wistfulness and praise toward us. I wondered if like us he thought of the days when we were all beginning to write, had no prospects, were young, hopeful and very poor—of the conversation in our little house in Sunnyside where we made good talk and fine plans for the future without having to take drinks. Jim full of violence against almost everyone now—longs for a house in the country. Couldn't we start a colony somewhere? Full of frightful sentiments about the war.

Little bits of news that cheer me up—not much. The *Harvard Advocate* asked H. to contribute to their anniversary number. John G. Fletcher is coming to have lunch with us tomorrow which will be a break from intolerable solitary worry and boredom.

February 17, Tuesday

Had dinner with the Kenneth Fearings last night. They live in a dark dismal railroad flat in the West Nineties now. A place however much cleaner, roomier and more carefully furnished than their other places. In fact this place marks K.'s first step away from Bohemianism. K. is maturing rapidly, reads more—but drinks as much as ever. Alas it's the vice of our generation. We had a pleasant time, that easy, much longed for—now much appreciated—conversation of old friends who have many memories in common. There was a mild pleasant warmish rain and I felt less ill than usual. K. and H. drank too much and when we got home (for the first time), H. decided to skip a class the next day.

We bought some new lamp shades for the living room. It's amazing the difference they make in the room. They add a new light and charm to the too shabby room, and certainly lift our morale. One may readily advise the tired housewife that if she can't afford a new hat she might buy a new lamp shade or chair cover for her best room.

Wonderful weather today. A warm mild-colored wind blowing in from the sea. Nostalgia, keen and fresh. In the evening a gray sky slashed with orange and rose. Grant's Tomb bathed in this cloudy radiance of dark and bright, of wind and water.

O God! How beautiful, how peaceful, how delightful, how full of happiness this world can be.

February 20, Friday

Heat flashes in my head. Frightening but the doctor says due to a slight nervous disorder. Very discouraging. I am so impatient to get to work, to be able to move around, to plan, to *work* above all.

Dunstan Thompson visited us last night, very thin and charming, full of gossip. Said that C. Aiken had sent him a long obscene insulting letter on a review in *Vice-Versa*. That man has grown old in petty literary feuds and his work shows it. William Roth, the young Californian who is running the Colt Press, visited us, a handsome quiet boy. It was a pleasant evening. But a drink or two went to my head and I talked too much.

When Horace comes home I feel safe and peaceful again. D. T. is the only one of our friends who makes me feel easy, gay and cheerful.

February 23

Heat flashes and customary attacks when I attempt going out. O dear and so much work that I *must* do.

Ran into Al Hayes* the proletarian poet at the Sea Cove Restaurant. He reminded us of many things that we had forgotten, and of some we didn't know. Reminded us of an occasion when Archibald MacLeish organized the "proletarian" poets, invited them to his home and offered them his leadership. Said Hayes, "He talked 'ideals' and we asked, 'How are we to earn our livings?' " A gloomy sad lot they were, those "P.P.s" (proletarian poets)—a period that to us looms sad and dark, because of the great waste of talent and idealism.

Came home. Listless and sad. Listened to music, read L. Untermeyer's new anthology, which includes me. My poems seem too delicate, too smooth.

How tactful L. U. has been. Our book [*History of American Poetry*] seems to be too harsh and unsophisticated. Well he has been decent to us, and he may be wiser than we are—in his kindness.

War news dreadful as usual. A foolish tactless letter from E. J. thanking H. for kindnesses, saying that she is not a bootlicker. We don't want bootlicking. We want human warmth and kindness. Long silence from M. R. The talk with Al Hayes depressed me, bringing back such memories. How helpless, childish and naïve we were!

Unable to read, write or think. Head full of poems which I can't write. Long for adult, normal companionship. Dear H. kind but very busy. A good doctor would help but it's so expensive and I haven't the energy to drag myself out.

Did I ever turn up my nose at Emily Dickinson? Fool that I was! What creative energy she had, what good health she must have had. How much she got out of such a narrow life. Well is my life broader? I don't think so. Yes, but I have more opportunities. Perhaps, but I'm not sure. She had her roots in Amherst, economic and social security. It's the custom to underestimate these advantages.

The *children,* my *work,* and equally *Horace's work.* These are my great reservoirs of feeling—my life in fact. But I must pull myself together and build up myself, integrate myself. It's about time. O God make me well! And give me strength to keep on working. Give me work I love. Give me some connections with the human race.

So many soldiers in the street, so many different kinds of uniforms. It brings back faint early memories of the last war; the years between have disappeared, and only those bleak early years seem real again. The rest was a hallucination. The same cold air, the same Fifth Ave. full of soldiers.

February 24, Tuesday
    The usual cold gray February morning. My heart sinks with loneliness, weakness and cold. Horace has gone back to work, the children to school, and the house rings with silence.

Last evening Klaus Mann called. He had had trouble with his magazine again. Such a charming, ineffectual, scatterbrained person, the sort of son great men produce, I suppose to their grief. But he has lovely manners. He had just heard of the suicide of Stefen Zweig in Buenos Aires and was somewhat upset. It is a dreadful tragedy. He (Zweig) was an intelligent writer if not a great one. I never liked the high-toned abstractions of his school, the mixture of sex, mysticism, Freud and Goethe, but he *was* an intelligent and feeling person. The tragedy of the refugees is indeed heartbreaking. It adds another dark stain to the darkening world. Klaus M. said that Zweig was a real pacifist. He grieved over the German dead as well as over the English, etc. The war had become an obsession with him. He never became reconciled to exile. He missed his country.

Poor H. has a bad toothache, thinks it may be an abscess. It adds to my worry and gloom. He worked on a poem all weekend, very powerful, grim and depressing. It makes my heart sink.

February 26, Thursday

Had a strange dream the night before. I am not an admirer of Elinor Wylie but I dreamed that she came to me and presented me with a beautiful emerald cut into the shape of a rose. I noticed that though the stone seemed newly cut the setting was worn and old. But it seemed the more beautiful for that, though the gift embarrassed me. I saw E. W. looking at me. She was still beautiful though worn and ill and sad. I pinned the brooch on a sash I wore at my waist. Then we sat down on the bed and she confided in me that she was in great domestic difficulties—that she had married Oscar Williams! and wished she hadn't.

Wonderful weather today. I walked out and all was light and heavenly air. Cold and windy but full of April sweetness—the false spring weather that sometimes happens at this time. But best of all, oh best of all I felt *almost* well, able to breathe, able to walk, able to plan again.

March 2

Heat flashes and congestion in my chest. I'm concerned now that something *is* wrong. After all even hypochondria is a form of illness. It's a symptom of *some* disorder. My dislike of doctors which is a compound of repulsion and fear begins again. O God make me well, make me capable of work and friendship and Life. In looking over K. Mansfield's diaries which I once found interesting and now find painful, I ran across the sentence, "The enemy is my body," and felt a deep bond of sympathy. How can one work if one is only half well? The sick body poisons the mind, the sick mind poisons the soul, and one is prevented from working from one's best center, from being one's best self.

A birthday party at Jim Farrell's. J. affectionate as he has been recently, the crowd fantastic. Aging actresses (friends of Hortense's), baby doctors, Jim's doctor, Hortense's doctors and psychiatrist friends, the remains of the Trotskyite literary front, three ugly pregnant women, Jim Putnam, who brought his favorite Macmillan author of the moment, repulsive and noisy and drunk. I ran into Leonie Adams again who told me Bill Troy couldn't come. Leonie's attitude towards me full of the old patronage, bewilderment, a little resentment. I talked to her with a little less respect and more self-confidence than usual. She became confidential, even a little bitter, defensive. I don't know why I ever thought of her as a remarkable intellect. Her comments on poetry I thought were downright foolish. But I heard Bill Troy's voice behind them, that fine sterilizing mind of his, guaranteed to shrink up any tender flower of the spirit. I told Leonie she had really had a comparatively easy time of it—almost all praise from the beginning, all respect, and even a little cult. She disagreed. She *had* received *one* unfavorable notice from Yvor Winters years and years and years ago and she never forgot it. She had talked about it to me in the past and she still remembered it. I wonder what she would have done with the abuse and filth poured upon Horace and myself. What a small selfish narrow little world she moves in. Leonie is undoubtedly the best in her set—but Troy with all the encouragement, the advantages, all the pretensions in the world hasn't been able to do a thing. He has gotten innumerable sabbaticals from Bennington—and nothing written. Naturally the chief cry of reproach against us of that whole sterile gang is "How much you write," or, "How facile you are." The eunuch putting on airs of superiority to the virile man, the barren woman telling the fruitful mother of fine children that childbearing was cheap, and a little vulgar.

But I may have been cruel to Leonie who is a fine poet. The poor woman didn't look well. Her hair is now grayish—only at a distance does she reflect that elfin charm and distinction that attracted me so.

March 3, Tuesday

Wakened this morning by a wild thunderstorm. Jo ran into our room crying, "Oh I think we're having a hurricane. Do I have to go to school?" The night before H. and I had broken our nondrinking rule. For a while my spirits lifted and H. seemed gayer, less tired. He then told me about something that he had kept from me, news of what looks like another betrayal. Instead of comforting him, I lost my temper and scolded him. "Oh why do people do these things to *you*, of all people?" Went to bed upset and in the morning I felt as if I had taken a powerful narcotic. Felt conscience stricken about dear H. who left for the school early, and when he didn't return at his customary hour I became panicky. Telephoned the school and they said he had left very early which frightened me. I saw a horrifying empty world without him and my fault too. Perhaps he had decided not to come home. I no longer believed in his love for me, for I did not believe I deserved it. Went out into the cold street, damp heavy air, looking for him, couldn't find him, returned home in a panic, my heart beating very fast, almost hysterical. There he was in my room, looking well and cheerful, like himself, and I burst into tears, fell into his arms. I've had my lesson anyway.

The noise of aeroplanes, breaking into the awful silence of the day. Then a wave of love and peace when the children come home from school.

Must give a poetry reading Thursday on the radio, a frightening thought. I hate poetry readings. I don't like to be read to and I don't like to read my poems aloud either. But I promised ages ago. Oscar Williams has also announced us for a poetry reading for the MacDowell Colony. I don't think I'll have the strength and H. says that a production of *Dido*, the Purcell opera, will be put on at the college and that he *must* attend.

How one hates to admit that one is growing older. But today as Horace was going over admissions for S. L. College, I came across names and pictures of young girls whose mothers were the glamour-girl celebrities of my youth and whose pictures (sometimes with these young girls as babes-in-arms) I cut out from the rotogravure sections and pasted in my scrapbook. They all seemed Beautiful, Fortunate, living the Ideal Life. Through their children's comments in the applications I get flashes of what their real life was. I am beginning to understand Michael Arlen's dream world of *These Charming People*, after all a popular book in my generation. Only a foreigner looking up in a mystical dream could have imagined these people. They were of course not people but the private Daydreams of Arlen. Yet I can never say I longed for frivolity, great gaiety, great admiration—the longing on my part was for peace, security, love, freedom to be one's best and travel so as to widen my very limited horizon. And O yes—a longing for some unattainable beauty most of all.

March 4, Wednesday

A sad letter from Bryher in England. She who had been so accustomed to traveling all over the world—Lapland, Finland, Iceland, Egypt, America and all Europe—must feel the keen suffering of the changing world as much as anyone in England. A book I sent her as a gift a little before Christmas arrived three months later—all the civilized swiftness of communication broken down! Teach me O God to be at one with your difficult, living world—not to shrink too much, not to suffer too much.

My heart full of love and hope and worry and pride for H. Preserve him, bless him, and may posterity admire and love him and know his true worth. But why *posterity*? Surely someday in our time the good recognition will come.

March 5, Thursday

Horace went to an air raid meeting held in our apartment house. Says that two air raid wardens claimed to have secret "tips" that a real air raid would take place in about two months. Nowadays the thought of spring is mingled with pain and fear and horror.

Oscar Williams called. Very amusing when he is with us, but when he leaves we feel a little defiled as if we had shrunk to his level. Some secret resentment against *me* especially. He is under the frightful delusion that we have enormous *power* of some sort. I say a *frightful* delusion because we haven't any and the charge of having power made against people who haven't it is a dangerous one. The world says "politician" and our work suffers from hysteria and prejudice. Curiously the word "politician" has rarely been used openly against MacLeish and Tate and Mark Van Doren* who have had and still have real literary influence. But they are too deeply entrenched. An ugly disturbing business. Oscar never forgets a slight or an injury and to fail him in one of his schemes is enough to have him as a violent enemy for life—though the failing may have been innocent or unconscious. The frightful advertising slogan conversation, the unconscious cynicism. Enough of that now! If I was only well I could cope with anything, I feel. Perhaps I could even find O. W. amusing.

Horace will work late at the college and not be home till ten in the evening. To have dinner without him is a great grief to me.

Reading Jane Austen's *Mansfield Park*. Again struck by the peculiar worldliness of her mind. Yes I can see why Crabbe was her favorite poet. It's a sensible eighteenth-century mind. She has read Dr. Johnson and has laughed at Rousseau. There is no foolish period "sensibility" about her. She has rejected it thoroughly, as she has accepted her society thoroughly. She sees through it, but she accepts her universe as it is. Everyone's income is carefully noted. Money is so important, and even her most virtuous heroines make very well-bred efforts to obtain it. "He is so handsome, so genteel and has 5,000 pounds a year." Jane Austen is indeed, to use a period phrase of her own day, "the best bred, the most genteel and sensible female in literature." But what a sense of life as it really is, of human beings as their society has made them. Another curious feature in her novels is the sensible, "respectable" father and the foolish contemptible mother of so many of her heroines. The women were married for a certain kind of good looks and money. The women in that class (unless they had too much of the wrong "sensibility") married for security, position and "reasonable" love. After marriage the emotional dissatisfaction and disintegration set in. There were servants and nurses and the little accomplishments were not enough. Their minds were stuffed full of social fears, taboos, emptiness; all their creative and mental powers had gone out to find and get a husband and later this horrid arid spirit was directed to their children—to find husbands and "situations" for them. One can imagine the ugliness, cruelty, smallness issuing from these pleasant parks and charming manors—a social ugliness emanating especially from the *women*. And in the middle of the nineteenth century, even earlier, this particular class (the upper-middle) became the real *ruling* class, the empire builders, the world from which many of the prime ministers came, the arbiters of taste and morals. Those frightful clergymen full of sensible platitudes and unimaginative reading, those arrogant dowagers and crawling genteel poor relations, those "spirited" and selfish young men who go from country house to country house and assembly after assembly in sheer boredom, those timid, sensible frightened young girls suffering because they cannot approach their man, the ferocious young women who scheme, suffer, commit crimes to get their man (the man with the big park and the 10,000 pounds or 5,000 pounds a year). It's not even a pure passion. For the pounds and the park seem so much the man that even Austen can't disentangle them.

March 7, Saturday

An unusually warm day. Very ill in the morning and after dinner and drinks with the Jim Farrells last evening. Jim full of persecution complexes about the Communist Party. It's become an identification mark of the writer who came up in the 1930s. The revelations as they come out from time to time are really shocking and worrying. Both Jim and Hortense seem sad—and I suspect lonely. Still he is well established, his work in certain quarters very much admired—it seems so much.

Took a bus ride to town with Joanna, very lively, pretty and gay. We met Horace in front of the Forty-second Street library looking a little guilty because he had bought a new English ash walking stick at a sale. My poor dear, he *needs* a stick badly and he has bought almost nothing for himself.

Waiting for Horace to come home. The hours drag. I wait for his footsteps—his breathing—this long day at the college must be very exhausting. I feel ready to burst into tears with loneliness and worry.

Worry about mounting expenses, the war, the loneliness, the limited strength. Our street is wonderful to look at lately but it seems harassed by the loud violence of the wind, eaten into by the bitter cold.

Saw the *Normandie* lying on her back in the pier as we drove by in a taxicab last week. A sorrowful sight, another symbol of the *waste,* the tragedy of everything now. All this beauty, this speed and luxury to end like this so foolishly, so differently from what one might have expected. It's like the delicate power and grace of France that seemed so fragile and yet strong. Alas the strength was deceptive.

March 14, Saturday

Horace has received the leave of absence from the college and a thousand dollar stipend. This shows the esteem and affection the college has for him, for they are not throwing money away these days. He was despondent for a long time feeling that the stipend or leave would not be forthcoming.

A party at the William Rose Benéts. Felt ill but went through it all with as much ease as I could summon.

Gave a radio reading of my poems on March 12. Dear little Pat went with me. My breath seemed short and I thought I did badly but the few people who heard me said I did well. Little Pat said, "Don't tell me *you* were nervous. I was so nervous I paced the floor." A nice girl-poet [Eve?] Merriam conducts these affairs, was formerly in the advertising business. There was a period when poets came mostly from the colleges, from the newspapers or the clergy. Now a very vocal group seems to have come from the advertising agencies.

March 15, Sunday

A telephone call from Muriel asking to call. A pleasant surprise. A quiet pleasant visit with Ted Wilson on Saturday night, and dinner at the Sea Cove Restaurant with him. The taxi drive back on a chilly drizzling night, the lights on the river, the heavy but cold air, the smooth flow of the motor on the black pavement—all things sinking into the memory.

Mary Colum telling H. at the Benét party, "I'm a tough Irish girl." H. retorting, "I'm tougher than you are" and turning his back on her, not disguising his dislike. She turned to me and said, "Oh dear! Young men used to like me once." M. C. also saying to me, "What a beautiful brow you have. People keep telling me that you are a Russian Jewess and I say, "Oh no, she has the most *Russian* face I've ever seen. After all Russian Jews are not real Jews." This made me silent and I wished I could be as rude to her as my usually polite Horace was.

March 19

Chest congestion again. O dear and I was so much better a few days ago! Gloomy company—one of the *Partisan Review* editors, clever and sensitive, full of persecution complexes about the Communist Party and MacLeish who he feels will suppress his magazine. Went to bed depressed. Sleepless night, foolish letters in the morning upset us again. I do so want to avoid the tainted souls of the 1930s. ___ infected me with his fears.

Went out in the little park here last night to see Pat driving his bicycle with remarkable speed. Stunning looking, rosy and gay in the wind.

The army and navy uniforms everywhere. The only touch of war. Lovely weather now, a new sun coming out, piercing the winter gloom and cloud. Lost my temper with dear H. again this evening, something I vowed never to do again. Plan beautiful poems every day which I cannot write down. The study seems too dark and close. The typewriter seems inaccessible, the artificial light gives me a headache, so I excuse myself.

Dinner with the Carl Carmers on St. Patrick's Day. Utterly charming socially. They seemed to have had a good time with us, but their manner is so perfect that one doesn't know. They listen to what you have to say with an air of passionate and avid interest, which is flattering and stimulating especially to a person who has been alone with his or her thoughts for a long time. After they left one wondered how much of it was delightfully good manners and which part was real. I like them immensely. Such a relief from the disgruntled, the outcast, the greedy who follow us around. To meet a contemporary, an equal, a man or woman who *offers* favors and does not ask for them. It's a joyful relief—a rare experience for us.

Have been reading Swedenborg's *Heaven and Hell*. The sweetness, simplicity, purity of his style and manner, the exact, matter-of-factness of his visions and insights. He was I suppose the spiritual forefather of Blake.

A pleasant talk with M. R. on the telephone. Impossible not to like her, difficult and disappointing as our friendship has been. We have a *rapport* anyway. Her qualities of mind and imagination appeal to me. I can be witty and gay with her as with no one else and we have so many memories in common now. But the breach is deep too.

Read in the *Times* a few days ago that the London poor still congregate in the underground shelters finding it more congenial and pleasant than home—the company, the sandwiches, the medical attendants. Only the poor and lonely know what that means, how natural and cheerful it is. The communal life for the very poor *is* a blessing one must be able to afford, and then culti-vate a taste for personal privacy, the snobbish selection of associates, the Pri-vate Life. No one cultivates the elderly anonymous poor, the tired mothers, the lonely youngsters who have no money for amusement and no place to en-tertain and few opportunities to meet other young people. And the getting together for companionship in danger, need, and excitement must add color and warmth to dull, starved lives.

March 20, Friday

A strong shaft of light has fallen on the steps of Grant's Tomb. Looking from my window I see that familiar landmark, half in brilliant hard cold light, half in shadow. A faint green tinge in the grass but the trees are stripped, cold, desolate. It seems that only a miracle will make them green and alive again. But of course that miracle is spring. It will come again; we know that with in-vincible faith. If only such an iron, secure Faith could console us about other things.

Working on an essay on John C. Ransom and the Fugitives. An interest-ing bit of writing to do but my eyes are strained and I find it hard to concen-trate. An enormous amount of reading necessary.

H. forgot to pay our gas and electric bill in time and I learned that the gas and electricity has been shut off. These things upset me to the point of mad-ness, especially now when I look for light everywhere. Must write in little Pat's room which is very sunny and has been fixed up with a pretty new desk and re-arranged furniture.

March 21, Saturday

Went last night with H. to see Noel Coward's *Blithe Spirit*. Nothing was available in seats but a box tier and as H. insisted on buying that I felt a child-ish awe and pleasure, saying to myself, "This is felicity." The kindness of H., the fact that he was able to give me these luxuries, something that in my youth seemed wildly unattainable. The play extraordinarily light, gay, graceful, so-phisticated in a way that made Alex Woollcott or George Kaufman seem clumsy, vulgar, or heavy. Very airy indeed, the plot and chief character (that of a madman) very much like Yeats' "Words upon the Window-Pane," made light and fluffy and commercially successful. It's as if the spirit of the Restoration dramatists had now reached its final stage of shallowness and attenuation, even the wit too frothy and unmasculine to be lasting. But it was a delight, the characters, especially of the madman, beautifully done and the subject matter holds me too much—much too much. Felt well enough but on the way home I had a nervous attack, sickness, nausea, weakness, palpitation, difficulty in breathing—the old thing, a desire to weep, to beg somebody for help. H. began to talk of *his* nervous spells, his difficulties, to nag me, and for a while I thought I would go hysterical. He is not of much help. One friend, one outside friend, would help and I haven't any and to ask for help would drive away any acquaintance I have.

March 26

Joanna very pretty in her new gray flannel suit. Quick, argumentative, fearfully opinionated. No doubt at her age I would have been the same—if I could have gotten anyone to listen to me. I learned the humility and the deep self-effacement of the very poorest at too early an age and H. learned his through physical handicaps and his too beautiful, almost Chinese fine breeding.

Daily we see the British Empire crumbling before our eyes, dying almost unlamented. Wilfred Blunt said in his journal that the twentieth century would see the end of the Empire—we all felt this in our bones and yet could hardly grasp the thought it seemed so unbelievable. What a remarkable man Blunt was, one of those tremendous failures that touch the imagination. He was also a forerunner of that other strange Audenesque hero—T. E. Lawrence.

March 28

Reading all I can of Rilke through difficult German, through flat translations, anything to catch that elusive spirit that seems to speak to me with more intimacy than any other poet of modern times. Nor do I always find him attractive. I read him often more out of need than love. He alone soothes, heals, talks to me. He lived the true poet's life, the sort of life which if offered to me I would be too frightened to take.

Visited the Rousseau exhibit at the Museum of Modern Art. Saw the wonderful wooden gypsy again with the immense toy-like tiger, the large, warm tropical canvases full of pointed almost human foliage, thick with tigers, golden oranges, frighteningly human monkeys with blue eyes and decadent civilized faces. I am one of the few people who can't quite think of Rousseau as a true primitive. Like his 18th-century namesake he has the forced naïveté of the overcivilized world from which he came. Some of his canvases remind me of the tropical poems and Ethiopian landscapes and images of Edith Sitwell in her African poems. The same consciously bizarre simplicity, the bright harshness of tone covering an ultimate grace, smoothness, elegance, and decadence, a *formal* simplicity.

Visited the Central Park Zoo with Sonia Sekula* and Horace. Lunched at the cafeteria in the fresh new-spring sunlight. A gay sight the children, the young girls and boys with their spring buoyancy, the elegantly dressed women, the brightness falling on every face. Visited the animal cages but the odors overcame me. I admired a lovely little ocelot, such a dainty little cat tiger—and animals all immense and strange and new to me. The constriction in my chest bad and I was glad to get home.

March 29, Sunday

Raining all day, and then a very slight wild downrush of thin snow that immediately melted into rain. Heavy air that clogged my nostrils and I found it difficult to breathe. The customary Sunday full of dishwashing and silence, Horace being at his typewriter and I did not wish to disturb him. My father visited us, always a strain. A rush of once frightening, now sorrowful, strange memories out of a world that always appears in my nightmares. Father charming, wistful, full of elaborate stories. The children find his English difficult to understand and are a little afraid of him, though he is gentle with them. This pains me but it *is* natural I suppose.

Am glad that H. is too absentminded to notice how awkward and eccentric I am becoming. I discover that I sit now always with my hand on my heart in a desire to stop it from beating too loud.

Perhaps a change will do me good. I remember Sonia Sekula saying that one always has an instinctive feeling, a revelation when it is time to leave a place. I felt that way about Bronxville; now perhaps the other change will work out. After Sunnyside I never felt as if I had a real home, uncomfortable as that little house was. Yaddo for a short time filled a great gaping need and colored my poetry for some years—even now its landscape returns, its fountains, corridors, terraces, rose gardens, statues, artificial waterfalls.

Thoughts of travel, my deep longing and love for it and my physical inability to be a good traveler. In all our travels, however, we took our dear children with us and this may have added strain though we loved having them with us. But we always traveled with very little money and my anxiety-love for the children always made me feel guilty about exposing them to discomforts. The children always have seemed to me like precious beautiful jewels put in the hands of a person who is too poor to wear them; like something superbly rare entrusted to one who can never find the setting for them they deserve. I felt our poverty for their sake, my shabbiness, our *different* appearance which perhaps my morbidity overestimated. I wanted them to have the normal gay time of children traveling with ordinary parents.

Horace reading Faulkner's new book of short stories, *Go Down, Moses.* He read a few passages to me, strange and beautiful. As strange and beautiful as Melville or Poe. He is the *only* American novelist writing today whose work I admire and truly respect. I like his lonely, deeply imaginative spirit.

March 31, Tuesday

Horace returned to work again after his short Easter holiday. The house lonely without him, though my little Pat is now home on *his* Easter holiday and is a comfort. I'm not getting better. I don't know where to turn.

H. came home late yesterday and I became worried about him. He had gone to do some research at the Fifth Ave. library and knowing he would return by bus, I waited for the buses stopping near the International House. I counted about twenty-five buses as I sat on the steps and people jumped out of them at our stop. I returned home at last as the air was cold and damp and counted buses as they passed our windows. Still Horace did not come and I turned aside in a panic. No sooner did I stop counting and looking than H. came in. He had arrived on the one bus I had not counted. Such a foolish thing for me to do but my nerves are shot to pieces. H. had run into an acquaintance and had stopped for a drink and talk.

A new colored maid—quite a procession—this one called Queenie Lee, who seems to be gentle and not too bad. I almost hired one called Magnolia

Hill, which would have added to our collection of odd names: Ozelle, Leola, Beulah. Difficult and nerve-wracking to break them in, and I dread the changes.

A strange sensation, that of being an employer. I don't like it and have an unaccountable sense of guilt.

Wrote one poem today (second draft) and started another which took so much strength out of me that I had to lie down. Everything I do seems loose, as if I no longer had the energy for the tight discipline. The purity of tone gone. Discouraged to tears.

Horace and Joanna went over to the Riverside Church to see a movie which tells how to put out incendiary bombs. Jo's enthusiasm about going very amusing. A movie is a movie to the children. Any kind is a treat.

April 4, Saturday

Pleasant afternoon. Went shopping with Joanna and bought her some pretty clothes for spring. She looked dazzling and dashing in her gray flannel suit, the Royal Air Force insignia in her lapel, her thick chestnut-colored hair falling down to her shoulders.

A pleasant afternoon and I felt much better. In the evening Ken Fearing telephoned asking to come down to dinner. He was very jolly telling Pat some amusing tall tales in the style and vocabulary of the Superman comics. Pat was delighted. But K. seems amazingly childish and immature for his forty years. He has not changed much in the last twenty years. The limited imagination and sensibility give me a sense of frustration. Will we never find a friend to whom we can open up *all* the facets of our imagination and intellect? The frustration limits and chokes us. K. has some unorthodox (to say the least) opinions. He thinks the Edgar Lee Masters of the *Spoon River Anthology* is worth a hundred Yeats' who he says is a bad conventional poet, etc. (The *Spoon River* is certainly a marvel.) He stayed late and I retired early, leaving him and Horace in conversation.

Today the illness returned. The morning gloomy and damp but sun, O the blessed sun, in the afternoon. Went for a bus ride with Horace and stopped at the Gramophone Shop to hear some music. Bought a small album of Lully for our record collection and then dined at Child's on Forty-eighth and Fifth Ave., very crowded, dark, noisy and hot. A large woman near us with a very thin small little boy made a dreadful scene with the waiter because he refused to wipe up some milk the child had thrown on the floor. She threatened to report him to the manager, and her voice—O, I do like gentle, well-bred, kind people. The waiter was obviously overworked. When she left (probably to look for the manager) the waiter turned to us and said despairingly, "Ain't she cruel?" It spoiled the meal.

I read the Gerstle Mack book on Cézanne. Informative, honest and rather dull. Cezanne's was a difficult but not tragic life. There was the ultimate victory that he foresaw before the end, a few friends who believed in him—and last but not least the private income that made it all possible—that made it possible to work and wait for the victory.

T. C. Wilson visited us last night, melancholy, had been drinking, wistful, affectionate. But with people so confused, or disintegrated, so unhappy, there can be little trust, fond as we are of him, concerned as we are for him. Has tried to go into the army or navy but hasn't been able. This adds to his sense of failure. Religion being out of the question, he has taken to Communism again in a rather furtive half-defiant way.

April 15
A birthday party for Horace on April 10. The Shedlovskys and Jim Putnam for dinner. Jim Farrell and Ted Wilson came afterwards. Farrell's behavior appalling, pleading with Jim Putnam to talk to him, ignoring the other guests, running after J. P. when he went into the kitchen, running after him as he was leaving. Oh well, I always knew that Jim F. was no Lord Chesterfield but as a guest he *is* a trial.

Made a visit to town all by myself yesterday. A psychological ordeal. I shall be as bad as old Ellery Leonard if I can't cure myself. I felt weak and shaky and in a frightful panic.

Must lead a more active life. Tried to work on the typewriter today. So ill I had to stop, revised three poems. Dissatisfied with my work, so delicate, so morbid, so without a center. I'm working for some greater firmness and strength and density, but my energy is limited. War news frightful.

April 20, Monday

Bad days. One dinner party with the Manuel Komroffs* and Jos. Shipley at a strange old house on West Forty-sixth St. in which one entered a business front and found oneself in a strange William Morris series of apartments. It had once belonged to Irving Berlin and had the stuffy air of refined heavy luxury of (say) 1906! I felt weak but bucked up by a drink or two. Talked well—too well. I frightened Komroff who is sentimental and flabby and full of that resentment against what he calls "literature" so characteristic of popular writers. It's what Muriel Rukeyser has called "the fear of poetry"—it's a real hatred, a real contempt, a real fear.

The next day a frightful cocktail party at William March's the novelist. An ornate apartment hotel on Central Park West. Many cocktails. Rich old men who spoke to me in a way that made me vomit. Obscene and old women. Ran into Oscar Williams who became violent against me and Horace. I lost my temper after trying to be conciliatory, a gesture he didn't understand. I do so fear hatred, fear it in my bones. Ill will has frightful psychic consequences. A wave of hatred and ill will poisons one imperceptibly. It floats like a thin wave of darkness toward you and discolors the air. It *harms*. But O. W. misunderstood my gesture of appeasement. I at last talked to him frankly and brutally. . . . Ugly, painful . . . sick . . . the next day weakness and despair. If I could only be well.

Real gold and April weather at last. But lately I've been through the real midnight darkness of the soul—the greatest I've ever known, the deepest darkest. What troubles me most is that even my dearest H., though he disguises it, is passing through a period almost akin to a loss of faith and morale.

Walked out in the sun awhile then tried to do shopping. Almost impossible because my heart began to pound and I had to get home. Sat on the International House steps and remembered that dreadful summer day when X was supposed to visit us and didn't. It killed my deep love and faith in X but it almost killed me too. Thank Heaven X can't make me suffer anymore—but there are a few people who still can.

April 23, Thursday

Telephoned M. R. who had burst in on us telling us of her undying friendship and of her desire to be of assistance to us. In the evening she telephoned again to tell us of another stroke of good luck (which she gets almost annually) and then I told her that if she would give me a few hours of her company and would take a short walk in the park with me it would be of great help, that it was my only chance of shaking off a growing claustrophobia. No answer—except to say that she would call me up sometime next week when she wasn't busy, etc. These things don't help to make me well.

April 28, Tuesday

A nice letter from dear Bryher today. What a loyal, sweet friend she is. Her news of the war, her accounts of wartime England are invaluable to us. Her continual interest and affection.

Unable to work and no longer try. Drifting pain-darkened frightened day. To cast out fear to stand up straight to simply go on as usual is all one can do— all my wish.

H. talking wistfully of his hope that the draft board might find him useful for the war effort and really draft him. He looks so frail when he says this. It breaks my heart. So frail, eager and anxious to do things—like a small boy wanting to enlist.

Reread a little Poe the other day. It's the fashion to sneer at him, to dismiss him. Yet there is more of a real horror, a real American horror, the true artist's horror of a hostile environment in his work than that of any other writer I know. No, not even Baudelaire got that real darkness, loneliness, fear of the poet in a world that does not want him. After all Baudelaire came from a rich, rooted environment, knew for a while the things Poe only dreamed of, was in a sense the inheritor of a richer culture. The [Rufus Wilmot] Griswolds are in power now as always, more solid, even more powerful, more respected, less provincial. They are called Yvor Winters or Mark Van Doren—or many college professors one can name. They are better read, better educated than Griswold [literary executor of Poe] but fundamentally the same.

April 29

The William Rose Benéts were here. Bill was delightful, such kind, good manners, it did my heart good. To be treated with gentleness, courtesy after the boors and barbarians who almost literally knock you down if you say anything that you are not expected to say and who sneer at you for stupidity if you say nothing.

For the first time Bill Benét has the upper hand in a marriage. Marjorie a little dazed, humble, worshipping, frightened by what she considers the intellectual brilliance of the family she has married into.

Expecting the Shedlovskys for dinner. H. has invited the M.S. people who bring me to the lowest level of depression. I did so want to see Ted and Beatrice alone.

I must clear my mind, purify my soul, wrestle, struggle and pray to keep my heart and spirits up, to keep irritation, suspicion, anger, disappointment far from me.

I cannot read Gerard Manley Hopkins' letters without love, reverence, admiration. How fortunate Robert Bridges was in having such a friend, such a mind near him, such a deep love! I reread some of Bridges' shorter lyrics again; the impression is always the same, a fine, a marvelous ear, a conventional smug mind, intellectual rather than intelligent, and a bad clumsy diction. A touch of the Pre-Raphaelite somewhere. Even in the beautiful elegy on the lady whom the death of her betrothed (or beloved) killed one feels that the poem is a perfect literary exercise, a recreation rather than a new poem, the result of much reading rather than real feeling. And when the poem should be most Augustan as its form *demands,* when it should be most like Pope, it becomes more and more in its imagery like a Pre-Raphaelite picture. One can almost see the illustrations done for it by a member of the Pre-Raphaelite Brotherhood.

April 30

Wrote a letter to ___ which instinct told me to put away. ___ is the one friend I have depended on and his reputation for loyalty is notoriously bad. But the letter horrified H. (justly) when I showed it to him. Such a neurotic display of intimate confession and to a person so shallow, as anxious to avoid unpleasant thoughts as ___. Such a document of indiscreet statements, too dangerous indeed if anyone else ever sees it. I wrote it as if in a trance and I was glad that I kept it and showed it to H. I destroyed it, thank God. But I have no strength left to write another letter, the letter I *should* have written.

Read Thomas Gray's letters, very slow, very fine they are, affectionate, shy, intelligent, witty in a slow-blooded way. One sees the organism that alone could have produced the slow, grave, sad, careful music of the great elegy, the man who was able (one of the very few) to keep the affections and arouse the emotions of a Horace Walpole.

[May] 5, Tuesday

Horace phoned me today to say that he had received the poetry award of $1,000 from the National Institute of Arts and Letters. Rukeyser had received recently a $1,000 award from the American Academy of Arts and Letter—which is which God knows. But it made me so happy that I almost became ill with excitement. I can no longer stand excitement of any kind. Sad because we want to celebrate with somebody and there are few friends we know to whom we dare tell of a stroke of good luck. It's one of the saddest lessons we've had to learn. Not only the money but the way the letter was worded cheered us up for it said that the award was not a prize but recognition of fine not too well rewarded services to literature. Also the thought that there is an unknown friend or well-wisher is a great joy and gives one infinite comfort.

Bill Benét got the Pulitzer which pleased us mightily as Pepys would have said. It will delight Marjorie and it will do wonders for Bill who is such a charming person and has given so generously and gracefully to others. One remembers what he did for his brother, for Elinor Wylie, and his generosity to other people he liked or who touched him.

Saw Jean Cocteau's *Blood of a Poet* movie at the strange little Thalia Theater last night. Very exciting, very brilliant, full of beautiful things. It has not "dated" a bit and yet somehow somehow it *is* a period piece. I can't just explain why. Certainly that sort of thing can't be done today, and won't be done again I feel.

May 7

Small almost unreasonable worries that I can't shake off. Difficulty in working, in thinking—even reading. Took a long walk near the river, deliberately overcoming a fear of walking out so far. Must conquer panics, one by one.

The uses of tradition. Am more and more convinced that unless one can completely revivify a tradition it's no use working in it at all. To do a little better what has been done well is not enough. Life, freshness, movement, awareness of one's own time (yes, I agree with H. there); one must learn these or one is lost.

May 11, Monday

Always a little sad when Horace's weekend holiday ends. Little work is done by either of us (and by work I mean writing) but it's pleasant to be together and the days seem shorter, less silent, less pain-wracked. We take long walks together in Riverside Drive park, looking at the water, drinking in the sunlight and I feel a little better.

Attended the exercises at the National Institute of Arts and Letters where Horace received the $1,000 award. M. R. there, seemed a little surprised at seeing us. H.'s award had not yet been publicized. The Academy and Institute members sitting on the platforms with purple and gold ribbons on their bosoms. Dignified faces out of old schoolroom pictures. I recognized Charles Dana Gibson in a wing collar and almost smart 1890ish costume, old Walter Damrosch who in profile looked like Gladstone, Van Wyck Brooks, the Benét brothers (Steve aged and ill, crippled I hear by arthritis), Louis Untermeyer, Thornton Wilder very nervous and shy and very nice to us, etc. Canby made a nice laudatory address about Horace as he gave him the award. Our old neighbor L. Mumford there, who made an address, still handsome but the golden hot potato voice that used to thrill me once no longer brought its response. Afterwards we went out into the garden for cocktails and it was pleasant to see the American Immortals crowding around the bar and drinking deep. Bill Benét very warm and sweet to us (he was I suspect partly responsible for the award). Robert Frost walked in and was immediately pursued by M.__. Max Eastman* put on his charm for me and told me that he loved my work but that the best thing I ever did was the work I did as a young girl on the *Masses.* He said that he was never really interested in politics. "I'm fundamentally a poet," and I said, "I don't doubt it at all." At which he offered to send me his new book of poems, or rather a long narrative poem to be issued soon called "Lot's Wife." Queer echoes from the past. R. torn between affectionate remarks to us and queer spurts of malice. These prizes arouse enmities. The letters of congratulation are very few—and almost none from old friends or friends we have counted on.

Dear Joanna bought me some beautiful red roses for my birthday and little Pat bought me some rather ornate handkerchiefs edged with imitation lace. I treasure them and almost burst into tears. I feel undeserving of such lovely fine children.

T. Wilson visited us. Very pleasant and good conversation. His father's recent death leaves him a comfortable income and I felt (I may have been wrong) that he was more cheerful than usual.

May 14, Thursday

Went for a walk in the park with Jim and Hortense Farrell. Hortense wheeled little Kevin who is an extraordinarily beautiful child, fair curly hair, big blue eyes. Hortense almost in as bad a nervous condition as I am. Jim gloomy and embittered. A lovely spring day on the Drive, a clear golden sun. Sat on the Child's Restaurant terrace and had some drinks. Came back feeling very uncomfortable, though for a while the talks, the drinks, the fine weather made me feel better.

Jim Farrell on St. Augustine: "He was really a dreadful person, always looking out for heretics to denounce and exterminate. But what can you expect from a convert?"

May 20, Wednesday

Tried to scrub floors today feeling that it is exercise I need most—that it would do me good. But I had to give up. I will try again tomorrow.

Max Eastman sent me his book, *Heroes I Have Known*. Strange that a person so charming, intelligent, experienced should always betray himself in his writings as a fundamentally commonplace person, but with great social gifts and a capacity for enjoying life that amounts to a real talent. One sees it in many of that crowd, their shallowness almost forgotten in that great gift of life, the valuable art of inspiring affection and enjoying life. John Reed had it, also Millay; one sees it in nasty old Arthur D. Ficke—the playboy revolutionary aesthetes. Naturally the sadness and even sternness of a Chaplin, a Trotsky, a Freud are not easily understood by him. The world is apt to be too kind to people like M. Eastman in their prime—and in old age too harsh. They then become like spoiled once-pretty children deserted in favor of a younger brother or sister.

With this page I intend to close this book and start a new journal beginning with the twenty-first of May. May the next year—Horace's sabbatical from the college—be one of fruitful and beautiful work, good fortune, old friends drawn closer, new friends bringing the widening stream of love and encouragement that we need. And may it record happiness and health for all my dear ones and myself. And above all may it record once in a while those strange strokes of sudden melodramatic good fortune that [have] never really deserted us even when our fortunes were at their ebb tide. Amen!

524 Riverside Drive, Apt. 21, May 21, 1942

I begin this new journal in hope, in the hope that it will record easier days, pleasanter hours. Last night Prof. Brebner of Columbia (the Canadian authority) and his wife who is at Sarah Lawrence visited us. They are interesting, pleasant, intelligent people but I was so ill and uncomfortable that I made poor conversation.

H. worried about conditions at the college which depressed me and the weather heavy dark and damp. It lies on my chest like a fog.

Donald Adams of the *Times* sent me the Dorothy Wordsworth journals for review. Such an opportunity! But my self-confidence and critical energy are, to say the best, now in abeyance. I will do my best but am so frightened. Still I do rise to occasions.

May 22, Friday

Rereading the Dorothy Wordsworth journals but in no mood for them. Somehow in my present agitated state, they brought no help, and I kept thinking, "What fortunate people." Wordsworth petted and sheltered by devoted females, his economic necessities always relieved by devoted friends and admirers, exactly the right surroundings for his work. Running like a thread through the book, a black thin thread through a tranquil white, one sees the then-unacknowledged results of the Enclosure Laws and the Industrial Revolution, the endless procession of agricultural vagrants, the starving children, the wandering beggars, the demoralized and brutalized poor, depending on the sensibility and sentimentality of the more fortunate for their sustenance. All this must have disturbed the pastoral beauties of Windemere greatly.

Horace disturbed by events in the college. How glad I am of that year off—may it bring good fortune, good health, real valuable work. He came home late last night and waiting for him impatiently I realized how much his mere presence, the touch of his hand, meant to me. Very lonely. Long for a visit from M. R. It would be delightful. But to ask her for a visit is the surest way to be refused. There is as much hostility in her attitude towards me as friendship. Some of it is my fault, but not all.

May 25, Monday

Went to an afternoon cocktail party at Harry Brown's.* The face of his beautiful new Powers Model bride so much like a mask because of exaggerated makeup that her undeniable good looks seemed unreal.

Frightful jitters. When I enter a room I shake all over. A few drinks help me but I become indiscreet and talk too much. Harry has just gotten a good job on the army newspaper, the *Yank,* and talked as usual about writing poetry for money. Young John Hay (a descendent of Lincoln's friend) and his bride, both good looking and not bright, were there. Young Hay and Brown were in uniform. Another young man in uniform (a Harvard man) was writing a book on *camouflage,* and dear Dunstan Thompson who always cheers me up. But it was a party of children and H. and I went home early having learned our lesson at other parties. Harry and his wife have a fine apartment on Park Ave., full of antiques and nice bric-a-brac. The money must be made by the Powers Model Bride for it all looks expensive. And yet one has the feeling of a large facade being put on. But I like Harry. He is intelligent, witty, good-looking, quick. The Beautiful Bride like all Beauties dull to talk to.

Late afternoon

Horace has gone to a cocktail party. I cannot summon up strength for these things and so stayed at home. Did some restless reading and walking in the little park next door, but there is no rest when there is unrest within. Read Dorothy Wordsworth's journals. Find it hard to concentrate and I'm beginning on the second volume of the new edition. The Grasmere journals are exquisite, a poet's eye, mind and sensibility.

May 27, Wednesday

Finished reading the D. Wordsworth journals and sat in the park for a while in the healing sunlight. But the park has become a prison and I know that the claustrophobia is not leaving me. It's a bad time for my poems too. Not only the coldest silence in years but real hostility. I myself cannot rage at this or be haughty. I know the limitations of my verse only too well and if one works in a backwash of literature, unless one can achieve miracles and wonders, one is in danger not only of neglect, but angry contempt. It was absurd of me to have put up a fight for my aesthetic. I should have worked and waited, cultivated physical strength, human activity, and then labored again to lift my poems into a fresher air, a broader sphere. I pray only for health, the well-being of my dear ones—and for a little outside word of love, kindness, esteem.

Dunstan Thompson called last night, but I am so shaky lately that I did not talk well. I like him so much. I would like to retain his esteem but felt I was childish and complaining. He is one of the few people I have a rapport with. But he is so young and one must with the very young inspire more respect than affection. For the latter, one must look for it among contemporaries. And who are our contemporaries?

The cure. "You must change your life." Yes the change must be deep through. It must go through the body as well as the soul. But one needs help, and so far there is no help from either doctor or friend. "Friends and lovers thou has put far from me."

"One does not go through hell in a hurry." True, but can one go through hell twice? Horace coming home from work is the one pleasant relief of the day. But I'm afraid of clinging too close to him. Cannot get down to work, my greatest trial; nor can I read. But it is life I have always wanted, not books. This invalidish existence is frightening. I want so to touch people, to share activities with them, to be a part of these stirring times, to do some war work, to share danger with others.

My greatest happiness in thinking of what I will do when I am well. Will I ever waste so much precious golden time again? Will I learn my lesson?

May 30

Dinner at the William Benéts. To celebrate his [Pulitzer] and Horace's award, the Benéts gave us a champagne and lobster dinner. We had read of it but never had had a C. and L. dinner. The champagne was a gift from his brother Stephen, 1928 vintage. It was all very very fine and W. B. was gracious and charming and Marjorie very sweet and kind. She looks so young and little-girlish to be a grandmother. The trip to town a frightful strain but I made it and it seemed an achievement. Going back was better but this morning the old trouble began. I think I know what my trouble is and that it's curable enough and that after a while I shall be better than I've ever been. But it all takes so long.

Finished the Dorothy Wordsworth review and think it quite good. But the strain of writing it was very great too. I felt as if I had climbed mountains and scaled high buildings and walked through an inferno doing the piece.

I should like to have a review every two weeks to do. The discipline would be good for me and earning a little money for the family would set me up.

June 1, Monday

Not particularly better and damp rainy weather does not help. M. Rukeyser visited us bringing parts of her Gibbs book, very brilliant and vital writing. We had a pleasant time, quite gay, like old times.

Yesterday Ted Wilson, Horace, the children and I had dinner at the Sea Cove. We were all at ease and gay and for the first time in ages I had an appetite. But the afternoon was bad, the evening a little better. A few drinks set me up but I'm afraid of getting to depend on them.

M. K. telephoned us about a house near Tappan. Good health and energy and faith for that precious year is what I need most.

News of the bombing of Cologne received everywhere with rejoicing. It's necessary—perhaps—but the wave of bloodlust and brutality sweeping everywhere all around, the destruction, the cruelty, is really something one doesn't want to think about too often.

June 4, Thursday

H. was asked to do the D. Wordsworth review for the *Yale Review* which was odd and amusing. I see where we shall have a surfeit of Dorothy in the family. All my taste at present runs to the healthy, the extrovert, the *do*er, the outdoor world of activity, an escape from the soul and its midnights.

An invitation from the James Johnson Sweeneys always pleasant, but I keep wondering if I can make the party and if I make the party can I carry myself with ease and lose track of the jitters.

June 7

Visited the T. Shedlovskys in Sunnyside for dinner last night. Seeing their little house, the backyard with the clothes tree, the rambler roses over the terraces, the staircase nicked by little feet running up and down it, I almost began to weep feeling as I do recently, so weak and despondent. It brought back our Sunnyside years, our Sunnyside house and the days so full of worry, trial, hope.

The Shedlovskys of all our friends are nearest to us in age and in economic circumstances. It makes a great difference now. And I like Beatrice more and more. Her restful common sense, her delicacy of feature and constitution and her loneliness as great as mine. Only she's not so restless.

Came home very late and awoke in the morning so ill that I felt as if I would at last give up and demand that I be taken into a hospital. But H. talked to me. I took some medicine and in the afternoon I felt a little better. But the heat was intolerable and my room seemed dusty, untidy, dark, and smells came in from the courtyard. To make it worse my last maid Queenie Lee left us. She was unkempt, dirty, irresponsible and destructive, but her rapt, ecstatic sensual smile pleased me after the sullen faces of the maids before her.

One beautiful day when the morning began in hope and ended in such a passion and fear and isolation I thought I would go mad for lack of human contacts. Sleepless night when my heart's pounding keeps me awake. Weldon Kees coming tonight from Colorado.

June 8

A cold letter from X—still not an indifferent one. I long for a wave of warm light and peace but one does not take Love as a medicine.

June 9

The Sweeney party a large affair, directors of the Museum of Modern Art, art critics, fashionable homosexuals, survivors of the Left Bank intellectuals of the 1920s.

Saw Eleanor Clark who is always amusing and attractive, and had a pleasant talk with Max Ernst who has a beautiful face, like Shelley grown old, very large blue eyes, a clear rosy skin in which the few wrinkles seem like a baby's not an old man's and a delicate slight figure. Malcolm Cowley suddenly kissed us when we left the beautiful river terrace and started for home, which surprised us. Horace said gloomily, "Malcolm is beginning to think of himself as a Russian mujik." Dinner out. Admired the beautiful neighborhood near the East River. Got home and went to bed, slept for a while, and then got up at midnight unable to breathe, the slowing-up rather than pounding sensation in my chest. Another half sleepless night and a morning full of depression. I got ill on the way to the Sweeneys' and dropped into a chair unable to breathe or talk. Most of this H. insists is purely psychological and will disappear slowly—but it takes a long time.

June 11, Thursday

Drugged sleep, due to the medicine I am taking, medicine which is I suspect partly a sedative. To be free of medicine and doctors, to move actively and sanely, usefully and calmly among the human race is my goal, my dream.

H. visited the Rockefeller Institute and dined with Shedlovsky and his fellow scientists. H. commented on the dignity, poise, assurance of the scientists, so different from academicians, or artists or writers. But Science is the modern profession, the scientist the most respected, admired and useful of all the learned professions, and the economic rewards are more solid, more secure. The scientist's respect for his work carries not only [his] own but the world's esteem and approval.

Perfectly alright until I step out of the house and attempt a long walk or a bus ride.

H. G. Wells interesting in his autobiography when writing on George Gissing, his contempt for the classical education which he insists did Gissing so much harm. And in some ways he is right. How alert, alive, how clean (in spite of vulgarity and occasional lapses in understanding) H. G. W. is compared to his backward-looking contemporaries. But Wells is unique, a journalist of genius, occasionally as in the *Time Machine* an artist of great imagination and power. His sex theories and comments really vulgar, but they influenced a generation and one saw it in its full honors in the Greenwich Village of the early '20s, in Max Eastman, Floyd Dell, Millay—and Edmund Wilson's *I Thought of Daisy.*

Notes for a self-cure:

1. Avoid the worries, the resentments that have caused this inferno. Remember this inferno and think yourself fortunate if well.

2. Try to write regularly prose or poetry remembering that it is through the writing alone, your one gift, that you can find and have found salvation.

3. Avoid excessive smoking.

4. When lonely think of your remarkable husband, your lovely children, and lift up your heart.

5. Keep working and moving, only be moderate in rest or work.

6. Cultivate cheerfulness even if for a while it is automatic cheerfulness.

7. Try to read and study in subjects outside of your customary line—physics, biology, any science you can get interested in. And there is always music. Above all get a routine into your days.

June 17

Returned from a weekend in Atlantic City. The garish ugliness of everything, the boardwalk full of expensive bad shops. But the change was a relief though I had to drag myself out, and the dreadful loneliness of crowds caught me and I clung to dear H. too much. The children delightful and gay, little Jo very responsible and sensitive but it was all a strain too. Traveling an ordeal to me, conscious as I am now of my strange foreign face. My clothes never look right.

My notes for a ring [engraving]: "Love and Longing."

June 22, Monday

The sad loneliness of Sundays. Horace reading the Dorothy Wordsworth journals, heavy heat pouring in through the window. In the evening went to Fifty-second St. and ate at an English restaurant, the Covent Garden. The food excellent but dear; still Horace liked the quiet of the place and the roast beef and Yorkshire pudding. Went back to Fifth Ave. to catch a bus but they were all crowded. The effect of the dim-out on Fifth Ave. very striking, a soft darkness.

We took our favorite extravagance, a cab, and drove back through the dim streets to Riverside Drive, a great luxury this soft closed view of the city.

The war news cannot be worse. The English as bad as the French. Hear that the coast of Oregon has been shelled: our soil seems so sacred, so untouchable, I cannot believe it! I saw the army and navy officers marching for ceremonies to Grant's Tomb. The sound of the drum arouses peculiarly atavistic feelings. Our officers and men seem so intelligent, such fine physiques that they seem invincible. As I drive through N.Y.C. our riches and our strength seem inexhaustible even in this the least American of cities—or is it the most American?

The *Atlantic Monthly* took H's beautiful poem and H. M. called us up timidly, furtively. Evidently her affection is not all gone and we have not fully lost a friend. But I must not forget my lesson—we must always patronize her a little, never quite treat her with too much confidence or as an equal. This I don't like. I don't like being a master or a slave. I don't like patronizing or being patronized.

My dear H.'s abstract, absent-minded kindness produces a fearful sense of insecurity.

Visited the Gotham Book Mart with H.—a hot, soggy late afternoon. Very weak, unable to stand, the shop dusty and close. Miss Steloff very nice and kind. Took a cab home, a great extravagance.

Read some of Matthew Arnold's *Critical Essays,* the Byron, the Keats, the Shelley, the Amiel. Very brilliant, that air of dogmatic authority taken over nowadays by T. S. Eliot, and in a smaller narrower way by Tate, Winters and their school. But *they* lack Arnold's scope, breadth and real learning and, curiously enough, his human passion. I can almost say his humanity. And how well he writes!

Dear little Pat at the radio again, absorbed and dreamy at all the noise, foolishness and horror coming from that box. It's an annoyance I share with many mothers today. I daresay it's neither better nor worse than the dime novels, the penny thrillers of my youth.

June 25

Beautiful rare days, the mild golden weather of June. The air, the streets, the park, the weather, everything seems to proclaim the beauty of life. If one were only well, if one could dismiss the war (which one can't) how happy we could be!

A visit from William Phillips, the *Partison Review* editor. His narrow bright little mind so small, so sad, so limited. Always feel depressed; it's as if unconsciously he dragged forgotten ghettoes, old sorrows and persecutions around him. I don't dislike him—on the contrary—but I have nightmares after he leaves.

H. not at home this afternoon. I miss him very much. I love him almost too much. One must not concentrate one's affections too closely on one person. But I thank God and my lucky star for having brought him to me.

Today not a good day. Yesterday I was a little better. When I am well again I shall be so much gentler, wiser, more tranquil and useful. I will work hard and well. New symptoms today.

Writing a letter or using a telephone has become difficult. This journal is my only consolation.

Almost a year of idleness and melancholy. I am looking forward to seeing the doctor tomorrow. One needs help and advice so badly. I am sure there is nothing seriously wrong; a little help or advice will set one on the right road.

Matthew Arnold on Clough: "In the saturnalia of ignoble personal passions of which the struggle for literary success in old and crowded communities offers so sad a spectacle he never mingled. He had not yet traduced his friends, nor flattered his enemies, nor disparaged what he admired, nor praised what he despised."

William Phillips denouncing Robinson Jeffers or rather sneering, "He's such a provincial, that's what I dislike most in his work." W. P. had never left N.Y. except for vacations in Conn.!

June 27, Saturday

Saw Dr. Penner the other day. As usual he was very encouraging and I left him in good spirits. But after dinner I heard a drum beating outside our window very loud and disturbingly. Got up from the table after the drumming had stopped and felt a throbbing and beating in my ear and head as if a hundred alarm clocks were let loose. Frightened by it; it took hours to get rid of and in the morning my left ear was still sore.

Kenneth Fearing called last night, was very gay and charming. Age cannot wither nor custom stale his infinite juvenility. Though forty years old he still looks like a schoolboy; he still works, thinks and feels like a schoolboy, which is also reflected in the flaws in his very original work.

Reading a fascinating manuscript edited by a Prof. Clark of Texas University. The journals of Mary and Percy Shelley copied from the original journals (of which I've only seen excerpts quoted) and which seem to be at the Huntington Library now.

First impressions: How young! My God how young they are!

Second: How rich. Oh God! How rich they are! There must have been unlimited sums of money at their disposal. How much they read! It beats even *our* endless reading. How much leisure they had! Shelley utterly charming and humorless. Something about Mary that I hadn't noticed before that she too had much charm and grace, in fact sometimes a delightful youthful coyness. She must have (in her youth at least) been something of a "cutey." And what a serious, studious little "cutey." Compare to the charmlessness of the Wordsworths.

June 29

We are leaving for Milwaukee this Wednesday. Rather dread the long trip, the loneliness, boredom, shyness that overcomes me in those difficult holidays. Don't know a soul in Milwaukee anymore and have a feeling that nobody is very wild to see *me*. How pleasant it would be to visit somewhere, someone who is full of delight and pleasure in seeing you! At one time I knew that feeling when visiting X's city and I thought that for a while he felt that way about seeing me. I always feel that where there has been a falling off, a failure in love, it is due to some inadequacy on my part, some foolishness, some weakness.

Expecting Rukeyser for dinner tonight. Wonder if she will come in time. I enjoy her company more than anyone's—alas I cannot depend on it.

To remember. What Rilke said of psychiatrists: "It is true that they can cast out the devils, but they cast out the angels too."

July 5

Shorecrest Hotel, Milwaukee, Wis. Sunday. Left N.Y. on the first of July and arrived in Milwaukee on the second after a not too difficult trip. Thought of the many trips we had taken with H. and the children and now they blend in my memory and faded procession of visits and I grow old and tired contemplating them. H.'s father has gotten us a very comfortable small apartment in a very pleasant apartment hotel. It's almost luxurious. He has taken us to fine restaurants, one magnificent place near the Juneau Hotel where we remembered that one year Norah Hoult and John Sweeney (calling on us from Chicago) took us. That seems ages ago and yet may not have been so long ago. But how pleasant and gay the talk was, and remembering that we once had such friends! such company! I wonder why we had not held on to them more eagerly, been wiser, shrewder, more capable of retaining as well as *giving* love. How immature we are still, how long it takes us to learn simple things!

A party at M. R.'s (last week) in honor of little Carson McCullers the novelist, who uses her extreme youth as a weapon. I've never seen anyone so youth-conscious, so aware of its value.

Jim [Horace's brother] and Nancy's children are charming. Yesterday we visited Josephine [Le Mieux, Horace's sister] and her children at their pleasant farm at Waukesha. Louis Le Mieux took us over his garden. It seems a pleasant, useful life. They have books, a fine house which they are improving, the children are all delightful. They have their church and music (and gardening and pictures). It's not on the highest level but on a *good* level. I thought of our feeling of homelessness, the viciousness and moral horror of so many of the people we know, the compromises we have to make to have friends at all, the devouring ambitions, the humiliations, the small triumphs, and wish that I at least could have had a smoother less hectic background for my dear children. But this is a hectic ugly horrible world. Why attempt to build another shadow world beside it and hope to disguise the violent reality? One of Josephine's boys is now grown into an extraordinarily handsome fellow—little Tom. Very dark, graceful, gay, French in appearance, an air of great distinction.

Am reading the Norton translation of the Rilke *Sonnets to Orpheus,* and comparing the translations with the German. For the first time in reading Rilke I can find nothing stimulating or exciting to me. The whole work seems too involved, too abstract, without any real feeling, a little pumped up, a trifle insincere. It is hard to believe in his grief, or that the dead girl meant anything more than a peg to hang his new sonnets on.

Rereading Dryden. Beautiful vigorous diction, a strong manly mind. Amazing lack of charm, though some grace of expression.

July 6, Monday
Horace went on a visit to his half-brother John who is ill. H. returned despondent and irritated. In the evening H.'s father came and we dined together; expensive rich meals which the old man insists on paying for. He's the most charming and generous of men. We are very grateful, for I admit that I keep worrying about our expenditures in this "Year of Grace" when we must watch every cent.

The luxurious comfortable houses, the pleasant landscape, the quiet of Milwaukee makes it a very pleasant place to live in. The people look well fed, have excellent physiques, good complexions. But an air of stodgy dullness over all. At nine o'clock in the evening the streets are deserted. No taxis can be found, even the movies are not well attended. All culture (or almost all) in the hands of women. The public library (one of the best in the country) hardly patronized by the wealthier classes. Fine houses with many cars in the garage and no books anywhere. The children active, lively, argumentative, exhausting. I seem to sit all day waiting for a long conversation to be finished, a long dinner to be terminated. Agonies from some queer form of nervous indigestion. H. is not fond of walking (my only exercise) and the result is little exercise. I can do no writing though my mind is full of things that must be written. No contemporaries of ours seem left in the city.

July 11, Saturday

The hotel in a beautiful section of the city near the lakefront. Fine old houses full of dignity and comfort shaded by thick elms. The streets very quiet under a bright sun. This is one of the most pastoral and charming of cities. The public library superb, the best I've ever visited, a delightful reading room and the selection of books done with intelligence and taste.

A kind letter from L. Untermeyer that gave me a feeling of security and pleasure. I'm really fond of him and superstitious about him.

This has really been a nice vacation and I for one would not mind spending our whole summer or sabbatical year in this city. But it *would* be lonely and far away from places where we can earn some money.

Visited the Ellery Leonards* at Madison. Madison has become impossible, a small town now sprawling over into an inchoate small city. Old landmarks gone, filling stations everywhere, cheap shops, ugly new buildings. E. L. and his wife Charlotte both unwell and lonely but delightful as ever. We had a pleasant time and we introduced him to Jo and little Pat. Ellery was enchanted with Pat and thought Jo very pretty. Hated to leave the Leonards'; so many memories rushed in on me. In the evening little Pat became ill because of the long trip and excitement but was better in the morning.

As usual L.'s conversation very good when off from his phobias but as I have a few phobias of my own these days I don't mind.

July 14, Tuesday

Bought a pretty new suit for Joanna and a new jacket for Pat. The streets were hot and saturated with heavy sunlight. Cannot get over the quiet even tempo of Milwaukee. H.'s aunt Martha visited with us. The children were gay and talkative. It was pleasant to sit back and watch the scene.

A birthday party at Horace's Uncle John's (his eighty-sixth!). The charming old house on Jefferson St. Uncle John still soft, graceful and charming. Some resemblance to my dear H. in the graceful charm but without H.'s keen hard brilliance—and flash of genius. The Skeleton in the Closet, Cousin Paul, taken down to visit with us—a frightening object because his conversation is full of crazy flashes—things that are almost very good. His fat swollen hands, his "literary" conversation, his ageless face, his evident conception of himself as a young man and his childish air—he almost convinces us that he's not fifty-six or more. What thin thread does divide the fine space between insanity and genius? Thought with horror of what his loneliness must be; the sick need friends more desperately than others. But in the long run we must earn our friends. Poor P. alas can give nothing—has never given anything.

The children have gone to the zoo with their Aunt Martha. It gives me pleasure to see H. and the children surrounded by relatives who love them for themselves and because they are themselves and it takes the rootless feeling away—at least for them.

Notes. "There is a term *ittakkirri* meaning 'all gone, completely vanished,' used by the Japanese contemptuously to express their feeling for verse which tells all and leaves nothing to the imagination." – Lafardio Hearn

"It is just the province of culture or right education—is it not?—that it shall train the mind to breathe easily an atmosphere foreign to its native habitat." – P. E. Moore on Crabbe

August 3, Monday

Returned from Milwaukee feeling a little stronger and pitched into housework too strenuously. Then little Pat sprained his ankle and in lifting him from one room to another I strained my back. Days of agony and helplessness followed. To be in that dark foul airless bedroom unable to move has been one of my old nightmares. Utterly discouraged. H. had to keep the Harvard appointment for his reading. I got a nurse for me, another fearful expense. But the care did me a great deal of good, a little nursing at the right time would have saved me in the past—but of course I couldn't keep the nurse long. Still my back is better now. I move slowly and painfully. A sore throat adds to my depression. I want so much to be strong, active, alert, helpful.

T. C. Wilson writes us from the army. He has enlisted in the air corps. Marcia Silvette writes us an account of the Peterborough Colony, foolish as ever. Yet these colonies were the only places where we could get a summer holiday cheaply and get work done. But the Peterborough Colony did me a great deal of harm last year. Silvette's friendship very charming and touching. I feel like the statesman who found a fiend devouring him and said in surprise, "Why does he hate me? I've never done him any favors." I say, "Why does she like me? I've never tried to please her; nor does she owe me any debt of gratitude."

Troubled about the children, about money, about doctor bills, about my inability to work, about Horace, about my inability to keep or make friends, about my bad health, and the fear that most of it may now be hypochondria—which is a disease too.

August 5, Wednesday

Moments of soft sweetness in the air that gives me a lift. When I take our very short walks with H. I feel full of hopes, of plans, of poetry, but inertia and weakness come in. My back has healed very well and rapidly, but my shoulder and throat are now sore. Difficulty in swallowing and a pounding in my head, probably due to my old sinus trouble. Become despondent for my spirit is now ready, alert and anxious to help the body. It chafes at my lack of physical strength.

Waiting for a visit from Christopher Lazare. Last night young Howard Nemerov* called bringing Horace a bottle of Irish whiskey. There seems to be a general rumor everywhere that H. drinks Irish incessantly. In fact, he can't afford it and drinks very seldom, only when we have company and we have company very seldom. H. N. in the Canadian Air Force, a handsome, bright boy. Something fundamentally uncongenial to me in his temperament, though his poetry has a sort of dry intellectual vigor. He reads Donne over and over again and Donne and the seventeenth-century metaphysicals have now been used and reused till I feel that they ought to be given a rest. They are no longer a fresh or revivifying influence.

The war news ferociously bad. I avoid reading the newspapers. Every day a parade passes our window, either army or navy, the band playing, the drums beating. I find myself unnerved and weeping at the sight. I can't pump up exalted sentiments.

August 8, Saturday

News of the execution of the six saboteurs captured recently. Immediate military execution. I watched the people's faces as they read the headlines, a look of unbelief, disgust, horror—not to be mentioned. No sympathy for the saboteurs but a feeling that all this ugly horror is not real, has nothing to do with American life.

Visited Eleanor Clark at Palisades, N.Y., and looked at a house in that lovely country. Eleanor read part of her novel to us and gave us dinner. The dark descended fast and we saw few houses. The long bus ride home an agony. The cold, the chill, the loneliness of the country as the dark fell down.

Visited the movies last night for the first time with H. and little Pat. *Sergeant York* and Chaplain's *Gold Rush*. Discomfort in throat, ear and back exhausted me but pleased to be able to sit through it all. Slowly, slowly, I shall return to normal life. *The Gold Rush* seemed somewhat dated even a little arty though Chaplain is always a delight. His exquisite sensibility, his fine courtesy, his astonishing distinction. *Sergeant York* much better than I had expected. Some of the innocent emotionalism (especially in the revival scenes) of a poem by Vachel Lindsay. The Cordell Hull episodes marvelous war propaganda. In fact the propaganda excellent and characteristic of the present war. No lush patriotism or flag waving, but grim, almost cynical resolution and desperate necessity recognized and assumed almost wearily.

Reflections on a life of E. Allan Poe, a new one by Arthur Hobson Quinn:

1. Never realized how well known he was in his day.
2. The poverty real and I cannot understand those who try to prove that his drinking habits were negligible. Perhaps a little drink was a great deal with him—but he never avoided just the amount that made a wreck of his life.
3. The frightful letters to Mrs. Clemm, so pathetic, childish and a little vulgar. She may have done him a great deal of harm. Quinn quotes a frightful letter from Mrs. Clemm to Griswold that almost gives him (G.) a modicum of justification. In that letter Mrs. C. offers in return for favors from Griswold to Poe to see that Griswold would get favorable reviews on his books from E. A. Poe—open bribery! In fact her whining, her begging, her interference with his literary integrity made an unfavorable impression in certain quarters and aroused snobbery in the powerful Bostonian clique. J. R. Lowell's comments on Mrs. Clemm full of patronizing annoyance and haughty benevolence are very characteristic. The fearful literary women are very much the same today though their badness is in a more modern style. Are B. L., T. J., H. E. (I'm not

giving them correct initials) any better, less foolish, than Mrs. Ellett, Mrs. Lewis, Mrs. Sigourney, Mrs. Osgood (who had a nice streak somewhere and was judging from her portraits rather pretty) or Sarah Helen Whitman, whose poetry now and then does have a flash of something that is not quite rubbish? But she *is* foolish, and provincial and frightfully immature for her age at the time of the Poe affair. The nonliterary women in his life almost as bad. The foolish, grisly letters of "Annie" to Mrs. Clemm, Mrs. Allan's letters to her husband beginning "Dear Hubby" are on a level with Mrs. Clemm's and she had more social and cultural advantages. The cultural level of literary America (aside from the rising Boston crowd) was as appallingly low and greedy and competitive as it is today! After all genius is rare, the slick journeyman always in demand!

The Poetry. The split between Poe's ordinary life and his world of imagination and creation! Compare with Baudelaire's. What Poe needed was a Guggenheim Fellowship to Paris at that time. If he had only met Baudelaire! But his work would have lost that pathetic, awkward innocent amateurish quality that gives it a certain flavor of its own, a period *American* flavor.

"The City in the Sea" and "The Sleeper" still move me immensely. It's the mood, the wonderful images, rather than the writing, which is loose and flabby and falls apart on analysis.

August 14, Friday
House hunting in the country in a pouring rain. Row after row of suburban houses near Nyack. Frightful suburban faces, a Bronxville without its real prosperity and smart glitter. Ugly houses, expensive too, and one had visions of further loneliness and isolation and no strength left to compete with difficult furnaces, etc.

Saw Eleanor Clark in the country. She seemed in the gray-green light of the rainy afternoon very wistful, graceful and beautiful again. She was dressed in shorts, a blouse and a raincoat and looked well in a costume few women could carry off.

A journal *does* encourage morbid introspection, egotism. And yet it is a comfort for me!

Looked over the poems in my manuscript book. Utterly dissatisfied. They are weak and self-pitying. This is not what I meant at all! Difficult to do any work but as soon as I get a return of strength I shall work and work.

August 21 (our wedding anniversary)

"When any fit of anxiety or gloom or perversion of mind lays hold upon you, make it a rule not to publish by complaints but exert your whole care to hide it. By hiding it you will drive it away. *Be always busy.*" – Johnson to Boswell. And yet what would a Freudian say to this? Submerge, suppress.

Depression when all telephone calls I make do not answer. . . . Absurd but a feather brushed across my cheek will make me break into weeping.

Another quote from Boswell's *Johnson:* "If you are idle be not solitary, if solitary be not idle." But work . . . work, work alone in a solitary eternity is not what I desire—detestable as idleness is . . . one must not step out of the life-stream, lose track of human voices, human activity; one must have human beings around.

Horace out in the country looking for a house with Bob Tallman.

Expecting our dear valued friend Theodore Shedlovsky* of the Rocke-feller Institute for dinner. Teddy and Bea are now among our oldest, our most mature, our most heartening friends. How few they are!

August 22, Sunday

One should keep a silence in this journal till one is able to write as a nor-mal human being again. But one must go on hoping, praying, trying not to be a burden. I seem to have lost interest in everything even my work but a little peace of mind will help to restore everything. The talk with Shedlovsky helped me a great deal, the affectionate kindness was a joy. But he made another ap-pointment with us for Sunday to which I looked forward and he didn't keep it. His excuse was reasonable enough, but I keep wondering if we exposed too much weakness, too much loneliness, too much need. Nothing drives people away faster. But Ted seems another kind of person.

A night of agony. Horace impatient. Am avoiding all medicines and reme-dies, all drugs.

Visited the country (Palisades) with Horace. The bus ride difficult but I made it. A charming house, a little too artistic when I longed for more comfort, but conveniences and comfort cost money. This place is charming, very cheap, the country enchanting and full of associations to me. Under normal circumstances everything would be a hope and a delight. This illness has lasted too long and if it is *not* an illness still it's an illness.

Reading Boswell's *Johnson* with comfort and pleasure. But it's true that most biography deals too much with the great, the fortunate, the successful. One needs more memoirs of ordinary people or people who have not made many friends or known great good luck.

August 27

The great need, the great want is now so obvious that I cannot even pray for it. And my present state of health makes it even more difficult. One had dreamed of so much, almost achieved something and now. But something very tough, very powerful and strong in me says Endure! Endure and all will be well.

May God send his blessing on my dearest Horace. Joy and blessing and love to him on all sides, good health, long life and rewards and honor. He has been an angel of kindness to me and having him I have no right to complain, for I've been rarely fortunate.

Muriel coming to dinner tonight. A visit from a friend is a red letter day. But one longs for mature, adult companionship.

Horace's poem will appear in the *Atlantic Monthly* soon. And he's doing an essay on Samuel Johnson. He *does* work under handicaps and never complains.

August 29, Saturday night

Jim Putnam visited with us this afternoon. A friendly face cheers me up a great deal and makes me feel better. I do not know how fond he is of us, but he's kindly and not too indifferent. Muriel's visit a queer one. She evidently forced herself to stay longer than she might have done, was flattering, amiable as ever, but—still I was so happy to see her I found myself weeping.

A new doctor who is giving me some hope. I will see him Monday for the final verdict. Once my fears are dispelled I can face the world again with new eyes. I begin a new world, a *vita nuova*, again. Everything will look clean and cheerful and hopeful again. A little more warmth and hope and I can begin to write again.

Better this evening after a bad morning.

A kind nice letter from old John Gould Fletcher. How I wish he would live near us! We haven't heard from the people whose house we want to rent at Sneden's Landing, but I feel that we shall and that in a new house, in new air, I shall recover completely. Today the weather was dark, dank, and gloomy. It affected me as always and I thought of old Sam Johnson's comment, "How low is he fallen who is dependent on the weather for his health and happiness."

September 2

Great discomfort. Tried to see a movie but found myself sunk in depression. The new doctor says he has discovered a slight glandular deficiency which he can work on and so help me get into normal life.

May this journal reveal soon even if slowly a sure turn for the better. Have not heard of the Sneden's Landing house—at least no definite word as to whether it can be rented at our price. If I can only earn a little money to help Horace fix up the place, pay the damn doctors (how I dislike them all) and— feel that I am no burden.

As for the doctors I feel with Virginia Woolf in her wonderful study of the nerve specialist in *Mrs. Dalloway*, I am like her Septimus in their presence. Their contempt for the "aesthetic" mind may be justified but it's hard to bear. To say that you are a poet is to be labeled as a freak at once, their suspicions aroused.

A wonderful flush of sunlight across this page as I write.

September 4

New medicine which I shall start taking hopefully. God is still with me I know and feel it.

My dear Horace had a bad fever last night which kept me awake in alarm and worry. Slightly delirious he kept talking of Dr. Johnson on whom he is writing an essay. In the morning I called a doctor who looked so much like the early Louis Mumford that Sunnyside nostalgia arose. Horace was much better this morning, for which great blessing I thank God. In the afternoon I went to the doctor with Joanna accompanying me. One must have faith in them and I shall try to believe.

Unbelievably hot day. My soul felt sticky and ugly with pain, impatience, sadness.

Muriel Rukeyser called and visited with Horace when I phoned her about Horace not being well. It was sweet of her; after all she has been more decent than most friends—which I'm afraid is not saying a great deal.

Muriel telling us of an aunt of hers who went insane and when they called to take her away ran to the radio and said, "President Roosevelt I appeal to you!"

September 9, Wednesday

Cold rainy day. Nervous tension. Difficulty in walking and yet a something that makes me feel the crisis is over, that now I will be well. Wish I could earn some money. Idleness, morbidity, I must throw them away. Think of Joanna's beautiful clever face, little Pat's enchanting golden atmosphere. The new house in Sneden's Landing, Horace's new books, the books I will write, the new friends, the laughter, the gaiety, the warmth, confidences, tendernesses, the good years ahead of honor, peace, and love and good work. Writing all this I feel close to tears, my sense of humor in conflict with that wild hope and desire.

The visit from Norman Pearson last week. Norman very thin and looks unwell but so gay and charming. With him a slow drawling fat young man who turned out to be Theodore Roethke the poet.

The next day a visit from Ted Shedlovsky and Jack Sweeney quite pleasant.

The grayish air, the falling leaves in the blue-yellow light, my favorite season.

Cold—yet not indifferent letter from X—how his love would have lifted me once. Now it has served life's purpose, like an old cistern that once held water and is now full of dead leaves, dried, flowers, ashes—more terrible things perhaps.

I must be getting better for I dream of traveling again. Dublin, the Wicklow hills, Glendalough. I should like to see that again. Florida, Colorado, New Mexico.

I could have been happy in Milwaukee if only we had a pleasant house and a number of friends near by. It is a lovely city and full of Gregory roots. Those roots that keep one from being homeless or rather *feeling* homeless and lost.

It will be nice having a room of my own to work in. It will make I think all the difference in the world. Joanna is now using Horace's typewriter too— three people using one desk, one typewriter. It is to put it mildly—very difficult—but most of all for dear H. whose year this is.

September 11, Friday

Treatment growing vigorous. Hope and pray it may do good. M. R. here yesterday with Klaus Mann. The latter's eyes wild and dilated, as if he had been taking drugs. His conversation as always charming foolishness. M. R. at her worst and shadiest, but she's been having a few blows and disillusions, the first serious ones in a career that started too smoothly at too early an age. Felt sad and sick at her attitude toward Charles Madison at the house. M. unusually attentive to him. After all he's a publisher. Had to take my short walk in the park and asked her if she would take it with me. Asked it with more curiosity than hope. As usual she had an excuse and as usual I took my walk alone.

September 19, Saturday

My father-in-law moved me to tears by sending me a birthday check and a kind note. To be remembered by anyone with kindness makes me weep a little. Kindness is so beautiful, so rare. It is true that I'm uncertain of my birthday but I've always given September 12 as an official date since people demand an official date, and if one can't do it for them get angry. I'm fairly certain of the year—and I say this knowing that it sounds odd.

Klaus Mann's new autobiography. Poignant, touching, occasionally charming—very often embarrassing.

Simply unable to summon up the ability and discipline to write. For the first time I can sympathize with Leonie Adams in her long period of silence now and understand it. And I think I know why her hair went gray so suddenly.

September 22, Tuesday

We are moving to Sneden's Landing on Thursday. May it bring us good fortune, good work, and cheerful minds. May it find me in better health.

The x-ray report quite favorable but the pain continues. The doctor feels that he can set me straight again. I shall become like one of those dreadful elderly ladies who can talk and think of nothing but their ailments. My fear and distrust of doctors as great as ever. My great desire is to get free of them. Once ill we fall into their power. We fall into that vast, complicated, bewildering, tortured network of helpless dependence and pain. Have written almost nothing except in this journal. Have even lost my pleasure in company. I let the world drift by till it becomes a black shifting shadow.

Palisades, N.Y., Sneden's Landing, Brearly House, River Road
September 30, Wednesday

Words cannot express, nor shall I make too detailed a record of the agony, the strain of moving, the packing and unpacking, the discomforts so difficult to bear at this particular moment. Found that the water had not been turned on. Then the furnace leaked, then the floor began to give way in Horace's study. But how beautiful, how beautiful this country is, the most beautiful country in the world, the silver Hudson, the autumnal coloring, the clear blue air.

Went to town today and in spite of great difficulty in breathing felt a little stronger. The children happy and set up by their new schools which are very nice indeed. I take long walks. A few years ago this life, this country, this delightful rackety old house would have filled me with ecstasy. I love it still but find walking and feeling clearly difficult. Some neighbors have been very kind. With good health all would be pleasant indeed, and the Riverside Drive apartment of last year a bad memory. But I know this year will bring health, content, good work.

October 3, Saturday

Chilly long evenings. Horace working in his cold rather crowded study. The long dark roads, a feeling that I shall never get to know anyone here, a feeling that I make a queer impression and that I shall never be part of any community. Too proud to make advances and besides know that advances of this sort are not always the right thing. After all one must learn to be solitary. But I wish that good writing, good health, mental and spiritual, might come yet—and I can't quite feel that. I have had too much loneliness. My poetry is at its lowest low. Complete silence or contempt and sneers.

Eleanor Clark has taken little Pat to the movie tonight. Quite a treat for the poor child who is still unaccustomed to the country.

The morning walk to the post office a delight. The clear fresh air, the slow gold and red changing of the foliage. But H. is beginning to complain that it's too much for him. He says that writing or rather using a typewriter is a *physical* difficulty and takes all his energy.

Lovely, lovely landscape, my favorite landscape, but difficulty in enjoying it. Handicapped by lack of a car for walking is difficult. Illness arouses impatience on all sides. Terrified at the expense, and the flood of doctor bills though I go for treatment and help as little as possible. Hope and pray that this precious year will not be wasted, that I will not be a burden to my dear H. who has been so kind and patient.

October 12, Monday

Brilliant autumn weather, the leaves full of light and color. The children have found friends and seem pleased with their school. H. and I have not been so fortunate but we make friends slowly.

Two very young neighbors, the girl a lovely blonde Italian, the boy Harvard, old American stock, fancy prep school, indescribably dull, and stupid and badly educated and literary in a pretentious way. He has a habit of asking heavy schoolboy questions in the manner of a dull-bright student. They are rather poor, not popular in the neighborhood and dear H. wastes hours of beautiful, profound, scintillating talk on them. But he gives of his best to everyone. The girl is very charming and young and likable and has been kind and helpful.

The houses here enchanting, lost in the wood, or dropped by some artist's hand beside the water and shaded by deep trees. A certain air of attractive shabbiness and antiquity rare in this country. But the Hudson is a noble classic river and adds distinction to every house on its bank.

I long for the company of mature people, people of our age, of our generation. But as D. T. once asked in writing a review of Horace's last book of poems, "Who are Mr. G.'s contemporaries?" We seem to be surrounded by children asking for lessons—but no friends.

The hardships of war slowly, slowly creeping in everywhere.

H. saying to me, "You have aged faster than anyone I ever saw." Perfectly true which made the remark more cutting, though it was made in a passing fit of irritation.

The walk to the post office. It seems almost impossible. My breathing is too difficult but later especially going back in this dream scenery, this Innes landscape radiant in yellow, orange, gold, the leaf strewn lanes, I feel better. This is the life, the house I've wanted for years. If one were only in glowing health to meet this beauty, this bounty of God.

October 13, Tuesday

Sat in the charming kitchen basement with Horace last evening drinking a sour vinegary California Burgundy the S.'s had brought us last Sunday. We had no real firewood and in the damp growing chill we lit some kindling wood and paper and for a moment had the illusion of a bright crackling fire. Went to bed chilled and uncomfortable again and the cold fell on my chest.

Horace and I terribly pleased at getting checks for our poems in Untermeyer's anthology. Together we earned $35, the price of a longish review for the *New York Times*. If only these things came a little more often.

October 14, Wednesday

Indescribably tranquil lovely weather. The silver flash of the Hudson among the gold and greens and oranges and crimsons.

Kindness of neighbors. Horace's fine Dr. Johnson piece completed. The children happy at their school. Now if only I could be completely well and at work again even at those poems of mine, liked by almost no one. Alas is my dear H. with all his brilliance, ardor, scope, better off?

October 30, Friday

Feel that I may have been too cross with my dear Joanna who is at that difficult age, half child and half grown woman. I lose my temper with her because she seems so adult at times and then so little-girlish, so full of decided opinions, sometimes brilliant and mature, sometimes so silly.

The landscape here is beautiful, but Nature alone cannot heal me as it almost could have done—ten years ago.

Dear Horace so kind and patient and intent on his work. Such *courage,* manliness, sweetness, so much sadness overcome. I become angry and impatient at the world not for the blows I have received but for the few rewards it has given him.

James Farrell and Hortense visited us. Jim in an uproar because the American Library Association has banned his book in Engand, for the duration of the war anyway! He blames MacLeish, the Catholic Church, and the Communist Party!

Hortense's personality so typical of the actress—so many personalities, so many moods that one wonders which is the real one, which Hortense is really Hortense. A hysterically devoted mother. Jim now calls her "Momma," which sounds odd. Little Joanna commenting on her appearance said, "Hortense does not look so well; she seems so emancipated." This puzzled me till I found out that Jo meant emaciated.

November 2

A pleasant tea at our neighbor Elizabeth Shipley Sergeant's house. E. S. S. is one of the few people who aroused in us a feeling of affection and warmth, a feeling that some connection existed, that all wires had not been cut.

In the evening H. and I had a gloomy talk on our literary prospects—continued snide attacks on us which *must* hurt eventually, or what is worst, a complete silence which saps creative eagerness and courage. Had a nightmare again when I retired—the same one only sadder and more vivid. It lasted into the day. The execution nightmare, only this time H. was with me and my grief was that I could not go alone, and greater grief in knowing he was feeling the same thing. A queer feeling of fatalism knowing that we were guilty of nothing but knowing too that even proofs of complete guiltlessness would not help. A feeling of great love and tenderness and concern for H., and knowing it returned, for me.

All I have heard of James Joyce from friends and enemies makes me feel that as a person he was one of the finest characters of all men of letters in our time. His love for his family and his unashamed loyalty and concern for them, his hard labor on their behalf, his courage in poverty and illness, his gaiety and lack of spitefulness, his mammoth labors done with such love and patience.

Curious how many people mistake pedantry for intellect. A good mind is never a dull mind.

November 8, Sunday

Pleased and excited when M. Rukeyser's Gibbs book arrived. We have some interest in it for we introduced her to Shedlovsky who first talked to her about Gibbs and suggested the book to N. Pearson who helped her with the important Yale section. Full of brilliant flashes, half-finished sentences, intuitive penetration, Waldo Frankian ejaculations, real poetry. Whether it will be a best seller or not I don't know, but I think the book will have a long life.

Note added later: "1944. Have changed my mind—it's a dishonest book, I wanted to believe in it."

A comment. "He bore his misfortune like a man—he blamed it all on his wife."

The news from the war front so good that one keeps fingers crossed. When will this cruelty, horror, hatred, evil stop? How long, O God, how long?

November 19, Thursday

Saturday a rush of invitations from the neighbors who seemed curious to meet us. It was very nice and a little puzzling. I felt and talked better and saw a number of beautiful houses, and a number of expensive houses that were not beautiful and made us realize that our charming little cottage, rickety and small as it is, is one of the most attractive places in the neighborhood. In the evening a drinking party at the home of Nichols, a drama critic on the *New York Times*. Eleanor Clark came in escorted by three or more Norwegian refugees, an amusing sight. Our host (Lewis Nichols), Harvard, an ex-student of Hillyer, looked so much like the Lautrec portrait of Oscar Wilde that when after not remembering his name and referring to him in a whisper as "the Toulouse-Lautrec portrait," everyone caught the reference and began laughing. Naturally, I was embarrassed, but Nichols laughed too.

A cold sharp frost that penetrated the whole house and went through our bones. We tried to make a wood fire in the fireplace but nothing seemed to burn. The furnace worked badly but outdoors in my warm clothes the air was pure and sharp and stimulating. It strengthened and supported me. The whole landscape glowed with vitality.

November 24, Tuesday
A frightful tea at the X's last Sunday. Dull dowagers simply bloodthirsty about the war. One feels they enjoy it immensely, that they would be sorry to see it stop. I had very little to say and the conversation of their dull males, heavy, pompous, prosperous, equally dull. I never get along with rich people. I never shall.

November 28
Sharp cold weather, all the memories, all the illustrations felt and seen in childhood rise up as I walk through this charming little town. My health seems better and a walk in the crisp clear air usually raises my spirits. This is a great blessing. And one gets fond of this shabby old house in a way one never gets fond of a city apartment. But I know that it is only a matter of time before H. will begin to long for the city.

H. dreary and abstracted, few calls, letters, telephones. Too many of these are a trial, but too few (to those whose position is as precarious as ours) is to say the least a little worrying.

Unsatisfactory visits with neighbors, usually elderly, rich, or successful popular theatrical artists. Delightful visits to an antique shop near the post office. We buy humble old family photographs (of the handlebar mustache period) usually enshrined in fine heavy old-gold frames. We dispose of the ancestors and use the frame for a folder of the School of Fountainbleau reproductions that Joanna has. Framed, the pictures look quite grand, an air of elegant voluptuousness and intense but refined richness—very French. There is one of Diane de Poitiers in her bath, an Ingres-like brunette with her in the bath, who extends an exquisite long finger to touch Diane's nipple. It's very strange and yet because of the thick red curtains in the background, and beyond the curtains a dark corridor where a woman in red (a woman neither beautiful nor young) seems engaged in sewing, one feels that all is correct, right, beyond good and evil—yes, gay and pure—and a little bit domestic.

December 7, Monday

Dorothy Pennington (maid) arrived late this morning and as usual I felt a sudden panic for she is much too—too good. I feel lost without her.

Had lunch in New York with Mr. Abbott of the Buffalo Library who asked for our poetry manuscripts. We never save rough drafts and never bother with manuscript sheets (except to work from). Somehow the thought of people saving every scrap of their own writing for posterity seems so presumptuous and vain. The finished poem, the printed book ought to be enough. Besides there's something I don't like about betraying one's method of working, exposing the creative processes. It's like Samson explaining the sources of his power. I for one am superstitious about it.

As Abbott, Horace and I left the Russian tearoom where we had lunched we ran into Louis Untermeyer. Louis was very voluble and gay as usual. He was full of his new war job in the propaganda bureau. "I am not even allowed to talk to poets anymore. I must stick strictly to business and I must submit all my writing and radio scripts to the board."

"But what do you submit? What do you do when you ad-lib in your radio talks?" I asked.

"Oh, said Louis. "They ask for a rough draft."

His nervous effort to be witty, amusing at any price, as if he had to be amusing or die! I am very fond of him and we owe him more than one debt of gratitude and though he has the reputation of being a weathervane, I must admit he has been decent to us when it has not been to his interest to be so.

Did a little Christmas shopping and found it as exhausting as usual. The house chilly and I struggle with the fireplace. I've discovered vague pyromaniacal tendencies. When a fire starts up I want to throw everything I see in it. A manuscript of poems arrived from Dunstan Thompson (whom I like very much). I picked up the wrapper and said to Horace, "How glad I am to have his address at last"—and then threw it in the fire absent-mindedly. A small box containing a pretty pin of Joanna's met the same fate. By a miracle I recovered myself and rescued it in time. Only the box was singed a little. God knows what missing articles may have gone up in ashes!

December 11

Visited New York yesterday and I did a little Christmas shopping. Went to my doctor for treatments while Horace had lunch with Rahv and Phillips of the *Partisan Review*. The magazine is undergoing a reorganization and Rahv has married into money and Phillips now has a part-time job on *Time* magazine. Somehow when Horace talked of them my mind went back to Sunnyside memories and the Social Period of the Literary Front when we first knew Rahv and Phillips. Form and Content, Kenneth Fearing had nicknamed them. Horace had always befriended them but at a moment when Horace needed friends they had deserted him when they found out that he could not follow them to the Trotskyite camp. But they are changed now and want a literary-critical magazine—no politics, they insist. . . .

December 19, Saturday

Unable to write and full of panic and lack of self-confidence. One tries to blame bad health and too much isolation but no excuse will do. [T]he fault is in oneself. Few Christmas cards so far, but from curious people. One pleasant one from Hilda and Perdita Aldington. We have earned very little this year and I feel quite upset and worried and yet we cannot curtail the children's Christmas. The cold house and the lonely evening difficult. I have not been able to return neighborly hospitality which I must do, which troubles me but to tell the truth there are few people here with whom one wishes to be intimate and I cannot entertain on their scale.

James Farrell called up in a pleasing Christmas mood. A Swedish firm has brought out *Ellen Rogers,* reprint libraries are bidding for his other books and he has received $1,500 in royalties. It is true that he has not made the fabulous sums earned by Hemingway, Caldwell, Steinbeck, but he is in the enviable position of earning his living by his writing and yet never compromising; doing exactly what he wants to do and in the way he wants to do it. And no teaching, no hack work necessary.

Tried to shovel snow off the porch and stone steps and became so exhausted that I had to give up. More and more I feel my physical limitations with greater distress and anger. Why can't I do simple ordinary things well?

December 25, Christmas morning
In better health than last Christmas but still strained and nerve-wracked. As one fear and worry leave, another one enters. Childish disturbance over Christmas cards because of silence from those one wanted to hear from. Surprise cards from people we never expected to hear from. A delighted moment seeing the children open their gifts and we were so pleased to be able to be as lavish as on other Christmases.

Dinner with the William Rose Benéts last Wednesday at a fine restaurant, Mario's, where Bill dined with Elinor Wylie in the past. A magnificent dinner which I couldn't eat. Bill gracious, beautiful manners, great charm but he doesn't particularly like me. Marjorie effusive, kindly, full of pleasant compliments. A beautiful tree which Bill had dressed for his children, grandchildren, nephews, and nieces. Hundreds of Christmas cards, a testimony to Bill's universal and deserved popularity as a man. Bill showed me a beautiful early nineteenth-century edition of Landor's *Imaginary Conversations,* which had belonged to Elinor Wylie. She really liked Landor and appreciated Thomas Love Peacock, two fine writers nobody reads today.

Came home on a midnight bus and walked home on a dark slippery road. But the cold spell was broken and our relief was great.

December 31, 1942 (last day of a difficult not too cheerful year)
Yesterday I did a little writing—not much, not good, but my first "creative" effort in a long time. Violent rainstorms for the last three days and chilly winds. But today the sun came out all freshness and then gold light and a soft beauty and clearness in the sky, a faint-false spring glow in the air. Walking was a pleasure as I took my daily walk to the post office. Stray Christmas cards and

letters came in, one from Allen and Caroline Tate which puzzled me for the man has done us much harm, never an act of kindness or generosity and yet he seems anxious to retain our good will.

A Christmas party at our neighbors' the Hutchins, an elderly couple who have a luxurious house across our road. All the best second-rate company in Palisades, mostly elderly, wealthy and suburban. I was badly dressed and felt unwell and could not talk. We left early. H. fortified himself by a few drinks before he came and so was gay, charming, talkative.

Eleanor Clark dined with us last week. She drove over in a blinding rain storm bringing in for a moment the cold, the frost, the sleet of the night air. As always she was intelligent and pleasant to talk and look at. It is with regret that we heard that she was moving from Palisades early in the coming year.

1 9 4 3

January 14, 1943

One may start this year's journal with a thanksgiving for better health. I am not completely well yet but I do feel better for which I thank God. May the terror, the horror, the bitterness of last year never be repeated. My worst sin is idleness, an endless daydreaming. May I improve, may I never lose hope and courage and faith.

The cold has been so dreadful, heating this house so difficult that we've decided to call our house (for the winter at least) Valley Forge. We have done everything to endure this cold except leave our bleeding footsteps in the snow. Horace is struggling with his coal stove now. He has worked incessantly on a revised essay for his book of critical studies.

Ted Wilson called on us on a furlough from his camp in Texas, very handsome, silent and glum. He has given up all reading and even thinking. He spoke of the monotony of camp life and looked superb in his uniform. His depression was so great that we found it hard to talk to him. He stayed overnight and in the evening we had a drink at the Algonquin bar, full of the customary prosperous old gentlemen escorting lovely young ladies. Many soldiers there.

We have a few projects that we look forward to with hope. May they prosper. We need some good news now, some small victory.

My great difficulty is lack of self-confidence. I am beginning to trace that and a great part of my illness to M. R. and the suppressed unhappiness and worry about her since she was (aside from H.) my only intimate friend. But I can now, since my eyes are open, open a new leaf. I see her as she is, dangerous, resentful, jealous, untruthful, driven mad by ambition, vanity and guilt. Only affection made me so blind, and loneliness.

Worked at my poem this afternoon. Exhausted and had to rest.

January 15, Friday

Difficulties with the maid who is getting restless, hysterical, discontented. She threatens to leave. I need her desperately as the kerosene stove is a horror to me but I have become weary of her impertinences, rages, hysteria. My meekness has probably encouraged her to be as impudent as she wishes. And yet in many ways I have found her so reliable and valuable. If I had a gas stove and a little more strength I could almost find it a relief to pitch into my own housework. But the Book. When will I find the time and energy to do it?

A visit with Eleanor Clark last night. She is leaving for N.Y.C. today and we shall miss her company, her conversation. She told us some stories of her friendship with Louis MacNeice. It was evidently a real love affair. I hadn't quite believed that before. Told us of a time he had fallen asleep at her sister's house with a lighted cigarette and had set fire to the bed. Her sister who was then pregnant smelled fire and tried to wake him but he slept too soundly. At last she woke him up by pouring water over him. Eunice had a miscarriage afterwards and Eleanor's grandmother was furious. "Never let me see another poet around any of my granddaughters again." Also an account of how she had nursed MacNeice through a critical illness. Told with rare emotion. Some intimate recollections of Carlos Tresca. Said that Tresca's idiot step-daughter heard the news [of his assassination] over the radio and called up her mother by telephone. This was the first time Margaret de Silva heard the news.

January 16, Saturday

Christopher Lazare visited us full of wild, amusing gossip about everything and everyone. We enjoyed his company as always. He visits every place worth seeing, knows the queerest and most fashionable people and listens to everything. Unfortunately I had had a return of my breathing difficulties and deep attacks of despondency. Unable to eat with the result that my energies are very low. But Christopher is a pleasant guest and one is sure of a witty statement or a good pun being appreciated by him. He has lived on his wits or rather conversation for years and is now writing the book which no one believed he would ever write, a life of Lorenzo da Ponte, Mozart's friend and Casanova's. If he writes as well as he talks it ought to be good.

Joanna's shy eagerness to talk to young men. She dressed up for Christopher and looked so beautiful, so eager, so much a child, so near to a woman that I felt a pang for her. O I do so hope life will be kind to her and that she will find the nicest of young men. Today she went off to N.Y.C. to meet a girlfriend dressed in her red raincoat and beret. She looked so dazzling, so innocent, so conspicuous that I was troubled about her. She is tall for her age too. Had bad dreams about her. My concern and worry for the future of my darlings is becoming an obsession. God protect them. I wish we were richer, healthier, more famous and successful for their dear sakes.

The Life of Yeats by Hone arrived and I read it avidly, not being able to set it down. Not that the book is so good but that the subject fascinates me. What an ideal poet's life. How fortunate and rich in the right experiences, how fortunate he was in every phase of his career, how fortunate he was in his parents, his country, his friends, his relatives. Like Rilke who was the only poet of his time to approach him in genius he had an unrivaled opportunity to develop his great gifts. Will poets ever be able to live such lives again? With our changing world can there ever be any Coole Park to shelter poets again? The Yaddos, though attempted substitutes, are institutions anyway. They don't count, and the rich are now too frightened to help the arts.

I am grateful to Yaddo now for giving me a taste, a faint understanding, of what a Coole Park could be, of knowing at least in a way of what luxury and peace of mind can be like. But of course there were always the fears of being turned out of Paradise, the institutional air, and occasionally the feeling of being locked up in an expensive sanitarium.

January 18, Monday
Dorothy threatens to leave and I suspect will leave. I may as well pitch into the housework now and try to save money and do what I can. Depressed about

my writing and can't write anyway. I will do my best to keep the house in order, the washing may be a little difficult but richer women have to do these things too nowadays. But they have had more training in household arts than I. I never even knew that people slept in sheets till I was in my late teens. Horace was truly generous, unpractical and kind to marry me. I realize only too clearly now what the social taboos were and what my lopsided education and personality promised for a boy so frail, so delicately brought up, so fastidious.

A bad quarrel today at the dinner table. H. too lost his temper. Sorry for the children.

February 3, Wednesday

One really pleasant day in N.Y.C. two weeks ago with Horace. It was dark, damp, cold, but I felt well, better than usual. Went to work in the library and worked better than usual. Found to my joy and surprise some material I have been looking for for years and some new material I never expected to find. Such delights are pure and strange for they give me pure real pleasure. I know I shall not be able to put it to definite use, commercial or even literary. It is all like a delightful private message for oneself alone. In the evening visited with Jim Farrell and Hortense. Van Wyck Brooks was there, softer, milder, sadder, older, weaker than I remembered him after many years. I looked well, talked (I think) well. Brooks was courteous, respectful, really charming to me. I had become unused to such treatment and I opened up like a flower. The Farrells in a commotion over some slight illness of Kevin's obviously due to teething. Jim true to his naturalism kept showing me the baby's soiled diapers asking my opinion. Did they look natural, normal. I said wearily, "Oh yes." Hortense talking diapers and baby diet to Brooks who looked uncomfortable. His children are all grown up.

Dorothy our maid left suddenly about two weeks ago. Since then I've been lost in an orgy of heavy housework and am violently exhausted every evening. My conscience feels fine, but my back aches, my hands are chapped and sore and I never seem to get enough rest.

April 6

The house still full of chill and damp and the air gray, the river clogged with a thick gray veil of mist. But something in the smell of the still withered grass, something in the pale thin mist-colored skies seems to tell of spring, something inexpressibly lovely and hopeful.

Since I've written in this journal Horace has almost completed the anthology of *Elegies and Devotions* he has undertaken for the Viking Press. It was such fun collecting the poems, talking about them, rereading them over and over! I would pick up books during spells of hard housework and check poems and discuss them with Horace. It has been our only pleasure and recreation. I feel that the book will be very lucky.

A visit with Rukeyser in N.Y.C. Very flattering, affectionate and catty. She had brought May Sarton with her, a young poet who spoke with enthusiasm and praise of my poetry. The first praise I've had in ages. I felt embarrassed and upset but for a while I began to feel that I wanted to write again.

H.'s father generously offered to buy us a house and we want one here. We started looking. All available are ugly, or so expensive. Saw one in Tappan we liked so much but the price asked is prohibitive. Still we have not given up hope of it.

Our oil gave out and except for a fireplace fire we shivered yesterday in what was almost the worst cold of the year.

Much stronger and my housework and cooking done with more skill than I thought I had. But it's all exhausting. No time for my writing and though I am much stronger than last year I'm still suffering extreme physical discomfort.

My stepmother died suddenly and I visited my father in the hospital where he had to go soon after. Frightful depression always when visiting the full wards of hospitals, those cities of the not-too-well cared for sick. But the luxury wards frightened me even more. Depressed and worried about it all. Pangs of conscience which though I can justify to myself, I cannot shake off.

I ought to have done more for my father. And yet what could I have done?

The war shows signs of lasting forever. The rationing does not trouble me yet as we've always lived on short rations.

While it is lonely here, it is not as lonely as in the city and walking here is really a delight.

Had a pleasant visit with Norman Pearson who is going to England on a government mission—such a pleasant change, he said, from teaching English at Yale. Jim Putnam is now in Dakar as head of the Lend-Lease commission there. How the war is shaking up settled lives!

Interested in a young poet who visited us recently and said (he had grown up during the depression) that for the first time he found jobs plentiful and that he had the luxurious sensation of being able to pick and choose his job. He had been deferred from the draft because of a recent nervous breakdown.

April 8

No letters this week. I cannot get over my sadness at never getting any. H. however received a phone from the *Virginia Quarterly* asking him to do the *Quarterly*'s poetry and an unexpected review from the *Times,* all a help.

Last night while we were sitting in the basement dining room late at night we got a phone [call] and my instinct told me that no message received so late at night meant good or indifferent news. I was right. Horace received a telephone [call] announcing his half-brother Johnny's death. Everyone called him Johnny, unlike his uncle whom everyone naturally called John. He was a kindly jolly aboriginal Gregory. The red hair, the blue clear eyes, fond of drinking and sports, completely dependent on his father and though over sixty as helpless and humble and frightened as a child before the old man. He had lived for years in hope of the legacy which H. tells me would have spelled independence and pleasure to him. He had none of the family culture, dignity or manner, but he had the family pride, its ingrown affections, and could never conceive a life away from Milwaukee, away from his father. His children, though offered cultural advantages by their grandfather, flunked out of every school and sunk back into the proletariat. Everyone treated Johnny with affection and contempt.

House hunting today in the cold unnatural weather. A marvelous pre-Revolutionary Dutch stone house in old Tappan restored by a wealthy lawyer, a connoisseur of old houses. Full of antique furniture, the restoration perfect.

One was back in eighteenth-century Tappan—and didn't like it. One would as soon live in a museum. But it was beautiful in a way and a little frightening. You couldn't call it a cozy house or an intimate one, and the isolation gave me the creeps.

Lovely walk with Horace in the woods here. A truly beautiful landscape, civilized, soft, with a kind of well-preserved wildness.

April 19

A lingering coldish arrested spring. Have been laid up with the grippe, a bad exhausting bronchial one and am still far from recovered, but one must go on. Am negotiating for a house in the neighborhood. It has much charm but is in a frightful state of disrepair. But we should like very much to have it. Such red tape, such difficulty. The owner says that a number of the neighbors have phoned him urging him to sell us the place because we are such desirable people to have in the neighborhood. This pleased me very much for I long to be liked, to be accepted somewhere, to find a home somewhere, but it fills one with dread to think of what happens to people in this neighborhood who have not made the grade with their neighbors or incurred their ill will. Other people are bidding for the place (real estate is the big mania here) and are offering almost twice what the place is really worth. O dear, in things of this sort we simply *must* leave ourselves out. We can't compete with rich foolish people. The cottage (it's hardly more than that) is just made for us and people like us—if we could only have it, we can make it as attractive as our Sunnyside place. We understand that we shall have first choice on it and the agent says she will let us know on Wednesday the twenty-first which is our lucky day. I do so hope and pray that the news will be good that our offer can be accepted and that we can start decorating and repairing the place soon. God guide us here to our best good. If the house is destined to be ours let it be ours and may we know soon.

Raining all day, a windy cold cheerless rain. Couldn't go out and the lack of fresh air affects me. [L]ast night a neighborhood party at Mrs. Gray's, an elderly English woman (quite a character), to welcome her son Peter back on furlough from the army. Then to other neighbors, the Frosts, rather gayish and gaudy and hard-drinking. We enjoyed them.

We shall do a little more home-hunting tomorrow, a gloomy job and we expect very little. But hope is a wonderful thing—and curiosity. We have seen more fantastic horrors of houses set on the Hudson, regal in lavish ugliness, deserted run-down cottages, crowded villas, fantastic Victorian mansions done in dark brown panelings—and sometimes the queer people who live in them. I don't particularly like Nyack and its vicinity.

I do so pray for luck, sunshine and above all God's good blessing.

May 1

On the day after the last entry (the twenty-first), Mrs. Bauer our house agent telephoned us to say that we can have the house we wanted at our price. Full of charm, and with repainting, cleaning and a few repairs will be lovely. We were so happy and excited we have talked and thought of little else and have been digging into our savings for repairing old furniture, especially Horace's ancestral Chippendale desk, my comfortable old battered chaise lounge, etc. I can hardly wait to get into the house which we intend to call Gregory Place, even though it does seem a little tony for a small cottage.

Golden, brilliant spring weather, almost unbearable beauty all around us. The sun startles me in the morning and my garden is full of daffodils and narcissi.

Our new house has marvelous laburnum bushes and a fine but neglected garden full of white violets.

We cannot express too much gratitude to Horace's father. We are so glad not to leave Palisades.

A moment of pleasure in seeing Joanna and her friend Angie Hyde dancing to the radio music, trying out the latest dance steps. There is nothing lovelier in the world than a lovely, healthy, sixteen-year-old girl, gay and animated, giggling and talking.

Little Pat is staying overnight at his friend Mac Whitney's house and Horace is working on a review of T. S. Eliot's "Four Quartets" for the *New York Times*.

Picked up a number of valuable books at a second-hand shop here, among them Emily Dickinson's collected and later poems. In rereading them as usual all my prejudices melted. All one can say is, "Here is genius." She kept up vitality and freshness to the end.

A gay party at our house last Saturday. Some neighbors and Eleanor Clark and a Mrs. Allanah Harper, an Englishwoman who had edited a literary magazine in Paris in the '20s, full of anecdotes of André Gide, Jean Cocteau, Joyce, etc. It did me good. Everyone was gay and talked well.

May 9, Sunday

Rukeyser visited us and stayed overnight, leaving yesterday morning. Had a fantastic story of how she knew the "inside" of the Tresca murder, knew the murderer and had denounced him to the police already. The purpose of it all was to prove that the Communists had no hand in it, that the "commies" were incapable of political murders, etc. She has reverted to type and become a perfect C.P. stooge full of wild eloquence but never meeting your eye. H. very cold and remote with her and rightly so. But my old affection never dies. I am very fond of that flamboyant girl though my distrust is almost as great as my affection. But we *have* some rapport.

I have done no writing for ages and feel sad about it. The housework exhausts me though I do it fairly well now and in my few moments of leisure I have to sit down and rest. Perhaps settled in the new house I shall be able to work again. Horace has reviewed T. S. Eliot's "Four Quartets" for the *New York Times* and is doing an omnibus review of current poetry for the *Virginia Quarterly* and has a fine Poe piece appearing in the *Partisan Review*. But the important things are his books, none of which, with the exception of the anthology, he has finished. Feel rather depressed about it all. His energy goes into *reviews*.

May 15

Heavenly golden weather. I have never remembered a spring so brilliant, so full of light and sun. Our garden has come up in full glory with almost no aid from me. Narcissi, red and pink tulips, and an exquisite white lilac tree has flowered suddenly. It excites me and seems to be a drain on my nerves. I am accustomed to take in great beauty a little at a time.

Took a trip to Closter with Mrs. Haagenson our neighbor. Later showed her our new house where the painters were making progress. Beautiful rich flowing landscape full of golden shadows. We are spending so much on the house that it frightens us a little. So much going out, so little coming in. Horace working hard on the preface to his anthology—too hard. Pat Covici as usual a little difficult when we come to collect the money due us. O dear and Viking is such a rich firm!

Went to the Academy of Arts and Letters reception yesterday and came just too late and so missed the speeches. Heard that Albert Stoessel* the conductor had suddenly dropped dead while conducting on the platform, a few minutes before we arrived. Horace was surrounded by beautiful Sarah Lawrence girls who had come to see Bill Schuman get the music award, much to the envy of Louis Untermeyer who rushed in and joined us. He was affectionate and gentle to us again—such a queer changeable man. Said kind things to me about my poems. In the evening we dined with the James Sweeneys at a French restaurant and were joined by Harvey Breit* whose wife had just had a baby. We all celebrated by having drinks at the St. Regis. Sweeney full of Eliot's "Little Giddings" poem which sent him to reading Shorthouse's obscure classic *John Inglesant,* always one of my favorite books, a beautiful and mature book if there ever was one.

July 5, Monday

Gregory Place

I think that this is the first entry that I've made since we moved into our new house about a month ago. In the mental darkness and black crisis of the soul that I went through a year ago it seemed as if nothing could ever arise that would give me deep interest and pleasure again but this charming house, this lovely country has restored my interest in life. As a little girl I had picked this landscape and this part of the Hudson River country as a place where I would have liked to live and after so many pilgrimages, after so many destructions, I have the kind of house I've dreamed of. I ought to thank God for his gifts to me. Surely I ought never to feel as if He has forsaken me. My great grief is that nobody seems to read or like my poems and I feel even more so for the neglect into which Horace's beautiful work has fallen. I have done almost no writing lately but a little encouragement would do wonders.

Am doing all my own housework again. After a year of empty idleness the labor and even drudgery is good for the soul. But at the end of the day I'm exhausted. I rest for a few minutes and have to start work again. There is no time for reading, thinking, relaxation or even enjoying this exquisite landscape. I become depressed over the fact that now that I feel well enough to write and think and feel again I have no time to write.

A fairly pleasant party at old Miss Gray's (one of our neighbors, she's a sister of the famous writing Powyses), Louis Nichols (the *Times* dramatic critic), Lee Gröen, some musicians (who played rather amateurishly), and other neighbors. Rather interested in a good-looking White Russian girl, the wife of one of the socialites here who sang for us. Not a good voice at all, the sort of voice that is considered quite nice in a fashionable boarding school and which in a young lady is another accomplishment like watercolor painting or playing the piano. But her poise, her self-satisfaction, the rapturous faces of her relatives were interesting. She had all the mannerisms of a person who had always been greatly admired and had never doubted or tested herself in a larger arena. None of the murderous doubts and self-conflicts of real talent—or genius.

July 15

Wednesday is the one day of rest I have for then I have Marie a colored girl from Nyack to help me with the housework. I always plan to do some writing on that day but I find myself taking that long-desired walk in this heavy-foliaged enchanted country or simply reading or resting. The day passes like a dream, a thick summer dream, and the day is done. Tonight for the first time in ages I have the longing for outside company, a friend, a voice from the outside world.

Theodore Shedlovsky called on us last Sunday and it was delightful to have him here. He has become in many ways our oldest and kindest friend.

At Amy Jackson's we met a White Russian pianist who had lived in Paris for many years and has known Proust, Joyce, Paul Valéry. He had many interesting stories about Joyce whose terrific erudition overwhelmed him. He had once presented the pianist (Gourevitch his name is) with a copy of the *Portrait of the Artist*, inscribed to him, as Gourevitch was told, in Gaelic. Out of curiosity Gourevitch once showed the inscription to a Gaelic scholar who could make no sense of the inscription and insisted that it was not Gaelic. Confronting Joyce with this he had laughed and gone over the inscription with Gourevitch saying, "I thought you would discover my little joke soon." The inscription turned out to be in Russian but written in Latin instead of Greek characters! Such an elaborate joke it wearies the head. G. said that Joyce was a great admirer of Field the Irish composer who died in Moscow and influenced Glinka and Chopin and to please Joyce he often played Field for him.

The proof of H.'s anthology, *The Triumph of Life*, has come in. Such a beautiful book! I do pray for God's blessing on it, and may He send us what we've never dared to ask for a book before, a slight financial success! To be able to live on our writing!

I don't think I've mentioned before the latest acquisition of our family, our dog Tom Jones. He was a sick stray puppy who was hanging around the schoolhouse picking up scraps of food. We took him home, nursed him and now he's the most faithful, affectionate, playful little dog in the world. We love him very much. I've never believed one can love an animal so much. He runs after me in all my walks and I realize that I've never had a friend so devoted or so loyal.

July 28, Wednesday

The endless housework. Sweeping, dusting, bed making, cooking, dishwashing—and the evening draws on and I no longer have the strength to write. Long endless daydreaming at night—the flies and mosquitoes and the day is done.

Poor crazy Ezra Pound's dilemma. He was always an adolescent, a foolish and at times a precocious adolescent. The behavior of some of his disciples who now admit no merit in his work—shocking. Reread some of his earlier work and found it as fresh and exciting and beautiful as always, and *Hugh Selwyn Mauberly* is as good as the best done in our time. I hope he will get off easily—MacLeish who borrowed so lavishly from him ought to plead for him. Eliot I know will.

Our dog Tommy has convinced me that dogs have souls. I do so hope God has a special place in Heaven for them.

August 6, Friday

Had a maid in today to help me with the housework. Even then my mind was so taken up with little household details that when at last I sat down in our pretty back garden and tried to write I felt I could not concentrate. Began again and again and had to take a walk in the rich gold midsummer weather, unbelievably clear and beautiful. Weeded the garden and found myself uncomfortable because of an attack of hay fever.

Then went back to the garden and tried to write again. The garden is lovely with phlox in various shades of rose, purple, pink, cerise, white, violet. They spread a faint perfume over the air. I admired them and my mind wandered again. Then I picked up a volume of A. E. Housman's poems and again was struck by his purity, simplicity, inimitable dignity of style. He strikes off masterpiece after small masterpiece with ease and dignity of style, the perfection of grace. Discovered a remarkable poem I've never seen before and could have kicked myself for not having caught it in time for H.'s anthology which is now in press. It is a trifle more complex than his usual poem, and has a strange touch of ambiguous subtlety. It might have been written by an Eliot or a Rilke. The poem is in *More Poems XLIV* and begins "Far known to sea and shore." A magnificent last stanza. H. thinks the whole poem may be a translation from some obscure early Latin poet in spite of the references to Venice and Trieste.

Uneasy about the war now that victory seems closer than it has been for years.

A visit from the Weldon Kees, he being full of literary gossip. Better informed than many of the young writers but his conversation makes me feel out of it all and sad. Had a feeling that both of us are very, very unfashionable and unread writers. One now sees new names springing up in literary reviews and journals that are utterly unknown to us, a whole new generation one supposes. Nor under these names have we seen anything that points a new direction or shows unusual talent. But of course there is the war.

Visited N.Y.C. yesterday in a sultry heat. The streets, the shops crowded. At Lord & Taylor's I was caught in an air raid alarm and couldn't leave the store for about an hour. I then left to meet Horace in the public library and found them removing black curtains, air raid drapes, etc., all done with slow inefficiency. We had to wait for a half hour before being permitted to go upstairs. Found H. upstairs in despair because though he had been in the library over two hours, he had just gotten his books.

We both worked and as I looked up at the blank bended heads around me and felt the silence very heavy tears came into my eyes. So many years of my lonely wasted youth spent in this room, in this way. And I always wanted a little more life, a little less reading. But—

Prayer: Forgive my sins that be too heavily upon me. O teach me how to cast off their weight, strengthen, harden me so that I walk under the clear sunlight of God and neither sin nor feel the need of sins anymore. No, this prayer doesn't say what I want to say, my guilt weighs me down. I want to do penance because of my father and do not know how. "Honor thy father and mother." —but—no excuses!

With Harriet Monroe I lost my last, my best friend. I did not quite realize this at the time of her death, much as I felt it.

Churton Collins. A tragic career. Surely one of the finest critics of his day and yet who reads him now? An ungracious literary style and too much given to controversy added to the feline hostility of Sir Edmund Gosse damaged him in his own day, and his bitterness and strict standards, his heavy erudition, his conservatism (but was he more conservative than Matthew Arnold?) seem to leave him unread today. We picked up a second-hand copy of his posthumous essays at Dauber and Pine. A good essay on Dr. Johnson, a fine essay on Matthew Arnold.

August 21, Saturday

Our wedding anniversary. We had hoped to go to town with Ken Fearing and have dinner with him but he was giving a party and wanted us to be there instead. But at the thought of the long trip to Greenwich Village, the heavy drinking, the people Ken gathers around him, the long ride back, my flesh rebelled. I stayed home instead, feeling rather depressed anyway. The Geddes Smiths took me in their car to Nyack where I did my marketing. A bright serene lovely day, but I felt drugged, heavy, sleepy. H. returned from town and brought me a pretty string of pearl beads. So sweet of him. The *New York Times* sent H. Oscar Williams' new anthology. To review it would be a foolish unnecessary indiscretion and though it is hard to turn down the small check we would receive for it, the book will have to be returned.

August 28

A sudden cold spell and rain falling all day. Such a rain, cold, damp, endless. Horace went to town and I was grateful for little Pat's company and Tommy our good gentle dog. But he is full of fleas (Tommy, I mean) and I run from his caresses. We must give him a bath, such a difficult job.

A heavy dull inertia has hit me again and even this lovely landscape doesn't soothe me. The housework endless, but the house looks lovely and I wish we had more visitors to show it off. I spend my days in housework, reverie, daydreaming and languor. I pray that God will not hold me to account too severely for my wasted days.

Received a letter from my publishers asking me about my work. I was so pleased and frightened too for I don't feel ready for a new book yet.

Read Eúgenie de Guérin's journals again. Such a strange out-of-the-world book. A curious touch of religious bigotry that troubles me but what a curious, sad, pastoral her life was. The personality charms me. She is a Dorothy Wordsworth of charm, grace and great talent. Her gifts spill over like dew on roses. And that rare thing, real purity, real religion, shines from out those pages. Feminine poetry of the most delicate and exquisite kind, the poetry of a distinguished and rare soul.

September 3

First signs of autumn in the air. The leaves beginning to fly, the air damp, mild melancholy, a faint touch of yellow and red in the thick dark foliage. Horace has started his work at Sarah Lawrence again. It was a little sad seeing him off in the morning. Soon my dear dear children will start going to school and the house will be empty. I dread the extreme loneliness and the thought of the winter cold. It has (compared to last year's nightmare summer and the horrid summer in Peterborough) been a lovely rich season. This lovely house, this heavenly landscape. If only our writings would prosper, if only a few friends would claim us, how peaceful how happy how good life would be. I thank God in all humility for never forsaking us, for always withdrawing His Hand when the punishment seemed too great and showering us with favors and so letting us know that His wrath is short, His graciousness eternal. "There are some," says Pascal, "whom he knows are but won to Him by kindness, others whom a mixture of harshness and kindness serve best (this is ourselves) and others who never turn to Him save when His Hand is heaviest." Dear God let your mingled reproof and Love be ours. Do not be too harsh.

Find in looking over my book manuscript that I have enough poems for another volume of verse. I should like to send it off and begin all over again. The title for this book (my fourth vol. of verse) will be *The Golden Mirror.* I have rescued a number of discarded poems which rewritten seem very good indeed.

The news on the radio pours out further hatred, destruction, death. And yet I would not be human if Hitler's downfall would not cause me real joy, real relief. Oh if I could only believe that these things will never happen again, that this world will be a better place—afterwards. It will be I'm afraid difficult to throw aside habits of cruelty, bloodshed. The Nazis have tainted the world. The stain spreads and will be hard to wash out—it infects even their enemies.

October 2, Saturday

Depressed because of the death of our neighbor Mrs. Hyde. I never knew her well but her sad aimless life, her dumb unhappiness, her lack of charm, her inability to gain love was always before me. She had the rare fortune of belonging to a locally distinguished family which to a person of her type was a great prop. There are some people whom one does not think of exactly as people but as leaves of a dynastic tree, unthinkable apart from the great tree that bore them and who when they fall lie obscured and buried beneath the maternal shade.

A frightful dinner given on the twentieth anniversary of Kafka's death by a Czech-refugee literary society. Unconvincing testimonials by old friends and acquaintances of Kafka's who seemed very much like the characters he half-satirized in his novels. A beautiful girl of the Mendlesohn family very blonde and German reading a Kafka fable with unbelievable archness. Kafka's old publisher Kurt Wolf saying to us, "I can't understand the interest in Kafka; he never sold in Europe, he never sells in America."

Rain and damp entering one's soul. A damp chilly soul is an awful thing to have. The landscape all golden light, crimson, purple, a luminous melancholy radiance. My respect for the not-too-much praised landscape painter Innes had gone up. It is he who best caught this wonderful landscape and made poems out of it. He is indeed the poet of the Hudson Valley scenery, one of our few fine artists.

October 10, Sunday

A bright fire in the fireplace which warms one room only. One steps into the next room and freezes. Upstairs the wind blows in and the cold chills the bones. A return of physical discomforts and continual stomach aches, such a discouragement for I had begun to be free of them. Nervous tension and sleeplessness.

H. has handed in his book of critical essays to Harcourt, the result of many years' labor and thought. The book has I think a beautiful title, *The Shield of Achilles*. I do so hope it will be a liked and fortunate book. H. has a contract for it but until we see the book in press we worry against reason. I do so pray and hope for it, and that it will be fortunate through God's grace and Horace's beautiful writing I feel in my heart.

A colleague of Horace's who had lived nearby and used to drive H. in her car to the school has left the college and the commuting problem begins. The thought of getting up at five in the morning in an icy-cold room after a bad night's sleep depressing.

The landscape more beautiful than ever. A fading haze of brilliant colors. The air dreamlike and soft, a poignant sadness over everything.

November 1

Handed in my new book of poems to Macmillan last Wednesday. To be called *The Golden Mirror*. It seems such a frail, thin book to throw down the great presses today, a candle in the wind, a flame in the storm, a penny in an enormous slot machine. But I feel that there are some fine things in it and I hope a few people will feel it with me.

Tuesday a frightful rain storm. Horace and William Carlos Williams gave a reading in the N.Y. Public Library and in spite of the storm about one hundred people showed up. H. peaceful but nervous. Williams curiously undignified, full of the "rebellious" attitudes of the 1920s. I don't mind rebels but it is important to know what one is rebelling against. Williams unlike Yeats has grown into a foolish but not passionate old man. His new work seems cute, full of silly whimsy, and a dated "artiness."

We had a few drinks with Muriel R. and her friend May Sarton who directs the library readings and had dinner with the Charles Madisons. I was soaked to the skin and stayed overnight at Muriel's apartment. The steam heat of the city was as uncomfortable as the damp cold of the country. I suffered keenly. When with M. my heart goes out to her in warmth. I forget all my resentments, all the bad treatment we've received. Only afterwards I become angry again feeling that I've fallen into every trap laid for me. C. L. speaking of M.'s warm personality said contemptuously, "Oh yes she's like a great big Yiddish mammy singer." I had to laugh in spite of myself.

We had dinner at our kind charming neighbors, the Lewis Nichols'. A few drinks and I become indiscreet. I have no small talk. And my poise is uncertain. I feel as if I shall never make any friends in the community.

Note. Quotation from Tennyson on literary squabbles:

> Ah, God! the petty books of rhyme
> That shriek and sweat in pigmy wars
> Before the stony face of time
> And looked at by the silent stars.

> And strain to make an inch of room
> For their sweet selves and cannot bear
> The sullen Lethe rolling doom
> On them and theirs and all things here.

November 16

Damp, cold house. Coal difficult to get but after much trouble I found a "Comfort Coal Co." (the name charmed me and I phoned them) and got a ton of coal. We work at the furnace but little heat, little hot water comes up and the cold chills my mind, my limbs, my spirits, my soul. Horace spends his teaching days at Bronxville for commuting is too much of a strain now and I rejoice that he is in a warm room for these few days. But I rejoice Wednesdays for he returns that evening and I usually fear that one more day of his absence would be insupportable.

November 23, Monday night

Cold evening, wind, the fires going badly in the furnace, continual nervous indigestion, depression. I smoke too much and eat too little. Horace is away at Sarah Lawrence and the evenings seem unusually heavy and depressing. Tomorrow I give a reading of my poems at the Public Library and I feel nervous, distraught and a little guilty as if something very private, very secret indeed, very painful must now be exposed to a curious, hostile public. I am getting to the state when I hate to get up in the morning and face the day—a danger signal. One does not even dare to approach God for help so deep is my hopeless depression.

The growing cost of living and Horace's small salary. I torture myself trying to make ends meet and keep expenses down but it's nerve-wracking and far from easy. The little extra funds from outside literary work almost nonexistent—but perhaps later—one piece of hopeful news. I asked L. U. and R. H. if I had any chance of a $1,000 grant given by the Academy of Arts and Letters to some poet—both seemed doubtful of my prospects and I had given up the idea. But suddenly, without warning, both R. H. and L. U. wrote saying that the chance was not a hopeless one. L. U. sent me a copy of a letter recommending me that was so kind that I almost cried. It made me feel that even if nothing came out of it all, this letter alone would almost be a recompense. Kindness, goodness, sympathy, a pleasant look and I shake with emotion. It is all too rare. I don't know why but I hope for the grant and feel that it is not impossible that I shall get it. And if the award is given at the time when my *Golden Mirror* appears, I shall be lucky indeed, though I'm sad about the book, feel it could have been so much better with a little more real leisure, better health. I've just begun to learn to write.

November 30

Chilly sharp days all taken up in endless household details. Went shopping in Piermont with my kind neighbor Mrs. Haagenson and took Tommy our dog with us. The automobile ride was a wild adventure to him. He seemed frightened and clung to my heels when I shopped in Piermont and jumped out of the car with passionate relief when we got home.

Horace and little Pat went to see the Paul Robeson *Othello* this Saturday and both came home thrilled and excited. Horace almost overwrought. He became bitter and unhappy and gave me a dreadful evening.

My reading went off very well. The audience was very large. Everybody said nice things. I know I looked and read well but my heart seemed to go too fast. I was really frightened. Padraic Colum read after me. Both he and Molly Colum were amiable and polite especially to Horace but they had treated us so badly in the past that I couldn't exchange polite small talk and found myself unconsciously making one faux pas after another to Mary Colum. Queer figures from the past showing up and asking for autographs. I drove home with Elizabeth S. Sergeant and Mrs. Haagenson and the next day went down with a bad grippe.

This house is taking too much strength, time and even money. How to keep warm *is* a problem.

I can hardly wait till Horace comes home on Wednesday night. In the evening of Monday I say, "Thank God this day is over." On Tuesday I say, "Thank God, only one more day now." And on Wednesday I wait eagerly for the six to seven o'clock bus that brings him in.

December 18
Patrick has his little friend Mac Whitney staying overnight at our house. Pleasant to hear their voices and to see their bright boyish faces, to hear their whistle, their laughter, to hear their quick little feet.

Joanna sitting under our great portrait of the Sibyl while mending her clothes—a pretty picture.

Macmillan sent me a contract and an offer of a $100 advance, a smaller advance than last time and a contract with a disturbing last clause which Jim Putnam (who has come back to Macmillan) says is simply written into all wartime contracts. Also some reports of the readers of my work which were very nice. In one of the reports I recognized Untermeyer's style—really warm and kind and perceptive. I felt quite touched. I had not expected kindness from either of the men—Jim or Louis.

Horace received nice treatment from Harcourt Brace too and a check for his last book of poems. *The Shield of Achilles* is now in press and we pray for its lucky reception. *The Triumph of Life* on the whole has received grudging praise or hush-hush from the press but somehow—somehow I believe the beauty of the little book will sink in, will inspire respect and admiration—will set a new tone.

Had dinner with Christopher Lazare at the Murray Hill and Horace and I stayed overnight at the comfortable very musty little hotel apartment. Pleasant conversation though C.'s corruption runs so deep that my soul shudders. But he has a gay witty mind and talks very well. Is convinced that all great writers and artists share his vice and was full of obscene anecdotes of Henry James' sex life, which he got from an elderly gentleman who was once intimate with James. I didn't believe a word of it. Amused and surprised me by a violently hysterical attack on Max Beerbohm who he says lacks real human depth and what a decade ago he would have called "social consciousness." It seems that Beerbohm (according to L.) had in his essay on Strachey gone the limit in bad taste and inhumanity. His insults and comments on the "common man" said L., were indecent. "As for me," said L, flouncing out of the room in a rage and draping his Chinese dressing grown around him (and this in his shrill feminine voice), "I adore the common man." We laughed so loudly that L. looked startled then laughed too.

December 29, Wednesday

Extreme cold and a furnace that doesn't work so that to get up in the morning is a gloomy difficult affair. However, a walk in this country among these good kindly people does one good. God directed me to this place I'm sure.

Have been invited to a New Year's Eve party by our favorite neighbors, Dr. Haagenson and his wife and the Lewis Nichols. The Nichols have given Joanna a job minding their children when they go out to see the new plays. She is very proud of earning money for herself and sets out on her job very proudly with Tommy at her heels.

1 9 4 4

January 3, Monday, 1944

Prayers for New Year's: good health for all of us, more friends, a warm sympathetic reception for *The Shield of Achilles,* and *The Golden Mirror,* a scholarship at Vassar for Joanna.

January 30, Sunday night

A dinner at the Shedlovskys. Beatrice lovely as ever. They now live in N.Y.C. in our old neighborhood. But I was tired and probably indiscreet. T. S. infatuated, completely swayed by M. R. She had written him a letter about us in the "I love them so much, why do they turn from me" vein. It's like the Lawrence-Middleton Murray mess. I understand now why Lawrence in reply to such another sleazy letter from Murray assuring him of his love said, "Your love is of no use to me." The fact is she doesn't really love us at all—but is full of guilt complexes—the most dangerous of all feelings and the person who has it for you must not be treated as a friend. Besides her last poems fill me with horror and disgust.

Dear Tommy our dog was hit by a car and limped home bleeding and broken. Poor thing. For days he sat before the living room fire (we've just gotten some wood), languid and so mournful like Tolstoi's little princess in *War and Peace,* a "Why have they done it to me?" look in his eyes. He seems better today.

Joanna seventeen last week. We got her a few pretty gifts, a sweater, a lovely reproduction of a Picasso of the rose period, a Buxtehude record book, and a Koestler book. All this seemed too little—we are too poor for our desires for our children. Jo is writing an application for a Vassar scholarship. I say my prayers and hope for her. Her school grades are very high.

January 31, Monday evening

Horace away at the college tonight and the evenings so heavy, damp and difficult when he is not here.

Drew an outline for my next book of poems. I want to make the next book stronger, deeper, wider in scope and less frail and feminine. My mind is so full of new poems and half-formed plans for them that I become quite ill. My brain works quickly, burns with inspiration, but my body is too sluggish— I can't summon up *physical* strength. I'm not satisfied with *The Golden Mirror* but a few poems in that book seem to me to be an advance over the last book.

Thinking over the John Jay Chapman letters, a fascinating book. I've read and reread it many times and am struck by that vivid, alert, brilliant personality. One should have liked to have met him—in fact I remember meeting him at some Poetry Society affair when I was very young. He got into some argument with Siegfried Sassoon over the war and I thought him a stuffy old gentleman. But I would not have appreciated his distinction then. And there *was* something loose and incoherent in his character—a final integration always missing—a final understanding. His dislike of Henry James, his refusal to read Edith Wharton's best novel, *The House of Mirth,* his limited appreciation of poetry (and his own poetry shows his lack of real feeling for that art) robbed him by a quarter of a half inch of real greatness. His English counterpart was Wilfred Blunt, but Blunt was more the man of action. Chapman was more the thinker—and yet how much more?

February 18

A telephone call from George Davis, formerly of *Harper's Bazaar* now of *Mademoiselle* magazine, offering me $100 for a poem for their May wedding number. It's the sort of thing I've sneered at other people for doing but I thought of Mozart who never refused a commission, of little Pat who needs new clothes so badly, of Horace for whom that $100 would help so much.

And who am I to put on so many airs? I did the poem—Davis seems satisfied. So far the check hasn't arrived but it will come I suppose. The poem I did was the first poem I've ever printed that I felt wasn't the best I could have done—the only poem I've ever printed that people might say was bad—certainly it's not my most distinguished. But it has a nice music and style.

Aside from the *Mademoiselle* request, I got a letter from my old friend Robert Hillyer asking me to give one of the Morris Gray poetry readings at Harvard. The sum paid will be $50 and expenses for the trip. Horace when he gave the lecture got $100 and expenses. But these little things give me a feeling that all my poems have not been written in vain.

In N.Y.C. yesterday. The city very beautiful and dreamy in a gray damp mist. Ugly brick slum tenements along the river front softened by silver damp mist—it brought back childhood memories of sadness, fear, loneliness, bewilderment—everlasting reveries.

March 13, Monday
A gloomy, difficult visit from Ted Wilson home on a furlough, impossible to get him to talk, his unhappiness penetrates us. He is a staff sergeant now in the aviation intelligence division.

March 19, Sunday
Had dinner with the Weldon Kees Friday. It was very pleasant and warm. And I hated to return to the house without heat and to my gloomy thoughts.

Surely there has never been a time when the literary scene has been so foul, so corrupt, when almost no great literary figure is seen on the horizon to cheer and guide, now that Yeats and Joyce are dead. Perhaps Eliot is the one figure now and Picasso in painting and both are exposed to a barrage of hatred, abuse and slander. The influence of the refugees is now beginning to be felt in the more pretentious little magazines—and the influence on the whole is not a happy one. What is one to do with people who prefer Werfel to Thomas Mann? Brecht to Rilke? Or those who prefer Allen Tate to Jeffers? Robert Frost to Eliot?

Endless housework, exhausting and (it's no use deceiving myself), *distasteful*. But I have no right to deceive myself, my family *need* my services there, the public does not respond enough to my poetry to make it possible for me to give myself up to it with a clear conscience—to afford a maid. Still it is the one talent I have that is death to hide.

Consolations. Dear Tommy our dog with his cute tricks and his unquestioning affection, our good family life, our real love for each other, an occasional check for some piece of work well done, a kind word not from the source we may have wished but from some unexpected quarter, a kind word here and there, a friendly smile, this pretty house, a gleam of sunshine, a hope of spring, a kind letter very occasionally, a good book to read in a quiet pleasant room, some wild unexpected hope.

Fears. One deep unspoken one—then the war which is beginning to shake me more and more with grief, horror and doubt—the silence, silence, silence, sneers and hatred that greet each new book we write, the silent phone, the empty mailbox, the unanswered letters. But from now on may we have nothing but good hopeful things to record—friends, warmth, hope, love.

Horace is reading Conrad's *Secret Agent* with great enjoyment and excitement. I am so tired after a housecleaning that I can't stop writing in this journal.

Memo. Avoid too great humility, too much gentleness with certain people.

March 21

The Shield of Achilles arrived today on the twenty-first, our lucky day, and I took it as a good omen. I know that my superstitions are laughable and that I shall be teased for them but they keep life from being too cruel and meaningless. *The Shield* is such a charming and distinguished little book. My hopes and fears for it go up very high. O for *once once* to have a universally praised and accepted book! God protect this little book!

Horace has been home from school because of a bad attack of flu. He frets and worries—if we were only not so dependent on the college. But I'm afraid of his getting worse and he couldn't go out in this the worst weather of the year, a raging snowstorm which froze the house in the morning.

April 1, Saturday

Went to New York yesterday with Horace and saw my doctor. Got another injection in the hopes that it would revive my strength and lift my spirits both of which are too—too low. The streets damp, the wind damp and cold, the lack of young men on the streets now striking and painful. When youth—when young men—are not seen everywhere and conspicuous a world seems dead or dying. Visited Harcourt Brace with H. to get some copies of *The Shield of Achilles.* The office seemed deserted except for old Mr. Brace who seemed weary and ill and kindly but perhaps all publishers feel weary and ill and kindly to their poet-authors—kindly because they feel benevolent at having printed them. Already H. and I have the plan of a new book which he does so wish them to sign up. And the next book of poems—that must be signed up. And one is so worried. It's our way of going on living, breathing—when one is writing, illness, loneliness, disappointments fade away—all is serene and as it should be.

The proofs of *The Golden Mirror* arrived. I was so pleased. It *does* look like my best book. I'm adding one new poem which I like called "The Haunted House." It seems both fresh and strange but it's a recent poem and one loves one's last poems as a mother loves her youngest children.

April 27, Thursday

Horace has been unwell and for a few days I was frightened about him but he seems better now. I see him off to the college looking unwell and my heart sinks but his school term is almost over. He says everyone has been kind to him and the college has granted him an increase in salary—much needed.

A week ago I went through with the Harvard poetry reading. I had had a bad tooth infection—two more teeth pulled. My throat sore, I don't know if I made a good impression. I had left H. ill. I was exhausted. F. O. Matthiessen, Theodore Spencer, May Sarton* and Jack Sweeney dined with us. Mrs. Spencer an exquisite silly mask, an embarrassing gurgle about Mrs. Conrad Aiken's paintings which the Spencers have bought at an exorbitant price—frightful, amateurish painting—bad drawing, bad color, art-student composition. And these are the Cambridge aesthetes whose judgment so many people listen to with awe and respect. Jack Sweeney visited me too—for once his rigid esotericism and aesthetic narrowness was a relief.

May Sarton full of the gossip about the Emily Dickinson papers which Martha Branch's executor wishes to sell to private collectors instead of giving to a library. M. S. full of public spirit about this. She is in her element writing letters to MacLeish, etc. I'm no longer interested in these things. Dickinson herself wouldn't have minded I'm sure—would have laughed sardonically. I doubt if there are any more good new poems—and another batch of the quality that has appeared in the latest publications would do Dickinson's reputation more harm that good. She is the greatest woman poet—Alas.

The Shield of Achilles has received a better press than we expected— prompt and prominent reviews. The praise is grudging but at least no sneers—not too much misinformation about the book—no personal abuse— more agreement than I thought possible.

Such a cold grudging rainy belated spring. Nothing but rain and cold and the lovely month of April almost gone.

Reading the Benjamin Haydon* memoirs with horrified fascination. What a good writer he was—and was he such a bad artist? Most of his contemporaries were small too—he had a right to despise them—Etty, Wilkie, Maclise, Hilton, Landseer. It's true he had no feeling for the better ones— Flaxman, Stothard. What he said of Lawrence's paintings was true and just. He did not value the best painters of his time and country—Raeburn, Turner. But he did lack an understanding of the smaller delicacies, fineness, taste. In this he was too *much* like the rest of the Cockney School of literature to which he was attracted. He was for his temperament curiously unradical in his art, too orthodox.

I now feel the Huxley preface inadequate. Poor devil! I can't help longing as I read of his difficulties that all will come out well—that after all he will do a masterpiece. Such courage (but curiously insensitive courage again), such faith—such flushes of good writing anyway, such a personality! What a good soldier he would have made! Such kindnesses as he received and of the wrong kind! A pension would have saved him—or an official lecturing job. And in the end the frightful humiliation that must have exhausted him at last. The book has given me a horror of debt, of too much identifying noble sentiments about my art with my own interests. Let me work so modestly and humbly as I can and trust that God and posterity will not be too unkind. I do not ask for wild praise, awe, admiration. Let it be enough if some of my books picked up carelessly will in the future inspire affection, interest, respect—which is asking a great deal. And Haydon's begging letters to God. I do that all the time. I'm sure more people do that than will care to admit it. Anyway this book of Haydon's is a moral document of great force.

April 30, Sunday

Correcting the final proofs of *The Golden Mirror.* I have never felt more fatalistic, more troubled about a book though I do feel that it's the best book I've done so far. It certainly leaves me dissatisfied and I feel incapable of judging it dispassionately. It's completely out of the vogue—the current fashions. And I haven't the least idea of anyone who might like it. Small as Horace's public is mine is even smaller. My only hope is in a miracle. It's as if one is going against the grain so far that I can't expect a word of praise. And the review sections are full of poets who can't get books published, and who will wonder why I can publish at all. I know of no critic who will care for what I do—since I'm neither "traditional," in the sense that the almost fashionable Yvor Winters group speaks of "tradition," or "esoteric" enough or smart enough and my personality in literary circles has not been a successful one. I've been too humble, timid, unpoised to have aroused confidence in myself.

May 3, Wednesday

The papers today carried news of dear Ellery Leonard's death—a great loss and it filled me with grief. He had complained of being unwell but he had always complained about his health and we had begun to treat it as a joke. This was unkind. He was one of my best friends, and how fortunate I was in his friendship, kindness, interest I never realized till very recently. I had dedicated my new book of poems to him and had looked forward to his expressing pleasure or interest. Alas—alas—he had seemed impatient to see the book and I thought he was teasing me about it—that he didn't believe it would come out but he must have suspected that time was short. His foolish phobias distracted people from his great gifts, his wit, wisdom, learning and real goodness.

In thinking of my dear friend Ellery Leonard's death I cannot help thinking of how such events while they do not exactly loosen our hold on life make death less terrible. For why should we fear to go where those whose friendship was an honor have gone before us?

O why do these things have to happen in the spring when Nature seems so lavish, kind and full of promises?

May 9, Tuesday

Spring in full force and beauty now, the peach and cherry trees in bloom in our little front garden, splendid because of the flowering quince tree and bleeding hearts, narcissi, forget-me-nots. My father on my mind and today I plucked up courage to write to him. If I ever pretend to virtue or to feel superior to other people let this sin humble me. This is indeed the "cruel" streak that M. R. tells people about me.

One of the few cheerful parties I've attended was last Thursday at Mrs. Murray Crane, given for the Padraic Colums. I looked and felt better and hid my tensions. Somerset Maugham was there. He singled me out for kindness and attention, a weary, subtle, charming and wise old man. Glenway Westcott handsome, curly-headed, witty, sophisticated, with Jacques Barzun whose distinguished, elegant appearance charmed Maugham. Marianne Moore looking very pretty and quaint and sexless and odd in a simple gray silk dress that was very becoming to her. S. Seidel Canby, the John Hall Wheelocks, etc., etc.—a very distinguished company and a fine dinner afterwards which I couldn't eat. Mary and Padraic Colum reading the "Cynara" of Ernest Dowson with a wild Irish wail explaining that Yeats used to read it that way. Westcott and Moore malicious about Dowson which rather offended the Colums who thought (we could see) that the poem was rather good. Earlier in the evening we dined with Louis Untermeyer who lives in a smart New York apartment now. He looked old and tired and had lost some of his wise-cracking brightness. In the throes of another domestic misadventure (his third) and I suspect that his alimony troubles have impoverished him thoroughly at last.

Horace is getting a daily letter from old William Carlos Williams about *The Shield,* urging him to assume literary leadership, etc. Wild raves against Eliot (a hate-love), ramblings about the *Partisan Review.* Well we are glad to have the book strike home and we love and respect old Williams but one longs for—a more reasonable appreciation. The book we hear so far has gone well.

May 18, Thursday

Heavenly sunlight. Our woods full of thick clumps of white violets, very pure, very frail, very tenacious. Something touching about their beauty. I thought of how beautifully H. D. had put them into poetry and wonderful if I could write about them in a poem as slight and yet so vibrant with life.

The days restless, agitated and nerve-wracked as if every moment was spent in some wearying nothingness. A poem I started full of good things but my strength and energy went toward the end and I didn't finish it well nor mold it into a strict enough form where every word would count.

Virginia Woolf's new book, *The Haunted House,* arrived and since it is a small book I skimmed it eagerly. So many perceptions, insights, feelings, that I have attempted to write down myself and many moving and beautiful touches. But after a while the book pressed down on my nerves and left me melancholy and irritated and psychically disturbed.

May 19

Idyllic weather. Such brilliant light, such fragrance in the air, such a high golden sun everywhere that I feel when walking out that Heaven's climate is like that. But I've had a bronchial grippe, weakening, depressing and unconducive to real work. H. is leaving for Cambridge tomorrow to make recordings of his poems. I was invited too but it will be too expensive and the grippe makes it difficult. If only I had received the Academy award my mind would be easier. One must be patient and resigned to these things and yet the encouragement to my work would have been a greater help than the money which we need badly enough. God teach me to submit to Your will. My sense of unworthiness is great enough. I need a little self-confidence and praise very much. When I go over the manuscript of *The Golden Mirror* I feel my heart sink. I don't know of a soul whose response I value who will like it. And when I glance over the last two books of mine they seem careless, stilted, slight—too slight to have a hold, too conventional to have a lasting appeal. And it's the lasting appeal I should like to work for.

A *Partisan Review* party last Sunday. An immense crowd of the usual people, as Horace said the crème de la crème of Greenwich Village intelligentsia—the esoterics and their camp followers out in full force. The apartment belonging to the Philip Rahvs ugly and expensive and full of smoke and dense thick air. Allan Tate with his arm around Mrs. Rahv. He looked ill and was very drunk. Louise Bogan, all beauty gone, the flabby fat of an alcoholic, her complexion a palish purple. Marianne Moore very polite and the bright birdlike shrewd look about her as always. Rich patrons of the arts, some second-rate publishers. Weldon Kees sitting with an air of rapturous devotion listening to Allen Tate addressing someone else. These things are almost the same from year to year and each year one wonders why one goes except that one is lonely and has been alone too much and the feeling is that a party, meeting people, is good for one. But it never is and, leaving without pleasure, stimulus, and with increased loneliness, we make a resolution never to go again and then hope springs eternal and we go the next year.

May 30, Tuesday

Returned a few weeks ago from another trip to Cambridge, this time with Horace. We made recordings, a frightful job lasting three hours apiece. Now our voices are recorded for posterity and one can only hope that Posterity will be amiable to us.

Joanna received an invitation to the Phillips-Andover prom from a boy who became interested in her through reading H.'s poem to her, a Billy O'Shea. As Horace said, "It isn't every boy who writes a letter to a poem"— of course Jo turned it down but it was amusing. The child has been job-hunting for the summer. I feel for her remembering my experiences at her age.

Never meet people now or pay a visit without a curious nagging feeling that I have made a faux pas or done something frightfully wrong. It's what is known as an anxiety neurosis and does not make for ease of manner.

A Henry James reading debauch. Like Kafka he spoils one for other reading.

Literary conversation. As boring as any other shop talk. How I dislike it and how few say anything worth saying. But there are a few people like old William C. Williams or Zabel or Horace among the people I know who communicate their own excitement and delight. I am tempted often with people who gush over poetry indiscriminately to say with Marianne Moore, "Poetry.

I too dislike it." And I really do these days. Only a handful of poets please me. The merely promising, the almost good depress me. Yeats, Eliot, Rilke, Hardy, a great deal of Pope and Dryden, some of Landor, some of Stefan George—that's about all. And I'm ashamed to admit how few of my contemporaries interest me—almost none.

And Henry James has given me the inspiration for one of my very best poems, "The Haunted House."

June 5, Monday

Such golden translucent weather that I grudge every minute not spent outdoors. White flowers in bloom—are they jasmine flowers?—tall golden lilies, rose-flushed honeysuckles, white and pink peonies slowly opening. They last such a short time—two weeks, three weeks, never longer than a month, and I grieve for them because the season is so short and I'm beginning to dread the thought of winter and the cold.

H. rewriting the poetry history book and I revised my piece on Louise Guiney. As I kept on writing I found that in writing about Guiney I was poking fun at myself. Her seventeenth-century mania is as foolish as some of my own period manias. Perhaps the sadder, darker, wilder, more fantastic nostalgia that devours me will save me from some of her foolishness.

Rome taken yesterday and the President's speech tonight very graceful and moving. But overcome with sadness and futility. O God take away our hearts of stone and give us hearts of flesh; teach us how to live our short lives in peace and love, in tolerance and humankindness, teach us to pity and protect the weak, both man and beast.

June 15, Thursday

Dream-soaked, useless day. After the housework which takes up the early part of the day, I run up to Horace's attic study and go over the revised chapter on our American poetry book with him and then read (for the poetry book), dream, walk, plan dinner and the evenings stretch out vast and lonely—except for the children's voices.

Thinking timidly of looking for a job—if I can get my teeth fixed—if I can overcome my street-crossing fears, my growing claustrophobia.

Saw *Othello* with Paul Robeson in the leading role. Went with Patricia Phillips. Extraordinary dense and rich play. Robeson's playing full of power, dignity and passion. Touched and excited but I felt ill, untidy and exhausted and felt I didn't make a good impression on Patricia who was disposed to admire me. I always break down now when I go out without Horace.

A telephone from Dudley Fitts to Horace—very pleasant. Amusing letter from Hilda Aldington and Bryher—nice to receive news from the lost world of Europe. A phone from Christopher Lazare which touched us.

No letter from X since he left the country. No regret exactly but a mixture of sadness, anger and something like grief. I have no illusions anymore.

Cast out fear, cast out remorse, cast out small gnawing thoughts. Let your heart and mind be a golden mirror—Yes the title came from God not myself.

Simply bitten by mosquitos and the damp seeping in everywhere. And I talk of Golden Mirrors!

June 16, Friday

Horace returned after a hot day in town trying to raise some money from Harcourt Brace. Bills mounting up steadily and no money coming in. My one extravagance is Leola the maid and an occasional trip to town. Cannot overcome worry and the worry causes a shadow to fall over this lovely little house. H. has been too optimistic about our ability to pull through the summer. I shall try to be as economical as we were in Sunnyside but we are not as young or as hopeful. If only our books would bring in a little money—so many of them now—and they bring in nothing. We are in debt to our publishers. The Haydon memoirs which I wish I hadn't read frighten me. I become afraid of overestimating my talents, of our ability to keep sailing along on hopes and a really deadly fear of getting in debt. I need dentistry badly too. I need shoes, underwear, a few little amusements badly—but we're afraid of buying anything.

Rewrote two poems today but with a sense of guilt. I ought to be earning money, doing something useful. My poems are such a luxury—and so few people read my books.

June 28

The news full of slow bloody victories. This war seems endless. I doubt if we shall see peace in our lifetime, a real stretch of peace. "Into what a century hast thou allowed me to be born oh Lord," as St. Polycarp was it? once said.

A visit from Christopher Lazare a welcome break. He brought a rare bottle of whiskey (we can't afford such luxuries now) and he and Horace sat up talking till midnight. He was gay, malicious, sensitive and in a good and characteristic mood. Even Joanna became amused and threw off her shyness and depression.

Another visit from Dr. William Carlos Williams and his nice motherly wife. What a delightful man and such a good gay talker. He made us laugh with his anecdotes of the days when he and Ezra Pound were students at Pennsylvania and how Ezra would drag him along when he wanted to pick up girls. He acted out Ezra's bold, bad antics and his own eagerness and timidity. It was well done. Williams told us that Ezra Pound was at one time engaged to H. D. He said he still has one of the announcements she sent out. She too was a classmate of Pound and Williams. He also told us what we had never heard before, that Wallace Stevens once worked as a reporter on the *Herald Tribune* and roomed with Witter Bynner.

William C. Williams told us that after the war he wants to turn the Rutherford practice over to his doctor son and get a place near us. The very thought was so pleasant that I felt the ice of loneliness melt around my heart.

Harcourt Brace saved our lives by sending us a check for $300. It is not quite enough but we paid up some pressing bills. Alas there are still quite a few more.

Horace is working on the Ezra Pound essay in our poetry history book— a delicate difficult job. His attic study is a very nice room now—the nicest study he's ever had. May it be a lucky room.

A long review of *The Shield of Achilles* by John Crowe Ransom. He said a number of very nice things about the book and the amount of space and the distinction of the reviewer were pleasant. No book of Horace's has been so widely reviewed.

June 30, Friday

A dramatic electric storm yesterday evening when all the lights suddenly went out and we sat in darkness for a while. This cleared the air and the next morning all was golden, clear summer weather. A beauty all around us so perfect that everything seemed like a world in a dream. The rambler roses in delicate clusters over the fence, gold tiger lilies warm as the sun. In the afternoon we had tea with our neighbor Marian Powys Gray, sister of the writing Powys family. A delightful old woman and her careless comfortable house and exquisite garden were very pleasant. Her roses are like no one else's. The walls thick with purple and white clematis like great colored stars, and yet she does weeding and heavy working in her garden not at all.

She told us about a new sister-in-law of hers, Elizabeth Meyers, who is writing a book about Swift and Vanessa—what an enviable book to do.

Visited with Amy Jackson who showed me a beautiful new book on Paul Klee done by the Oxford University Press. The Klee cult very strong in art circles I notice. I get so little response and pleasure from Klee that I'm a little ashamed of myself. Isn't it a bit like the poetry of Marianne Moore or Wallace Stevens, all craftsmanship and little emotion, scope or real depth—best appreciated by fellow craftsmen?

Tried to read Proust. It required too much leisure. Turned to read James' *The Awkward Age* but found it dull and the people like so many of James' people hateful and unspeakable. James will make a rabid Communist of me. And yet every now and then I find a sentence, a line, a phrase, a picture of unbearable poignance, revelation, insight and beauty through stretches of dullness. I'm saving *The Ambassadors* and *The Tragic Muse* for some special occasion. Horace's favorites.

Horace has been reading Maugham's *Cakes and Ale* and threw it aside. He said the unspeakable cheapness and the ugly spirit make him squirm. I thought the book had some good worldly wisdom—but H. is not wrong.

July 4

A quiet Fourth, the children at home and H. busy writing in the attic, now a very pleasant room. He dropped the poetry history book for a breathing spell—but simply changed off to revise a poem that he had written some time ago. We've spent the summer in a rather harassed quiet, tortured by limited funds, no amusements—almost no visitors. But the book is progressing. God stretch out Your Hand to bless it, and give us strength to finish it.

Horace got a letter from Marion Strobel of *Poetry* asking for poems—and so the long sad divorce from that magazine is seemingly ended. All things come to him who waits. Dillon being off the magazine helps I suppose. I haven't been asked yet but if my *Golden Mirror* is well received I *will* be asked.

Getting into Proust at last slowly and carefully. Marvel after marvel of delicacy and beauty and yet unlike James. As Proust's personality unwinds through the book one dislikes him with an almost physical repulsion. He is not charming or truly lovable, but extraordinarily interesting—which is the best substitute for charm.

What a curious personal achievement his book was. It could so easily have veered off into pure amateurishness. It is one of the great autobiographies of the world—fiction or nonfiction—so curiously French, so curiously Jewish too if one lifts veils and veils of meaning.

July 17, Monday

Leola the maid ill for the last week and I've been doing the housework and almost glad of the occupation. Except for the few heavy jobs, I do not find it too hard and I was glad of the chance to do without a maid for we were very low—terribly low on funds, almost desperately so. A feeling of fright and insecurity. Fortunately, praise to God, Horace's father helped us out this time and a load was lifted off our minds. But we have to be careful. Slow dark nagging worries and loneliness. I find it hard to talk to people—even Horace who is now deep in the poetry history book. His contribution is so much deeper and finer and larger than mine that I feel upset at signing my name to the book. All the credit ought to be his.

Golden warm weather after a bad heat wave. In the rich full completed ripe summer beauty one thanks God for this pretty little house. One loves it almost too much for there is something perverse in the love of inanimate objects.

The war news good enough to make us impatient for victory—for peace. Even in this country quiet, the thought of the war discolors the air, darkens the mind. If only these frightful sacrifices will settle the evils that have started the war and make future wars impossible.

July 22, Saturday night

Restless, dreamlike days. The weather perfect, warm, not too warm, rich and golden. But my mind is so discolored and I see all this beauty as if through half-shut eyes.

Our poetry history book progressing well—a difficult and unpleasant chapter done with dignity, common sense and tact (I hope). This is the piece on Millay, Taggard, Bogan. The second a hellish job because of Sarah Lawrence. No mention would arouse spite and complaints from that noisy and conceited woman; hypocritical praise would arouse contempt from people we respect—not to mention our own self-respect—and no praise is enough for these women who have more vanity than talent and half know it. Since they have lost all interest in the real problems of their art (poetry is now nothing but an excuse for publications or display of ego to them) the humility and self-doubt of the true working artist is always missing.

Visited with some neighbors of ours who live in the Sneden's Landing side, a Mrs. Parton, widow of a newspaper man, herself an old San Francisco newspaper woman, and her pretty daughter very shy and sensitive who is a reporter on the *Herald Tribune*. Dinner under a beautiful grape arbor, the grapes hanging in stiff glazed festoon as in early Italian pictures.

Guests, a few newspaper couples who live in Grand View. They were full of 1930s Communist jargon. Comment of one of the women: "How can people tolerate religion? A little psychoanalysis would cure any religious fanatic." Weird and fantastic concept of the religious and imaginative life. Their own spiritual background must have been empty and crude indeed.

The *Herald Tribune*'s Inita Van Doren phoned Horace yesterday and asked him to review a new life of Gerard Hopkins—thus breaking the long *Herald Tribune* ban—the second stone now lifted from the bad period. For recently Marion Strobel, now editor of *Poetry*, asked for and accepted two new poems of Horace's. I feel more relief at these things than Horace.

August 10, Thursday

Little or almost no household help and the days pass in heavy heat and exhaustion. Still the heat is not so unbearable as the paralyzing winter cold. My book arrived Tuesday—two frightful proofreading errors—my fault I think—very depressing.

Horace and I went to town yesterday and had drinks at the Algonquin bar with Christopher Lazare and Jim Putnam. Very pleasant. The bar full of theatrical celebrities—Christopher pointed out Peter Lorre and others. Max Eastman—with a lovely young lady and still full of the famous-beauty airs and graces of his youth—came up to our table. Afterwards Christopher, H. and I went to the Blue Ribbon and then to a little bar near Carnegie Hall where the drinks were cheap and the atmosphere friendly and pleasant. Those little "breaks" mean a great deal to me and dear Horace.

The poetry history book our only pleasure is getting along well. Marianne Moore now disposed of decently and beautifully I think and next Wallace Stevens. Each chapter is like a milestone crossed with great pain. Oh, I do hope we will get a little praise, a little recognition for this book. But praise or blame, the book will be as good, as honest, as fine as we can make it. And if God wants to reward us, He will find His own means to do so. As Hopkins once said, He has His ways and means of rewarding works which are meant to be blessed.

Dear Tommy our dog lying at my feet. Every once in a while he jumps up to catch a fly. He's a darling and his foolish actions, his simple affection, [are] a delight.

___'s hatred of Robinson Jeffers. Insists that he is a bad poet—and he surprised me by adding "And do you know I find Hart Crane passé?" These people like only the small, the pretty—and that only if it is esoteric enough—in poetry, Marianne Moore, in painting (at its highest level), Paul Klee. Picasso is passé of course. Well I no longer argue but one is overcome with weariness and depression.

Yet isn't an opinion based on taste like ___'s preferable to me than the other kind which prefers Millay, Steve Benét, Paul Engle in poetry, in painting Grant Wood, Benton?

August 15, Tuesday

Extreme heat very enervating and working over a hot kitchen stove my strength fails. After I serve the dinner I can't eat.

The children darling and good. I'm so discouraged and tired that writing is out of the question. Household help not only expensive but impossible to get. A little mental stimulus when I talk to Horace about the poetry history book. Today in speaking of the style of certain critics, so involved, tortured, unreadable, I said that they based it all on the Henry James version of the Bible. H. was delighted and used it in the piece on poetry he's doing for Allen Tate.

August 17, Thursday

Badly in need of my monthly injections—so completely exhausted that I can barely move. When I wake in the morning I feel as if everything is too difficult—too strenuous.

Violent thunder showers, a crash so loud, so majestic, so violent that it seemed to come out of a Greek play.

There are some things so painful, so difficult that even the most candid never speak about them—in fact to speak about them argues a certain lack of depth. But I shall never lack for a wound in my conscience, a sense of sin and guilt which will make me meekly silent to M.'s damaging lies. "No I'm guiltless of this," I'll say, "but there is a private sin greater than all this—for which I must do penance—forever—so have your say, let it all be part of my penance."

Of a romantic. "His dream-soaked, book-sodden mind."

A visit to Nyack today. Had my nails done and hair cut. A young girl at the beauty parlor who was proudly showing off a box full of gifts from Italy sent by her husband in the army. Such ugly things from that beautiful country. Purple-red silk handkerchiefs, a sky-blue petticoat with imitation lace, cerise-pink embroidered doilies, a rosary full of bright imitation jewels, green and red and pink blessed by the Pope, a number of cheap imitation mosaic brooches such as used to be sold at Woolworths. The girl's happiness so ecstatic. I envied her and her love which was still new and fresh. The refugee German woman who did my nails and her look of ferocity and suspicion as she looked at my ring, the ugly turquoise ring that Mrs. White gave as a gift to me on her return from Mexico in 1927. I've always kept it on out of superstition for it's a good luck ring and has two large swastikas on each side. Well the swastikas had a history before Hitler and will have another one long after Hitler and yet feelings being as they are now it is becoming disturbing and even foolish to wear it. This is not the first time I've received harsh looks for wearing that ring.

Chilly, the first exhilarating yet half-melancholy feeling that autumn is about to appear. News of the taking of Paris and Marseilles, the surrender of Romania, all the news so sudden. We become confused and wonder what the real story behind the story is. This bloodshed, cruelty, waste lies on my heart like a private sin, a personal guilt. One cannot even pray to God. I can't feel that He approves or cares very much.

August 21, our wedding anniversary.

I heard from Robert Hillyer about my book—the first and only re-sponse—very nice. I'm grateful to him. I'm afraid of reviews and don't want to see them. Hillyer praises me for not exploiting the war, of being the only poet who has not done so—alas it's for that that I expect attacks. The war is too large, too dreadful, too heartbreaking. I am not fit to touch a theme of such scope and tragedy—only a little of the sadness and terror bit by bit, al-most unconsciously, can appear in my poems. I have never been blind to my limitations only too conscious of them. If only God will send me a new friend or two for my book, I shall be well rewarded.

"Into what a century has thou caused me to be born O Lord?" I keep re-peating this over and over as so many do these days in their thoughts.

Monteverdi records played on the Victrola by Joanna. Unbearable, grave, heart-piercing music. I find my eyes full of frozen tears.

A fine walk with Horace to the post office. Golden clear weather and such gardens everywhere! Passed a local funeral—a neighbor, a man aged ninety-six, one of the old families here, the atmosphere as it should be of the mourn-ers grave and yet not uncheerful. H. saying, "It is a good thing to see so much of life even if one is not too happy."

Saw a book on modern poetry by a Prof. Wells of Columbia where I was called "virginal," "orchid-like," etc. These people can't realize that real feeling can be quiet. When they think of Passion it is in terms of the schoolgirl histrionics of Millay. Still it's good to be mentioned.

September 8

Horace's school has started which depresses me greatly for the loneliness becomes too thick and heavy. Today he has been working on a poem and is full of temperament. It's very hard on me. I write *my* poems by stealth and with a wild sense of guilt, as if I am working on stolen time.

Had lunch with Dudley and Cornelia Fitts at the Russian Tea Room— two cocktails and I got ill—couldn't eat. H. amiable, kindly as if he were talking to a wall. I'm getting angry but it's this abstract attitude for the human race that has saved him. But if I can't get a little more attention and human warmth—I shall never get on, I shall collapse—this frightful self-effacing life can't go on.

Tommy our dog refusing to eat anything when we left food for him and went to New York with the children. Began to eat when we returned late at night and such a welcome. Really if I were wise I would look for love only among dogs.

September 13

Poor Leola White our former maid died and the news upset me frightfully. I thought of her goodness, decency and patience under suffering and I hated this world again, its cruelty to the gentle and good, its waste, of its useless suffering.

Damp and rain and the dust gathers over everything. Every day the silence gets thicker and I keep losing my temper with those I love most—my only well-wishers and dearest loves.

The broken stove quite a problem. A roof that leaks, broken brooms not easily replaced, lack of energy, loss of confidence.

September 17, noon

Nightmares and sick dreams. Stomach disorders and the endless damp and rain accentuating everything. Began housework again after many hours. Some semblance of order, but this fight against dirt, dust and disorder is a losing fight and I'm not adequate.

A frightful dream about *Poetry* magazine. For a moment old and new memories arose in some poignant despair. I thought of writing it down, but a bad dream, a bad thought written down becomes a permanent evil.

This year an amazing growth of sunflowers in our neglected back garden, a marvelous sight growing without human aid and all the more beautiful for it.

September 18, Monday

Trouble with the hot water furnace, worries about my dear Joanna, my strength so low that I feel frightened at the thought of the coming winter. Worried over my aimless life, the silence and discouragement over my book has made it difficult for me to write, the isolation has affected me so much that I find myself talking to myself even when with people.

Great pleasure in reading Trollope's obscurer novels. Great rest for my nerves and I've affected Horace with my enthusiasm for him. Have read during the summer *The Duke's Children, Phineas Finn, Ralph the Heir, The Eustace Diamonds,* all fat two-decker novels, very refined, a very intelligent way of escaping reality I fear, and I must stop. But they soothed me, delighted me and kept me from a nervous breakdown.

The autumn chill on the air, a fresh clean smell in the air as if the hurricane had brought some breath of the ocean with it.

September 23

Chilly weather. The dread of winter growing on me. I do not feel very strong or brave. H. moody, kind and preoccupied and I feel ashamed of losing my temper with *him* my dearest, kindest, best friend.

Dined with the John Gould Fletchers who have arrived in N.Y.C. from Arkansas. They have a comfortable shabby hotel room in a queer forgotten once-nice hotel in the Nineties called the Wolcott, where Mrs. MacDowell of the Colony used to stay. As I grow older I'm ashamed of the longings I have for comfort, pleasant surroundings, even a little luxury and it seemed that a poet like John F. who had grown old in the service of the Muses ought to have had greater rewards open to him, a pleasanter place to live in. But he's really very fortunate. He's always had a private income. He can't get his books published and is bitter and despondent but as usual his conversation was delightful gossip, but gossip of the highest order and with some intellectual distinction.

John F. told us that Louis Mumford, whom I thought of as the healthiest and cheerfullest of men, suffered heart attacks all the time he was writing his last book. His son Geddes who is not much older than Joanna is now serving in the South Pacific—it gave me a feeling of weariness and age. How glad I am (and yet I have no right to be glad) that my firstborn is a girl and that Pat is still a child.

Note added later: "Geddes Mumford killed in action in 1945."

Edith Sitwell sent us her new book of poems, *Green Songs,* very beautiful. It lifted me up from my lethargy—real poetry, rich, mature, beautiful in every sense. It is on her and not curiously as I had thought on Eliot that the mantle of Yeats has fallen.

This has been a sad year for poets, or people concerned with poetry. Old Ellery Leonard my friend, Peter Monro Jack, Sturge-Moore, Ann Tietjens, J. P. Bishop, none of them happy or secure in their life work. Those who ought to know say Sturge-Moore was good. J. P. Bishop had everything a poet ought to have had for a good start, looks, physique, money, friends, sound position and I suppose talents. His friends made large claims for his gifts but said nothing when he died—but they are a *dirty* lot, E. Wilson, Bogan, MacLeish and the rest.

Minna Bodenheim described him as the most beautiful young man among the beautiful, well-groomed young men and incredibly smart young women who dazzled visitors in the old days on *Vanity Fair.* Elinor Wylie was one of them for a time and Nancy Hoyt in her foolish biography of her sister describes him and E. W. as being the belles of a Louis XVth costume ball in Washington when they were young.

The President's speech. That comforting friendly voice. It does become tiresome as the intelligent platitudes roll out.

September 25

If Jo can go to college and I'm lucky enough to get Pat into a prep school I won't have to spend the too difficult winters here. We can get a cheap place in town.

October 1, Sunday

Bitter cold. My health bad. Spent all day yesterday at the doctor's. Must return again Wednesday, a thing of horror to me. O why must I face these things over again? I must beg God again for favors for there is no one else. I do feel that He prefers us to help ourselves and in the midst of so much human misery why should He care?

Is it really true about the falling sparrow? Such dark shadows on the mind and I did so wish to end this diary cheerfully.

My book not badly reviewed. It has not so far been reviewed at all. And I know my faults so well that I always blame myself. If Horace has better luck I shall not complain.

This diary habit is a bad one. The time ought to have been spent on useful things. But it has relieved my loneliness and saved my sanity sometimes and has been a vehicle for thoughts I couldn't put into poetry—it has kept me writing.

October 2, Monday

Grateful to have Horace home. Bad dreams, pain—found myself weeping all night in discouragement, worry, despair. Must see a doctor Wednesday. If his test is not frightening I shall cheer up a bit. Nothing in the mail. The morning bad, the days difficult, the nights uneasy. A pleasant fire in the living room of some comfort.

Lovely, lovely weather, my favorite season. Sorry I can't enjoy it more.

Very pretty flowers in the front garden, white with a slight flush of purple. They're weeds and ought to have been rooted out and yet they're quite pretty. Lovely and graceful but weeds—like so many people in the arts.

October 9, Monday

Miss Lawler of Brentanos told me that my book is selling well. Was more amiable to me than she has been in years and a Russian woman who came up in the store and spoke to me of the book saying she had admired it and was recommending it everywhere—that it reminded her of Anna Ahkmatova—a poet for whom I really feel the deepest sympathy—it pleased me so much. But the press is pretty silent or abusive. Little things cheer me up so I make this entry.

So pleasant to see Horace laughing and talking as he is at this moment with Ted Wilson. The children very gay in the kitchen. A pleasant fire in the fireplace. The weather not too cold. Bless us dear God and send us health, useful[ness] and many years—more love, more cheerfulness, and more courage.

Reading Macaulay's *History of England.* I picked up a nice five-volume set for seventy-five cents. Fascinating and horrible book.

If I were a good girl I would give up keeping journals. It's a waste of time. It's too great a giveaway of faults that one ought to hide, but it does help me to clarify my mind, to gather my stray thoughts, to lighten loneliness, to pour out my heart.

This concludes the notebook manuscript of M. Z.'s journal, headed "May 1942- October 1944." The following year Joanna was to marry Ensign S. H. Zeigler (U.S.N.) and in 1947 Patrick was to leave for boarding school. With the children gone, Horace and Marya rented the house in Palisades and returned to New York City—first to Greenwich Village, then back to Riverside Drive. These were busy and productive years for them, though Marya felt herself increasingly detached from the emerging fashions in contemporary poetry. Her own work grew in intensity and seemingly in remoteness. Her Selected Poems *appeared in 1954, published by Grove Press. The Gregorys returned to Palisades in the 1960s.*

Biographical Notes

Index

Biographical Notes

Adams, Leonie (1899–1988): Poet. Never a prolific writer, Adams was subject to long periods of artistic aridity. Nonetheless, her work won the esteem of fellow poets, including M. Z. Her *Poems: A Selection,* published in 1954, was awarded the Bollingen Prize.

Barker, George (1913–1991): English poet. On the eve of the war he held academic posts briefly in Japan and the United States.

Benét, William Rose (1886–1950): Poet and literary critic. In 1924 he became one of the founding editors of the *Saturday Review of Literature* and remained with that publication until his death. Louis Untermeyer's eulogy sums up the man and his work: "To intensity he added integrity—and pervasive kindness. His poetry was the man: generous, sometimes too lavish, overflowing with forthrightness and brotherly good will."

Bogan, Louise (1897–1970): American poet. From the mid-1930s she wrote most of the poetry reviews for the *New Yorker* and thus exercised a certain influence on the critical scene. The Gregorys were not kind to her work in their *History of American Poetry:* "A fierce, almost frightening, rhetoric and an unguarded love of passionate pagan sentiment seemed to overwhelm her verse, especially in her later phases."

Breit, Harvey (1909–1968): Although he published one book of poetry and collaborated in the writing of a couple of stage plays, the major part of his career was spent as a staff writer for the *New York Times.* Breit was a columnist and assistant editor of the *New York Times Book Review* from 1948 to 1957, and it was in that capacity that he had frequent contact with the Gregorys.

Breton, André (1896–1966): French poet, novelist, critic, and one of the founders and chief proponents of the surrealist movement.

Brinnin, John Malcolm (1916–1998): American poet, editor, and memoirist. Helped arrange Dylan Thomas's American tours during the 1950s, and after Thomas's death wrote an account of the experience, *Dylan Thomas in America* (1955).

Brooks, Van Wyck (1886–1963): American critic and literary biographer.

Brown, Harry (1917–1986): Left Harvard in his sophomore year to work as a subeditor at the *New Yorker* and to write poetry. During the war, he served abroad as an editor of *Yank* and published a novel about the Italian campaign, *A Walk in the Sun* (1944), which became a best seller and subsequently a successful film. After the war he went to Hollywood where he wrote many film scripts and was awarded an Oscar for coauthoring *A Place in the Sun,* a movie version of Theodore Dreiser's *An American Tragedy.*

Bryher, Winifred (1894–1983): Daughter of Sir John Ellerman, prominent English industrialist and financier, she adopted the name "Bryher" at the outset of her literary career in the early 1920s. Although a woman of broad and intense intellectual interests, she was by temperament a shy and very private person who preferred to exert her not inconsiderable influence behind the scenes as a friend and patron of a number of writers and scholars in both Europe and America. Her own writings represent a distinctive personal achievement. An early book on the Soviet cinema *(Film Problems of Soviet Russia,* [1929]) is a pioneer study in the field, and her series of nine short historical novels, published between 1952 and 1969 and ranging in setting from Italy in the fourth century B.C. to London during the Blitz, reveal an informed concern with pivotal shifts in European history, as well as a strong belief in the enduring qualities of individual morality and courage. Bryher settled in Switzerland in the late 1920s and lived there for the rest of her life—except for the war years, when she elected to return to London. The Gregorys met Bryher during their first trip to England in 1934. She helped to finance their second English trip in 1939, subsequently supplied them with a modest annual stipend, and in later years helped to defray a portion of their heavy medical expenses. M. Z. never failed to regard Bryher's interventions as quasi-miraculous events, and beyond the sheer relief of the financial contributions, she prized the enduring and ever-deepening quality of the friendship. (For a personal account of Bryher's life during the war years, see her book *The Days of Mars: A Memoir, 1940–1946* [New York: 1972]).

Brzeska, Sophie: Polish-born companion of the French sculptor Henri Gaudier (1892–1915). M. Z. would have read about her in H. S. Ede's *Savage Messiah,* a joint biography of Sophie and Henri published in 1931.

Campbell, Joseph (1904–1987): James Joyce scholar and author of books on ancient religions and mythologies. Campbell became a member of the literature faculty at Sarah Lawrence College in 1934, shortly after H. G. He was one of H.G.'s favorite colleagues.

Canby, Henry Seidel (1878–1961): Editor, teacher, founding editor of the *Saturday Review of Literature,* and chairman of the Book-of-the-Month Club.

Carmer, Carl (1903–1976): American author, folklorist, and editor. He is perhaps best remembered today for his book *Stars Fell on Alabama* (1934) and his volume on the Hudson River, which appeared in the Rivers of America series in 1939.

Clark, Eleanor (1913–1996): In 1937 W. W. Norton published an anthology of younger writers entitled *New Letters in America,* edited by Horace Gregory, with Eleanor Clark as associate editor. At the outset of the war, Clark had published a few short stories and written reviews and critical articles that appeared in the *New Republic,* the *Kenyon Review,* and Klaus Mann's *Decision.* During the years 1943–1945, she worked in the Office of Strategic Services in Washington, D.C. In 1945 she published a novel, *The Bitter Box,* which enjoyed a critical *success d'estime,* and in 1952, a book of essays on Roman life and history, *Rome and a Villa,* which became a best seller. During the mid-1930s she was briefly married to Jan Frankl, Trotsky's Czech secretary. She later married the poet and novelist Robert Penn Warren.

Colum, Padraic (1881–1972): Irish-born poet, playwright, folklorist. A youthful participant on the Dublin literary scene during the heady days of the Abbey Theatre, Colum emigrated to America with his wife in 1914, and they subsequently became American citizens. He and Mary were familiar and interestingly incongruous figures on the New York literary scene.

Colum, Mary (1887–1957): Literary critic and author of children's books. With her husband, Padraic, she wrote a memoir of their Dublin days entitled *Our Friend James Joyce* (1959).

Cowley, Malcolm (1898–1989): American poet and editor, perhaps best remembered today for his nostalgic memoir about literary life in Paris during the '20s, *Exile's Return* (1934). Served as literary editor of the *New Republic* from 1929 to 1940.

Dahlberg, Edward (1900–1977): American novelist and critic. The Gregorys' acquaintance with Dahlberg goes back to the late 1920s, before the publication of his first novel, *Bottom Dogs* (1929). A self-proclaimed genius, he managed to persuade a number of prominent literary figures to join him in praising the quirky originality of his viewpoint and the wondrous eclecticism of his prose style. The titles of two of his most interesting books of critical essays are *The Flea of Sodom* (1940) and *Do These Bones Live?* (1941).

Diamond, David (1915–): American composer.

Eastman, Max (1883–1969): One of the most glamorous figures in New York's Greenwich Village spanning the years immediately preceding and following World War I, Eastman was an enthusiastic spokesperson for a generation of young radicals bedazzled by the new perspectives offered by the Russian Revolution, psychoanalysis, and free love. Though his faith in the Soviet experience began to fade in the mid-1920s, he retained his statuesque good looks and buoyant optimism. The titles of his two autobiographical volumes are *Enjoyment of Living* (1946) and *Love and Revolution: My Journey Through an Epoch* (1965).

Eberhart, Richard (1904–): American poet and teacher, with bachelor's degrees from Dartmouth and St. John's College, Cambridge. A prolific poet, he published some thirty volumes of verse between his book *A Bravery of Earth* (1930) and his *Collected Poems, 1930–1986*. He was the recipient of the Bollingen Award (1962), the Pulitzer Prize for Poetry (1966), and the National Book Award (1977).

Farrell, James T. (1904–1979): American novelist and critic. The Gregorys first met Farrell around 1930, while he was still working on the first volume of the Studs Lonigan trilogy. Farrell's energy, enthusiasms, and buoyant self-confidence were exhilarating if not always contagious, and their friendship endured over the years, growing into mutual sympathy and affection in their final decades.

Fearing, Kenneth (1902–1961): American poet and novelist. He graduated from the University of Wisconsin-Madison, where he and M. Z. worked together on the university literary magazine. In 1925 Fearing, recently arrived in New York City, was introduced to H. G. by the novelist Margery Latimore, and he in turn subsequently introduced H. G. to M. Z.

Ficke, Arthur Davison (1883–1945): American poet, born in Iowa and educated at Harvard where he was a classmate of Wallace Stevens and Witter Bynner. In 1914 he collaborated with Bynner in producing a spoof volume of "experimental" modernist verse that successfully hoodwinked a number of literary critics and reviewers. His own preferred verse form was the sonnet.

Fitts, Dudley (1903–1968): American poet and translator. After graduation from Harvard, he became an instructor at the Choate School, later at Phillips Academy, Andover. His *Poems:*

1926–1936 (1937) showed an original poetic sensibility and proclaimed much promise, but his future literary productions lay primarily in the fields of translation from the Greek and Latin classics and of modern Latin American poetry.

Fitzgerald, Robert (1910–1985): Poet, translator, and teacher. While a student at the Choate School, he met a young instructor, Dudley Fitts, with whom he was later to collaborate on a number of imposing translations of Greek tragedy, including the *Antigone* of Sophocles, which was dedicated to Horace Gregory. From 1936 to 1949 Fitzgerald was a staff writer at *Time*. His memorable verse translation of *The Odyssey* appeared in 1961, and in 1965 he was appointed Boylston Professor of Rhetoric and Oratory at Harvard. He delivered the commemorative tribute to Horace Gregory at the Institute of Arts and Letters in 1982.

Flack, Marjorie (1897–1958): Children's book author and illustrator, married to William Rose Benét. Her work, especially *Walter the Lazy Mouse* (1937), was held in high esteem by young Patrick Gregory.

Fletcher, John Gould (1886–1946): Arkansas-born poet, educated at Harvard and associated in his early career with H. D., Amy Lowell, and the Imagist movement. Never a popular poet with either public or critics, he nevertheless won respect for his technical versatility and the high seriousness of his subject matter. (Cf. *Fierce Solitude: A Life of John Gould Fletcher* [1994], by Ben F. Johnson III.)

Freeman, Joseph (1897–1965): Editor, poet, and social critic. He was founding editor of the *New Masses* in 1926, and a prominent anti-fascist polemicist throughout the '20s and '30s. His autobiographical narrative, *An American Testament* (1938), was an eloquent plea for social change that was widely read in intellectual circles in both America and Britain. His later years were spent working on a lengthy political satire in alexandrine verse that never appeared in print.

Garrigue, Jean (1912–1972): Poet. Born in Indiana, she received her M.F.A. from the University of Iowa and settled in Greenwich Village in 1943.

Hampson, John (1901–1955): British novelist, best remembered today for his first novel, *Saturday Night at the Greyhound* (1931), which narrates the interplay between a handful of people in a rural pub during the course of a single evening. His work has been compared in its meticulous prose style and half-suppressed homoeroticism to that of Forster and Isherwood; yet Hampson remained throughout his career little read and little known to the public. Horace Gregory included a short story of his, "Care of the Grand Hotel," in *New Letters in America* (1937).

Hayden, Benjamin (1786–1846): English historical painter. Hayden was a compulsive diarist, and his published diaries, spanning 1808 to 1846, offer a valuable historical portrait of the British art scene during the period as well as a human document of tremendous pathos. In spite of his high ideals, lofty ambition, and an uncompromising dedication to the art of painting, Hayden's technical skills as an artist always remained limited, and his imagination strangely deficient. The discrepancy between the grandiose scale and subject matter of his work and the banality of its execution became increasingly apparent over time, especially since the artist was committed to a genre of painting that was rapidly passing from vogue. Tormented by grinding poverty, the dissolution of youthful promise, and a growing bitterness toward the British art establishment, Hayden committed suicide.

Hayes, Alfred (1911–1985): Poet, novelist, and playwright. Wrote socially conscious verse during the late 1930s. During the war he served in the army in Italy and worked with Rossellini on the script of the film *Paisan.*

Hillyer, Robert (1895–1961): American poet and professor of English at Harvard. Although M. Z. liked Hillyer personally and was grateful for his appreciative response to her poetry, she found his repeated attacks on Eliot, Pound, and "modernist" verse wearisome and wrongheaded. Hillyer's papers, like the bulk of both the Gregorys' manuscripts, were left to the Syracuse University Library.

Holty, Carl (1900–1973): Painter. Knew H. G. during their youth in Milwaukee. Studied with Hans Hofmann in Munich during the mid-1930s before settling in New York City.

Hoult, Norah (1898–1983): Irish novelist and short story writer. The Gregorys may have met her first during their visit to Ireland in 1934. She came to New York City in 1937 and remained there until the outbreak of the war when she moved to London. Among her books are *Poor Women* (1928) and *Coming from the Fair* (1937).

Josephson, Matthew (1899–1978): Author of biographies of Rousseau, Stendhal, and Zola, as well as a number of books on the shaping of the American system, including *The Robber Barons* (1934) and *Sidney Hillman: Statesman of American Labor* (1952). His autobiographical book, *Life Among the Surrealists* (1962), recounts his years in Paris in the late 1920s and early 1930s.

Kees, Weldon (1914–1955): A poet whose reputation seems to have grown steadily in the years since his death, in part because of his romantic persona as a jazz pianist, amateur film maker, and apparent suicide. In their *History of American Poetry,* the Gregorys wrote in 1942, "His greatest debt was to the poetry of Allen Tate, and Kees' promise seems to be in achieving a balance between direct prose cadences and those of verse."

Komroff, Manuel (1890–1974): Novelist and biographer; president of the Author's League, 1941–1943.

Kreymborg, Alfred (1882–1966): A native New Yorker, Kreymborg was a prominent literary "rebel" during the heroic age of Greenwich Village, during the decades immediately preceding and following World War I. Poet, editor, and early champion of "modernism," he returned from a brief sojourn in Europe in 1921, where he met Pound and helped launch the literary review *Broom,* with his credentials as a mover and shaker confirmed. In spite of a steady production of poetry over the years, his reputation today seems destined to survive mainly through his position as an emblematic figure of the time.

Lazare, Christopher (1912–19—): Lazare was a familiar figure on the New York scene during the 1940s, where he frequented the upper regions of literary Bohemia. He made a precarious living as a reviewer for various publications, served as art editor for Klaus Mann's review *Decision,* and published several translations (among others, of E. T. A. Hoffman). He was a semiprofessional house guest, and earned his keep by his exceptional conversational skill, which was characterized by wit, a wide range of reading in several languages, and the ability to give dramatic shape to an anecdote. After the war he served in Germany on a cultural mission of the U.S. Information Service and died abroad.

Leonard, William Ellery (1876–1944): Scholar, linguist, poet, and teacher who was a friend and mentor to both M. Z. and H. G. during their undergraduate years at the University of Wisconsin-Madison. He held degrees from Brown University, Harvard, and Columbia, and did further graduate work at the Universities of Göttingen and Bonn before coming to Wisconsin in 1906. Although primarily known as a Latinist (his critical edition of Lucretius's *De Rerum Natura* is still prized by scholars), he also did a noted translation of *Beowulf,* and during the 1920s published a number of volumes of verse, as well as an autobiography, *The Locomotive God* (1927), remarkable in its time for its use of psychoanalytic techniques and its candor. His personal life was tragic. His young wife, whom he married in 1909, soon revealed signs of mental illness and committed suicide. Shortly thereafter Leonard became prey to bouts of agoraphobia, which kept him confined for the rest of his life to a five-block radius of his apartment. On his death, the obituary in the *New York Times* bore the headline: "Dr. W. E. Leonard, Famed for Phobia," before going on to list his impressive literary and scholarly achievements. M. Z. and H. G. visited him whenever they went to Wisconsin.

Lerner, Max (1902–1992): Journalist and newspaper columnist who wrote extensively on the American political scene. He was married to Anita Lerner, a colleague of H. G. at Sarah Lawrence.

Lewis, Wyndham (1886–1957): English painter, novelist, art critic, and poet. With Ezra Pound, he founded the Vorticist movement on the eve of World War I. He came to the U.S. in 1940 in the hope of earning a living wage. The experience is chillingly related in his novel *Self Condemned* (1955).

Mann, Klaus (1906–1949): The son of Thomas Mann, he tried his hand as a novelist, critic, playwright, actor, and memoirist before his death at forty-two in southern France. Shortly after coming to America after the outbreak of war in Europe, he founded a literary review of cosmopolitan outlook whose board of editorial advisers included W. H. Auden, Julian Green, Stefan Zweig, and Horace Gregory. He was a frequent visitor to the Gregorys' apartment on Riverside Drive.

Masters, Edgar Lee (1868–1950): Winesburg, Ohio, and Spoon River, Illinois, remain perhaps the two most notable geographical locations associated with the literary renaissance that swept middle-western America in the years surrounding World War I. Although Masters continued publishing both poetry and prose for the remainder of his life, his *Spoon River Anthology,* which appeared in 1915, suffices to sustain his reputation as an important figure in twentieth-century poetry. This collection of epitaphs of small town folks, from the local banker to the village drunk, has the rough-hewn candor and stark integrity of a rain-swept rural cemetery. Because this was the sort of peculiar masterpiece that defied imitation—even by its own author—it sets Masters strangely apart from the evolving literary scene.

McMaster, Helen (1897–1974): A favorite colleague of H. G.'s at Sarah Lawrence, McMaster earned her Ph.D. in English literature at Yale, shortly following the death of her husband in World War I. Her interest in literature was both broad and discriminating. She was largely responsible for bringing the Belgian novelist Marguerite Yourcenar to teach at Sarah Lawrence in the 1940s.

Nathan, Robert (1894–1985): Author of a number of best-selling novels blending romance and poetically charged whimsy.

Nemerov, Howard (1920–1991): American poet. After graduating from Harvard, Nemerov served in the Canadian and American air forces. His numerous books of poetry were to win him various teaching appointments and many awards, including the National Book Award, the Pulitzer Prize, the Bollingen Prize, the National Medal of Art, and in 1988, the Poet Laureateship of the United States of America.

Pearson, Norman Holmes (1909–1975): Educated at Yale and at Magdalen College, Oxford, Pearson taught in the English Department at Yale throughout his academic career and was chairman of the Department of American Studies there from 1957 to 1967. Although he was identified as an authority on the life and work of Hawthorne, his critical editions of Hawthorne's *Complete Letters* and *French and Italian Journals* remained lifetime works in progress. Nonetheless, Pearson was successful in acquiring the letters and manuscripts of contemporary authors for Yale's Beinecke Library and was on a first-name basis with many of the most prominent literary personalities of the day. During the war Pearson served overseas as a civilian in the Office of Strategic Services and received for his work a number of significant decorations, including the Medal of Freedom (U.S.), *Medaille de Reconnainance* and *Chevalier de la Legion d'honneur* (France), and Knight of St. Olaf, First Class (Norway). Marya and Horace became friends with him while he was still a graduate student at Yale, and they maintained close ties throughout their lives.

Pitter, Ruth (1897–1992): English poet. The traditional form and religious imagery of her later work kept her pretty much an outsider on the literary scene, though she was much admired by certain poets (including Edith Sitwell and M. Z.), and her *Collected Poems* (1968) won her the Queen's Medal for Poetry.

Prokosch, Frederick (1906–1989): American poet and novelist. His first book of poems, *The Assassins,* was published in 1936; his last was *Chosen Poems,* issued in London in 1944.

Putnam, Arthur James (Jim) (1893–1966): One of the last of an old breed of publisher's editors, Putnam was courtly in manner, gently cultured in a traditional way, socially at ease everywhere, and personally unambitious. He was very tall, with a deep voice, and his infectious laugh could always be heard floating above the babble of a crowded cocktail party. Though a hearty host, he could in intimate gatherings be a solicitous guest and a sympathetic listener. He was M. Z.'s editor and loyal supporter at Macmillan during the 1930s and 1940s, and though she sometimes wondered whether he actually had ever read a line of her poetry, she found his physical presence reassuring and came to regard him as a personal friend.

Richardson, Dorothy (1882–1957): English novelist. Her multivolume autobiographical novel *Pilgrimage* was greatly admired by the Gregorys, and H. G. published one of the first critical studies of her work, *Dorothy Richardson: An Adventure in Self-Discovery* (1967).

Rodman, Selden (1909–): Poet, art critic, and photographer.

Rougemont, Denis de (1906–1985): Swiss author of *Love in the Western World* (1940), an influential treatise on the origins of courtly love and its dissemination in late-medieval Europe.

Rukeyser, Muriel (1913–1980): American poet, born in New York City. While at Vassar College she figured in a sorority of aspiring writers (Elizabeth Bishop, Eleanor Clark, Mary McCarthy), commemorated in McCarthy's novel *The Group* (1963), and was the first of the group to achieve literary recognition when her manuscript of poems, *Theory of Flight* (1935), won the Yale Younger Poet's Award. That volume contained a poem entitled "Citation for Horace Gregory," and her next book, *U.S.A. 1* (1938) was dedicated to him. M. R.'s relationship with M. Z. was close, lasting, and fraught with strain.

Sarton, May (1912–1995): Memoirist, novelist, and poet. In her later years she became a feminist icon.

Schubert, David (1913–1946): Horace Gregory included an early poem by Schubert in *New Letters in America* (1937) and a selection of his work later appeared in *Five Young American Poets* published by New Directions in 1941. The Gregorys efforts to help foster his literary career were hampered by the young poet's increasingly fragile mental health. From 1941 he suffered a series of breakdowns and was repeatedly hospitalized (the diagnosis was paranoid schizophrenia). His death in 1946 was attributed to tuberculosis. A posthumous collection of Schubert's poetry, *Initial A,* was published by Macmillan in 1961, and in 1983 the *Quarterly Review of Literature* issued a volume containing all his poems as well as biographical and critical pieces on him by, among others, William Carlos Williams, John Ashberry, and James Wright.

Schwartz, Delmore (1913–1966): American poet and short-story writer. M. Z. found Schwartz's luridly self-centered poetry not to her liking, and his flamboyant—and self-destructive—personality repulsive. The antipathy was reciprocal.

Scott, Winfield Townley (1910–1968): Poet and essayist, born in Newport, Rhode Island. Scott Donaldson's biography, *Poet in America: Winfield Townley Scott* (1972), offers a cautionary tale on the emotional cost of pursuing a literary career during the 1940s and 1950s.

Sekula, Sonia (1918–1963): A Swiss-born émigré artist, influenced in her work by the surrealist and abstract expressionist artists with whom she exhibited at Peggy Guggenheim's New York gallery during the mid-1940s and early 1950s. She also had a one-woman show at the Betty Parsons Gallery. Reviewing a posthumous exhibit of her work, Hilton Kramer wrote in the *New York Times:* "Trying her hand at a lot of things—from small, intimate poem-drawings to big apocalyptic canvases, Miss Sekula seems to have evolved a truly personal style—though she often produced remarkable individual pieces. The promise here was—alas!—very large." She committed suicide after a series of mental breakdowns.

Shedlovsky, Beatrice (1902–1986): The Gregorys were neighbors of the Shedlovskys, first in Sunnyside, then in New York City, and the two couples stayed in close contact throughout their lives. Beatrice was a New Englander by birth and temperament, steady, intelligent, reticent. During the period of these diaries, M. Z. found Beatrice's quiet constancy and sincere sympathy a relief from the tensions of literary relationships.

Shedlovsky, Theodore (1898–1976): A graduate of M.I.T., and subsequently a biochemist at the Rockefeller Institute in New York City. Among Theodore's passions were classical music, chess, and late-night discussions concerning Life, Art, and the Foibles of Humankind.

Silvette, Marcia (1910–1998): Painter. In 1925 the Silvette family moved from Pittsburgh, Pennsylvania, to Richmond, Virginia, where Marcia's father and brother David established themselves as fashionable portrait painters. After studying at the Academy of Design in New York, she taught art classes at the University of Richmond and subsequently married a nephew of the Iranian consul in New York. In 1971 she was living with her husband in Geneva, Switzerland, and resided abroad until her death.

Stoessel, Albert (1894–1943): American conductor, violinist, and composer. After a distinguished career as a violinist, he turned to orchestra and choral conducting. He founded the

Julliard Graduate School's opera and orchestra programs in 1927 and directed them until his death.

Sweeney, James Johnson (1900–1986): Art critic and museum director. From 1935 he mounted a number of important exhibitions at the Museum of Modern Art, including a show of African Negro art, and one-man exhibitions of Calder, Miro, Mondrian, and Stieglitz. In 1952 he was appointed director of the Solomon R. Guggenheim Museum in New York City. His brother was Jack Sweeney, another good friend of the Gregorys.

Sweeney, John ("Jack") (1902?–1986): A member of the English Department at Harvard, Sweeney's special domain there was the Poetry Room in the Lamont Library, where he initiated an important series of readings and recordings by living poets. Learned, modest, unambitious, he moved with good-humored sympathy and grace among temperamental egoists. After retiring from Harvard in the 1960s, he and his wife lived in rural Ireland. His obituary in the *Irish Times* is indicative of the sort of response his memory evokes among those who knew him: "Sweeney dressed well, he was a fine host, and incomparable companion. Life and literature excited him. His students don't merely remember him: their eyes light up when his name is spoken. He had the qualities the goddess admired in Odysseus: he was civilized, intelligent and self-possessed." Jack was the brother of James Johnson Sweeney.

Tate, Allen (1899–1979): American poet, critic, and teacher. He was associated with John Crowe Ransom and Robert Penn Warren in the Agrarian group of Southern writers.

Teasdale, Sarah (1884–1933): M. Z. wrote the introduction to an edition of Teasdale's *Collected Poems,* issued by Macmillan in 1966.

Thompson, Dunstan (1918–1975): After graduation from Harvard, Thompson became a founding editor of a lively literary review, *Vice-Versa.* His first book, *Poems* (1943), published while the author was serving overseas in the army, was well received. The Gregorys wrote in their *History of American Poetry:* "The promise that his first book holds is of a line that links it to the work of the 'Romantic Traditionalists' of an earlier generation." Apparently this tradition seemed all too remote to the critical tastes of the postwar period; in any case, Thompson gradually withdrew from the literary scene and into private life in a provincial town in England. In 1965 he wrote in the twenty-fifth anniversary report of the Harvard class of 1940: "The most important thing that has happened to me since leaving Harvard has been the rediscovery of the Catholic faith in which I was brought up. . . . I could not begin to describe the peace and happiness which the practice of Catholicism has given me."

Troy, William (1903–1961): Critic and teacher whose reputation exceeded his production. His *Selected Essays* (1967) were published posthumously. He was married to the poet Leonie Adams.

Untermeyer, Louis (1885–1978): His astute and influential anthologies of modern poetry (particularly *Modern American Poetry: A Critical Anthology,* 1942) offer the present-day reader a valuable overview of the poetry scene between the two wars.

Van Doren, Mark (1894–1972): American poet and educator. A longtime teacher of English literature at Columbia University in New York, Van Doren was much venerated by his students, and came to be looked upon as an exemplar of down-east traditional wisdom.

Wheelwright, John (1897–1940): Poet. The Gregorys recognized his value as a rare original in American poetry and looked forward to his "discovery" by future generations of readers.

Williams, Oscar (1900–1964): Poet and anthologist. Edited the Little Treasury series of poetry anthologies for Scribner.

Wilson, T. C. (1918–1952): A young poet and critic whose intelligence and high seriousness attracted the interest of a number of literary mentors, including Ezra Pound and William Carlos Williams as well as M. Z. and H. G. It could perhaps be said that his acute critical sensitivities outstripped and eventually paralyzed his own literary endeavors. After serving in the U.S. air force during World War II, he inherited a private income and settled in New York City where he shortly, methodically, killed himself with alcohol and drugs. He left his literary remains and extensive correspondence to H. G. who subsequently turned them over to the Beinecke Library at Yale University. He was a close friend of the Gregorys, who were much shaken by his death and their inability to prevent it.

Winters, Yvor (1900–1968): American critic, poet, and teacher. Beginning amongst the Imagists, he subsequently rejected modernist innovations to become a forceful advocate of traditional verse forms and a return to conventional prosody. His most influential critical volume was characteristically titled *In Defense of Reason* (1947). Throughout his career he taught at Stanford University.

Yarmolinsky, Avrahm (1890–1975): Translated poems from Russian and German in collaboration with his wife, the poet Babette Deutsch (1895–1982).

Zabel, Morton (1902–1964): Literary critic and editor; professor of English at Loyola University in Chicago (1929–1946), then at the University of Chicago, from 1947. His books include *Literary Opinion in America* (1937); and he edited the Viking Portable volumes of Joseph Conrad and Henry James. M. Z. met Zabel during her University of Wisconsin days and always had for him a strong if ambivalent attachment.

Index